La Cucina Italiana

ITALIAN COOKING

La Cucina Italiana

ITALIAN
COOKING

A COLLECTION OF NEARLY 400 SIMPLE YET AUTHENTIC
RECIPES FROM ITALY'S LEADING CULINARY MAGAZINE

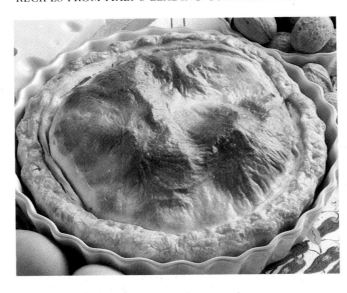

Crescent Books

New York ● Avenel, New Jersey

This book was devised and produced by
Multimedia Books Limited
32–34 Gordon House Road
London NW5 1LP

This 1994 edition published by Crescent Books,
distributed by Random House Value Publishing, Inc.,
40 Engelhard Avenue, Avenel, New Jersey 07001

Random House
New York ● Toronto ● London ● Sydney ● Auckland

Editors
Anne Johnson, Isabel Moore

Design
Kelly Flynn

Production
Hugh Allan

Copyright © Multimedia Books Limited 1993

A CIP catalog record for this book is available from the Library of Congress

Original recipes and pictures copyright © NEPI
La Cucina Italiana,
Via Mascheroni, 1–20123 Milan

ISBN 0-517-10288-9

10 9 8 7 6 5 4 3 2 1

Phototypeset in Linotron Sabon by
Northern Phototypesetting Co. Ltd., Bolton, UK
Printed in Italy by New Interlitho SpA, Milan

Contents

Introduction

Italian food and wines are second to none. Dependent on the best raw materials, Italian cuisine treats its ingredients with respect.

La Cucina Italiana is the title of Italy's leading cooking and home interest magazine. Every month, its pages display a marvelous selection of seasonal recipes and menus – some traditional, some newly invented and tested.

All the recipes and photographs in this book are reproduced by kind permission of the magazine. They accurately reflect the wide scope of the magazine, and the careful balance of the traditional and modern on which the magazine's expert consultant panel has always insisted.

In the pages that follow, there are recipes and ideas to suit cooks of all temperaments, from the simple to the ambitious, from the modest to the flamboyant. There are dishes, too, that will suit every possible occasion, from the family picnic to the biggest party, from the quiet dinner for two to the grand gala supper. All of life's possibilities are catered for here.

The climate range, neighbors, tradition and geography of Italy have developed marked regional variations in Italian cooking. In the north, butter is more widely used for cooking, while in the

south olive oil is more commonly used. Rice, grown in the north, is eaten there as a staple alongside pasta; coastal regions abound in seafood; while the delicious cakes and pastries of the north, not to mention its game, have a distinctly Germanic accent.

Apart from these general regional characteristics, there is a wealth of individual regional dishes, pasta, cheeses and drinks throughout Italy. To get to know Italian food is to get to know an entire world of cooking.

Essential pantry ingredients for Italian cooking are simple. Perhaps the most important one is olive oil — a lighter one for cooking and a heavier, fuller-flavored one for salads. The other essential is a selection of herbs, preferably fresh: oregano, basil, sage and rosemary.

Some of the recipes in this book call for special ingredients, which are readily available from the increasing number of Italian food shops. But don't let this put you off. If you can't find the precise ingredient mentioned here, substitute a similar cheese, fish or meat. There is nothing dogmatic about Italian cookery — the only real essential is your own enthusiasm.

Other than, perhaps, a basic pasta-making machine, you won't need any special kitchen equipment either. A large saucepan is a must for cooking pasta — one that holds 6 quarts of water for every 1lb of pasta. Apart from that, the recipes in this book can all be achieved with standard kitchen equipment.

Italian food, as well as being one of the world's most delicious

cuisines, is also one of the healthiest. Olive oil, pasta, rice, seafood, vegetables, salads – these are all staple ingredients in Italian cooking, and they are all blissfully good for you.

Packed with vitamins and minerals and low in saturated fat, this is a way of eating that is particularly beneficial to a healthy heart. It is no coincidence that Italians have a low incidence of heart disease. There are lessons to be learned here.

The Italian way of constructing a meal is to start with an *antipasto*, meaning, literally, 'before the pasta'; then a soup or pasta, though not both; followed possibly by a vegetable course; then the *piatto di mezzo*, meaning 'middle dish' or main course, of fish, meat or poultry, which is often accompanied by a salad, or more rarely a non-salad vegetable. Finally, desserts range from simple fresh fruit in season to elaborate cakes or *torte*. Cheese tends to be eaten as an *antipasto*, as a snack or as an ingredient of some other dish.

Some outstanding features of Italian food are the superb cured, smoked or raw hams; salamis; veal; pasta; pizza; and sweets: nougat, macaroons, zabaglione and, above all, ice cream are all famous Italian confections.

Think of Italian food and most people will immediately think of pasta and pizza. Pasta made with flour bound with eggs, oil or both, and possibly colored with spinach or beet, comes in all shapes and sizes, many of them regional specialties. Eaten hot or cold, with a classic sauce or one improvised from seafood, meat, cheeses, herbs, vegetables or oil, pasta is infinitely versatile.

Fresh pasta is easily made at home. A simple pasta machine, which is inexpensive and simple to use, will give you a more uniform result, but you can just as easily roll and cut pasta dough (about 4 eggs to 1lb of flour) with standard kitchen equipment. It's well worth the effort, because the end result is far superior to the dried, manufactured product. Fresh pasta is now more commonly available from delicatessens and supermarkets.

Pizza, once a hearty, all-in-one Neapolitan snack, has become an international fast food. It is a great favorite with all members of the family, young and old, and now appears in flavor combinations that the Neapolitans never even dreamed of!

Real Italian icecream is a delight far removed from its commercially produced namesake: a soft confection of pure fruit juice, sugar, cream and eggs. It is fairly simple to make at home and the delicious result is guaranteed to be worthwhile.

Italy is the world's largest wine producer and her population is high in the world's wine-drinking league, with 120 bottles per person per year. As well as being the home of the internationally known Martini and Cinzano, Italy also produces scores of other *aperitivi* and *digestivi*.

An increasing number of the very many Italian wines are becoming available outside Italy. Well-known names include whites such as Orvieto, Soave, Verdicchio and Frascati, and reds such as Valpolicella, Bardolino and Barolo.

Antipasti

For Italians, the best way to begin a meal is with an
antipasto – meaning, literally, before the pasta. This is a
dish designed to prepare the stomach for – and so
enhance – the main course. *Antipasti* can range from a
single item, such as asparagus in butter, to a selection of
delectable items beautifully and lovingly arranged on a
plate. Essential ingredients loved by Italians – fresh
seasonal vegetables, eggs and regional cheeses – form the
basis of this all-important first course.

Melon with Shrimp

Melone e gamberetti

salt
²⁄₃ cup dry white wine
1 small bay leaf
2–3 whole black peppercorns
2–3 sprigs fresh parsley
1 small onion, halved
12 oz fresh small shrimp
1 medium melon
2 lettuce leaves
²⁄₃ cup mayonnaise
2 tablespoons mustard
2 tablespoons tomato ketchup
1 tablespoon whipping cream
Worcestershire sauce
1 teaspoon brandy

SERVES 6
PREPARATION AND COOKING TIME:
ABOUT 1 HOUR

Bring to the boil about 1 quart of water, a little salt, the white wine, bay leaf, peppercorns, parsley and onion and simmer for at least 5 minutes. Add the shrimp, cook for about 4 minutes and then remove them from the pan with a slotted spoon, discarding the other ingredients. When the shrimp have cooled, peel them and place them in a bowl.

Cut the melon in half and discard the seeds. Scoop out the flesh, cut into ½ inch cubes and place in a bowl. Put a lettuce leaf in the bottom of each empty melon skin.

Prepare the dressing: blend the mayonnaise with the mustard, tomato ketchup, cream, a dash of Worcestershire sauce and the brandy. Test and adjust the seasoning to taste.

Mix the shrimp and melon cubes and dress with the prepared sauce. Divide the mixture between the two melon halves and serve immediately.

Christmas Pâté

'Delizia' delle feste

4 oz chicken livers
8 oz pork loin
1 medium leek, white part only
6 tablespoons butter
1 tablespoon olive oil
4 tablespoons Marsala wine
½ chicken bouillion cube
4 oz prosciutto ham
1 teaspoon white truffle paste
1 tablespoon pine nuts
1 small black truffle (optional)
a little gelatin dissolved in warm water
toasted bread for accompaniment

SERVES 6–8
PREPARATION AND COOKING TIME:
ABOUT 1¼ HOURS

Remove any traces of green from the chicken livers then carefully wash and drain them. Cut the pork loin into small slices. Finely slice the leek and fry in 3 tablespoons of the butter and the olive oil, taking care not to let it brown. Add the chicken livers and the pork, turn up the heat and allow to brown a little. Pour in the Marsala and crumble in the bouillion cube, stirring constantly.

When the Marsala has been completely absorbed, remove the pan from the heat and pour the contents into a blender. Add the chopped ham with the truffle paste and the remaining butter cut into slivers. Blend on minimum speed for a minute, then on maximum for a couple of minutes. Sieve through a fine strainer into a bowl and leave to cool, stirring from time to time.

Mix again vigorously with a wooden spoon to make the pâté light and fluffy. Heap into two earthenware pâté dishes and garnish one with the pine nuts and the other with slices of black truffle if you wish (you can leave it as is if you can't find a truffle). Finally, brush the surface with the gelatin, softened in a little hot water. As soon as it sets, cover the dishes with plastic wrap and refrigerate. Serve with toast.

LEFT: *Melon with shrimp.*

Salami Canapés with Fava Beans

Canapé di salame con fave

---

9 slices of white bread
18 slices of 'salsiccione' salami
4 oz medium matured pecorino cheese
4 oz shelled fresh fava beans

MAKES 18 CANAPÉS

PREPARATION TIME: ABOUT 30 MINUTES

Cut out two 1½ inch circles from each slice of bread and toast in a hot oven. Meanwhile, stack the salami slices, pressing them together. Trim the edges to make a sort of rectangle, then cut the salami in half to make two squares. You will now have 36 slices of salami. Chop all but 18 of the fava beans.

Grate half the pecorino and mix it with the chopped beans, then divide this mixture into 18 equal parts. Arrange two pieces of salami in a cross on each circle of toast. Place a little heap of bean mixture in the center, then fold up the ends of the salami to make a 'parcel'. Cut the remaining pecorino into circles and place one on top of each canapé. Decorate with the reserved fava beans.

Monkfish in Aromatic Oil

Pescatrice all'olio aromatico

---

1 piece of monkfish, about 9 oz, boned, skinned and membrane removed
salt and pepper
2 garlic cloves
extra virgin olive oil
a bunch of aromatic herbs (thyme, marjoram, rosemary, sage)

FOR THE COURT-BOUILLON
1 celery stalk
1 small carrot
½ onion stuck with 2 cloves
1 bay leaf
parsley stalks
dry white wine
black peppercorns
salt

SERVES 4

PREPARATION AND COOKING TIME:
ABOUT 40 MINUTES, PLUS MARINATING

Make a court-bouillon by boiling 1 quart water with the celery, carrot, onion, bay leaf, a few parsley stalks, ½ glass of wine, a few peppercorns and salt to taste for 30 minutes.

Meanwhile, slice the monkfish into ¼ inch thick medallions. As soon as the court-bouillon is ready, put in the fish and cook for 5 minutes from when the liquid comes back to the boil. Drain the medallions and arrange them in a fairly deep dish; season with salt and pepper.

Lightly crush the garlic cloves, leaving them whole. Heat half a glass of olive oil with the crushed garlic and the bunch of herbs, without letting it frizzle. Pour the mixture over the fish, cover and leave to marinate in a cool place for at least 12 hours before serving.

Chicken Tartlets with Peas

Tartellette con pollo e piselli

FOR THE TARTLETS:
14 oz prepared pie pastry
flour for dusting
dried baking beans

FOR THE FILLING:
5 oz chicken breast fillet
butter for greasing
1 medium shallot, finely chopped
salt and white pepper
dry white wine
2½ cups shelled peas
1 large tomato, ripe but firm
12 quail's eggs, hard-boiled

MAKES 24 TARTLETS

PREPARATION AND COOKING TIME:
ABOUT 40 MINUTES, PLUS THAWING THE PASTRY

Thaw the pastry. Preheat the oven to 350°F. Meanwhile, trim the chicken breast, then slice it diagonally into thin slices. Grease a shallow baking pan and scatter on the shallot. Spread out the slices of chicken breast on top. Season with salt and pepper, moisten with half a glass of white wine, and cook in the oven for about 10 minutes.

Cook the peas in boiling water until tender but still crunchy, then purée. Season with salt and pepper and

RIGHT: *Monkfish in aromatic oil* (top left); *Salami canapes with fava beans* (top right); *Chicken tartlets with peas* (bottom).

then leave for a while until cool.

Raise the oven temperature to 400°F. Lightly flour the work surface and roll out the pastry to a thickness of ⅛ inch. Prick it with the tines of a fork, then cut out 24 circles, large enough to line 24 tartlet tins. Line the pastry with waxed paper, then top with baking beans (to stop the pastry rising during baking), and bake the tartlet cases blind for about 20 minutes.

Meanwhile, plunge the tomato into boiling water, then remove the skin. Turn it upside down to drain out the seeds. Shell the quails' eggs and cut them in half. Take the tartlets out of the oven, unmold them and remove the baking beans. Divide the puréed peas equally between them and top with slices of chicken, half a quail's egg and a piece of tomato.

Avocado Appetizer

Antipasto di avocado

½ cup white wine
1 bay leaf
parsley
black peppercorns
salt
4 oz peeled small shrimp
a little mayonnaise
Worcestershire sauce
mustard
3 avocados
1 large lemon
Belgian endive

SERVES 6
PREPARATION AND COOKING TIME:
ABOUT 40 MINUTES

Heat ⅔ cup of water and the white wine in a saucepan, add the bay leaf, 3 sprigs of parsley, 2 black peppercorns and salt. Simmer for a few seconds, then turn down the heat and add the shrimp to the shallow boiling liquid, cover and boil for a couple of minutes. Remove cooked shrimp with a slotted spoon, drain well and leave to cool.

Put them in a bowl with a little mayonnaise, a generous dash of Worcestershire sauce and 2 teaspoons of mustard.

Cut the avocados in half and remove the stones. Using a teaspoon, scrape out some of the flesh and add it to the shrimp. Finally, stir in a few drops of lemon juice. Place the shrimp mixture in the hollowed-out avocados and arrange on a serving dish. Place half a slice of lemon between each avocado with some chopped endive. In the center of the serving dish, place half a lemon decorated with mayonnaise. Serve at once.

Smoked Salmon Domes

Cupolette di salmone

---

8 slices of white bread
8 oz smoked salmon, sliced
4 oz Belgian endive
2 oz button mushrooms
2 oz celery heart
salt and pepper
juice of 1 lemon
1 tablespoon white wine vinegar
¼ cup mayonnaise, plus a tubeful for decorating
⅔ cup heavy cream

SERVES 8
PREPARATION TIME:
ABOUT 30 MINUTES, PLUS CHILLING

Take eight small ramekins or molds about 3½ inches in diameter. With a medium pastry cutter, cut out eight rounds from the bread. Line the molds first with plastic wrap, leaving an overhang, then with the smoked salmon slices.

Trim the vegetables, rinse under running water and drain well. Dice finely and place in a bowl. Season with salt and pepper, lemon juice and vinegar and mix well, then add the mayonnaise. Whip the cream and fold it in gently. Divide the mixture between the molds, cover each one with a round of bread, then fold over the overhanging plastic wrap and seal it. Chill the molds in the fridge for at least 3 hours until firm.

Just before serving, invert the molds onto a large serving plate. Peel off the plastic wrap, then decorate each dome with mayonnaise, piping it straight from the tube. Garnish as you wish (we arranged wafer-thin slices of cucumber between the domes and topped them with small pieces of celery).

RIGHT: *Piquant peppers*

16

Piquant Peppers

Peperoni aromatici

8 small yellow peppers, weighing about 2 lb in all
3 tablespoons capers
4 large anchovy fillets in oil
½ garlic clove
a handful of parsley
pinch of salt
Tabasco sauce
Worcestershire sauce
1 tablespoon mustard
olive oil

SERVES 6–8

PREPARATION AND COOKING TIME: ABOUT 50 MINUTES, PLUS AT LEAST 2 HOURS CHILLING

Gently broil the peppers and remove the scorched skin. Halve them, discarding the stalks and seeds and flatten. Arrange in a single layer on a large plate.

Thoroughly drain the capers and chop coarsely, together with the anchovy fillets, the garlic and parsley. Sprinkle this mixture over the peppers.

Prepare the dressing by mixing together a pinch of salt, 2–3 drops of Tabasco and a dash of Worcestershire sauce. Blend in the mustard. When the salt has completely dissolved, add 5 tablespoons of olive oil and blend to a smooth sauce.

Pour the prepared dressing over the peppers, cover with plastic wrap and leave to stand in a cool place for at least 2 hours. This dish improves if left to stand and is best eaten a day after preparation.

Lobster and Avocado

Aragosto e avocado

4 oz lobster meat
2 ripe avocados
Worcestershire sauce
pinch of salt
2 teaspoons mustard
juice of ½ lemon
olive oil
4 crisp lettuce leaves

SERVES 4

PREPARATION TIME: ABOUT 40 MINUTES

Dice the lobster into ½ inch cubes and put them in a bowl. Cut the avocados in half lengthwise and remove the stones. Peel and slice them lengthwise then cut into irregular-shaped pieces a little larger than the lobster cubes. Mix the two together carefully.

Prepare the dressing: put a pinch of salt in a bowl and add a dash of Worcestershire sauce, the mustard and lemon juice. Mix until the salt has completely dissolved, then mix in 4 tablespoons of olive oil and continue stirring vigorously for a few minutes until the dressing emulsifies.

Pour the dressing over the lobster and avocado mixture, mix very carefully and leave for a few minutes. Place a lettuce leaf in each of four glass goblets and divide the mixture between them.

Lobster and Melon

Aragosto sul melone

1 medium melon
8 oz lobster meat
a small glass of port
⅓ cup mayonnaise

SERVES 4

PREPARATION TIME: ABOUT 40 MINUTES

Cut the melon in half and remove the seeds and fibers. Scoop out the flesh in little balls and place

LEFT: *Lobster and avocado* (top left); *Lobster and melon* (top right); *Lobster tarts* (bottom).

these in a bowl. Cut the lobster into 12 medallions (not too thick) and dice the rest. Mix the diced lobster with the melon balls, pour in the port and mix carefully. Cover the bowl with plastic wrap and refrigerate for about 10 minutes.

Arrange the melon and lobster mixture in four chilled goblets and place 3 medallions of lobster on top of each one. Decorate with a piped swirl of mayonnaise in the center and serve at once.

Lobster Tarts

Tartellette all'Aragosta

1¼ cups flour
pinch of salt
¼ teaspoon dried yeast
4 tablespoons butter
1 egg yolk
4 oz celery root, peeled
½ cup mayonnaise
1 teaspoon mustard
Worcestershire sauce
12 small medallions of lobster meat, weighing about
4 oz in all

SERVES 6

PREPARATION AND COOKING TIME:
ABOUT 1 HOUR

Preheat the oven to 375°F. Sift the flour onto a work surface and add a pinch of salt and the yeast. Mix, and make a well in the center. Soften the butter and cut it into pieces. Put these, the egg yolk and 2 tablespoons of cold water into the well and mix quickly to make a smooth dough.

Roll out the pastry to a thickness of ⅛ inch. Using a fluted 5 inch round pastry cutter, cut out six rounds. Put these into buttered tartlet pans or ramekins and prick the bases with a fork. Leave to rest and rise for 15 minutes. Line the tartlet cases with waxed paper, add baking beans, and bake blind for about 15 minutes until golden brown. Remove from the oven and leave to cool.

Meanwhile, shred the celery root and mix immediately with half the mayonnaise, the mustard and a dash of Worcestershire sauce. When the pastry cases are cold, remove them from the pans and place a little of the celery root mixture in the bottom of each one. Lay two medallions of lobster on top, then pipe on the rest of the mayonnaise and garnish with a few lettuce leaves.

Scallops with Salmon Trout

Capesante salmonate

---

8 oz salmon trout fillets
²/₃ cup light cream
salt and pepper
6 large scallops
1 shallot, peeled and finely chopped
olive oil
¼ cup dry Martini
6 scallop shells
1 slice of white bread, crumbled
butter

SERVES 6

PREPARATION AND COOKING TIME:
ABOUT 40 MINUTES

Preheat the oven to 400°F. Make sure there are no bones in the trout fillets, then pass them through a grinder. Transfer the ground trout to a food processor, purée at full speed for a few seconds, then mix in the cream and season to taste.

Rinse the scallops. In a shallow pan, sweat the shallot with 2 tablespoons of olive oil until soft. Add the scallops, season and cook briefly until lightly colored. Remove the scallops from the pan and add the Martini. Reduce the sauce until it has almost completely evaporated, then put back the scallops to glaze them. Turn off the heat.

Divide the salmon trout purée between the scallop shells and top with a glazed scallop. Sprinkle the scallops with breadcrumbs and dot with flakes of butter. Cook in the preheated oven for 7 minutes, removing the scallops as soon as they are well browned.

Arrange on a serving plate and garnish as you wish. To keep the shells standing firm, we arranged them on a bed of coarse salt. We decorated the plate with lemon wedges, cucumber rounds and a few lettuce leaves.

Melon Sorbet with Shrimp

Sorbetto di melone con gamberetti

---

1 medium melon
juice of ½ lemon
Worcestershire sauce
8 oz uncooked small shrimp, shelled
¼ cup dry white wine
1 firm, very ripe tomato
salt and pepper
9 fresh basil leaves
3 tablespoons olive oil
½ cucumber
6 cooked green beans

SERVES 6

PREPARATION AND COOKING TIME:
ABOUT 40 MINUTES

Halve the melon and discard the seeds, then scoop all the flesh into a blender and purée for 1 minute, or a little longer, until very smooth. Transfer the purée to a bowl with the lemon juice, a few drops of Worcestershire sauce and 1½ cups water. Mix well, then leave to chill in the refrigerator.

Cook the shrimp in a little boiling salted water and the wine for about 4 minutes. Drain and leave to cool. Dip the tomato briefly in boiling water, then quickly skin it. Remove the seeds and core, cut into strips and cut these in half. Put the shrimp and tomato in a bowl and season with salt, pepper, three torn basil leaves and the olive oil. Mix gently, cover and leave to chill in the refrigerator.

Meanwhile, place the well-chilled melon purée in an ice cream maker and churn according to the instructions. When the sorbet is ready, place two or three scoops in ready-chilled bowls. Divide the shrimp and tomato salad between the bowls and decorate with basil leaves, cucumber slices and green beans. Serve immediately.

RIGHT: *Baked mussels.*

Baked Mussels

Teglia di cozze

2 lb mussels
olive oil
1 garlic clove
7 oz frozen puff pastry, thawed
10 anchovy fillets
1 egg
3 slices of white bread
a small bunch of fresh parsley
pinch of salt
flour for dusting

SERVES 4–6
PREPARATION AND COOKING TIME:
ABOUT 40 MINUTES, PLUS THAWING THE DOUGH

Preheat the oven to 400°F. Thoroughly scrub the mussels, removing the beards and any impurities; discard any that are open. Wash them and place in a shallow pan with 4 tablespoons olive oil and the garlic. Cover and set over high heat until the mussels have opened (discard any that are still closed). Remove the top shell from the mussels, leaving them on the half shell. Divide the mussels into two equal portions.

Roll out the pastry thinly on a lightly floured surface and, using a pastry cutter or a sharp knife, cut out enough teardrop shapes to cover half the mussels.

On one half of the mussels, lay first a piece of anchovy, then a pastry teardrop. Press the edges of the dough firmly on to the shells with your fingertips. Lightly beat the egg and brush over the pastry covers.

Crumble the bread and rub it through a strainer. Place the breadcrumbs in a bowl and mix in the finely chopped parsley and a pinch of salt. Cover the remaining mussels with this mixture.

Arrange the mussels in rows in a baking dish, alternating the pastry-covered and crumb-covered ones. Trickle a little olive oil over the latter, then bake in the oven for about 15 minutes. Serve the mussels piping hot, straight from the oven.

Royal Aspic

Aspic regale

---

1 small onion
1 clove
3 large carrots
1 small celery stalk
1 garlic clove
2–3 sprigs fresh parsley
salt
12 oz chicken on the bone
2½ cups prepared aspic
1 tablespoon gelatin, soaked, added to an additional
1¼ cups prepared aspic
4 eggs
12 oz potatoes
about 8 oz zucchini
5 oz cooked green beans
2 oz canned tuna in oil
2 tablespoons capers
2 anchovy fillets in oil
½ cup mayonnaise
1 teaspoon lemon juice
1 large red pimiento
8 oz ham, diced
Worcestershire sauce
1 tablespoon tomato ketchup
oil

SERVES 12

PREPARATION AND COOKING TIME: ABOUT 1½ HOURS, PLUS AT LEAST 4 HOURS REFRIGERATION

Bring about 1 quart of water with the onion (halved and pierced with the clove), 2 tablespoons diced carrot, the celery, garlic and the parsley to the boil. Salt to taste and add the chicken. Half cover the pan and simmer for about 50 minutes.

Meanwhile, hard-boil the eggs, cool under running water and shell. Peel and dice the potatoes. Cook them in salted boiling water for about 12 minutes. Drain and dry them on kitchen paper, reserving the water. Cut the zucchini into ⅛ inch slices and cook in the potato water for about 10 minutes. Drain and spread out on a plate. Slice the remaining carrots and, using the same water again, cook for about 15 minutes. Drain and dry. Cut the green beans into ¾ inch lengths. Bone and skin the chicken and cut into thin strips. Leave to cool.

Finely chop the tuna, capers and anchovies. Place them in a bowl, stir in the mayonnaise and lemon juice and use the mixture to dress the chicken. Add 3–4 tablespoons of the cooled aspic.

Brush the inside of a round 1½ quart mold with the aspic, coating it three or four times and setting it in the refrigerator after each coating.

Slice the hard-boiled eggs. Using a pastry cutter, cut six tear-drop shapes out of the pimiento. Line the mold with some of the slices of egg, slices of carrot and zucchini, cubes of potato and tear-drops of pimento. Fill the mold with layers of the remaining vegetables, the chicken mixture and the rest of the slices of egg, pouring a little aspic on top of each layer. By the time all the ingredients and aspic have been used up, the mold should be almost full. Tap the mold gently and then refrigerate for at least 4 hours or until the aspic has set completely.

Meanwhile add the soaked gelatin to the additional 1¼ cups of aspic while it is still hot and stir until the gelatin has dissolved completely. Pour the mixture into a blender and add the diced ham, a dash of Worcestershire sauce and the tomato ketchup. Process until smooth. Pour the mixture into a 9 inch round shallow container which has been greased with a little oil. Refrigerate for a couple of hours to set. Turn out onto a plate.

Submerge the mold containing the aspic in hot water for a few seconds, dry it and then turn the aspic out on to the ham. Garnish and serve.

Tasty Toast Appetizer

Fette biscottate 'golose'

---

5 oz canned tuna in oil
1 tablespoon capers in vinegar
4 anchovy fillets in oil
⅓ cup mayonnaise
8 toasted bread slices
1 oz pimiento
a little fresh parsley

SERVES 4

PREPARATION TIME: ABOUT 15 MINUTES

Drain the tuna, capers and anchovies. Roughly chop the capers and anchovies, mash the tuna and place everything in a bowl. Add the mayonnaise and stir well until all the ingredients are blended. Spread the mixture thickly over the toasted slices.

Drain, then chop the pimiento very finely, reducing it almost to a pulp, and place 1 teaspoon on each slice. Garnish with fresh parsley and serve at once.

Little Savory Turnovers

'Crescentine' di grasso

---

1 sprig fresh rosemary
2 oz mortadella sausage finely chopped
2 oz salami, finely chopped
1 egg
1 oz grated Parmesan cheese
ground nutmeg
salt and pepper
2 cups flour
½ teaspoon baking powder
butter
½ cup cold stock (or use vegetable bouillion cube)
1 egg white, lightly beaten
frying oil

SERVES 6–8

PREPARATION AND COOKING TIME:
ABOUT 1 HOUR

Chop the rosemary leaves finely and bind with the mortadella, salami, egg and grated Parmesan cheese. Season with a pinch of ground nutmeg and a little pepper.

Sift the flour, baking powder and a pinch of salt on to a board and make a well in the center. Cut 2 tablespoons of butter into small pieces and rub into the flour. Add the stock a little at a time and mix to form a soft pastry dough.

Roll the pastry out thinly and cut into 3 inch circles with a serrated pastry cutter. Brush the edges of the circles with the beaten egg white. Place a little of the prepared stuffing mixture on one half of the circles then fold over the other half of pastry. Press the edges together and seal carefully.

Heat plenty of oil in a large frying pan and fry the turnovers until golden brown on both sides. Drain and dry on paper towels. Place in a large dish and serve immediately.

Gourmet Asparagus

Asparagi di bassano alla buongustaia

2lb fresh asparagus
a few parsley leaves
4 tablespoons butter
salt and pepper
4 egg yolks

SERVES 4

PREPARATION AND COOKING TIME:
ABOUT 45 MINUTES

Wash and trim the asparagus and tie in a bundle with kitchen twine. Stand the bundle upright in a saucepan of salted boiling water (the water should come about halfway up the asparagus). Simmer over a moderate heat for about 15 minutes, or a little longer if the asparagus are very thick.

Drain thoroughly, discard the twine and spread the asparagus out to dry on paper towels. Arrange in warmed asparagus dishes and garnish with a few leaves of parsley.

Melt the butter, season with salt and pepper and pour into each dish. Place 1 egg yolk in the center of the dish containing the melted butter and serve immediately. Each person should blend the butter and egg yolk to form a delicate sauce, and use this as a dip for the asparagus.

Sturgeon Cornets

'Cornetti' di storione

---

1 egg
a little fresh parsley
1 anchovy fillet in oil
2 green olives, pitted
1 tablespoon mayonnaise
salt and pepper
8 very thin slices smoked sturgeon
toasted wholewheat bread

SERVES 4

PREPARATION AND COOKING TIME:
ABOUT 30 MINUTES

Hard-boil the egg, then cool under cold running water. Shell and finely chop it, then put in a bowl. Finely chop a little parsley together with the drained anchovy fillet and the olives, and add to the egg. Add the mayonnaise and mix to a smooth paste.

Taste and adjust the seasoning, then spread the mixture on one side of each fish slice. Roll the slice into a funnel shape, sealing in the filling. When all the cornets are ready, fan them out on a round serving dish and garnish to taste.

Serve with slices of warm toasted wholemeal bread.

Salmon and Crab Rolls

Involtini di salmone al granchio

---

6 oz smoked salmon
6 oz crabmeat
Worcestershire sauce
1/3 cup mayonnaise
1 tablespoon mustard
Tabasco sauce
a little gelatin dissolved in 1/2 cup warm water
celery leaves
1 pimiento
2 slices lemon

SERVES 6

PREPARATION TIME: ABOUT 40 MINUTES

Divide the smoked salmon into 18 slices and spread them out on a large sheet of foil. Drain and squeeze the crabmeat well, then put it in a bowl, removing any filaments or bits of cartilage. Flavor with a generous dash of Worcestershire sauce, the mayonnaise, mustard and 2 or 3 drops of Tabasco. Stir thoroughly, then place some of the mixture on one edge of each slice of salmon and roll the salmon up tightly.

Arrange the rolls neatly on a serving dish and brush them all two or three times with the gelatin, refrigerating between applications to help the gelatin to set. Garnish the dish with celery leaves, pimiento and lemon slices.

Cover with plastic wrap and keep in the refrigerator until you are ready to serve it.

Stuffed Grapefruit

Pompelmi ripieni

---

3 medium grapefruit
2 kiwi fruit
2 oz Emmental cheese
2 thick slices ham
1/3 cup mayonnaise
Worcestershire sauce
2 tablespoons mustard

SERVES 6

PREPARATION TIME: ABOUT 40 MINUTES

Using a short, sharp knife, cut the grapefruit into halves. Separate them, scoop out the pulp and put it in a bowl, taking care not to include any pith. Peel the kiwi fruit, halve them lengthwise and slice thinly. Cut the Emmental cheese into matchsticks and the ham into short strips.

Pour off the juice that has run out of the grapefruit and mix the flesh with the kiwi fruit, cheese and ham. Put the mayonnaise in a bowl, flavor it with a dash of Worcestershire sauce and the mustard, and stir into the prepared mixture.

Fill the grapefruit halves with the mixture, and serve at once.

Egg Surprise

Sorpresa d'uova

---

butter
olive oil
1 small onion, finely sliced
flour
1 cup good meat stock
tomato paste
salt and pepper
4 eggs
1 thick slice ham

SERVES 4

PREPARATION AND COOKING TIME:
ABOUT 35 MINUTES

Heat a knob of butter and a tablespoon of olive oil in a small saucepan and lightly fry the onion until transparent. Sprinkle with flour and add the boiling stock in which half a teaspoon of tomato paste has been dissolved. Bring to the boil, stirring constantly. Lower the heat and simmer for 3–4 minutes. Purée and return to the pan. Check and adjust the seasoning to taste.

Hard-boil the eggs, cool under cold running water, shell them and cut in half lengthwise. Arrange on a plate, curved side up, and coat with the prepared sauce. Garnish each piece of egg with a diamond of ham and serve warm.

RIGHT: *Stuffed grapefruit* (top);
Salmon and crab rolls (bottom).

Terrine of Sole

Terrina da sogliole

10 oz sole fillets
2 egg whites
salt
a pinch of paprika
1¼ cups whipping cream
2 oz pistachios, shelled and skinned
a small bunch of watercress
12 slices smoked salmon, about 7 oz
butter for greasing
toasted white bread, for serving

SERVES 4

PREPARATION AND COOKING TIME:
ABOUT 1 HOUR 20 MINUTES

Wash and dry the sole fillets. Chop finely and rub through a coarse strainer to make a very smooth purée.

Place the purée in a bowl and, using a wooden spoon, gradually mix in the egg whites, a little at a time, adding salt to taste and a pinch of paprika. Stand the bowl in a bowl of ice and continue to work the purée (you can use an electric beater), adding the cream in a steady stream until the mixture is smooth and aerated.

Chop the pistachios. Trim, wash and chop the watercress, then mix it and the pistachios into the fish mixture. Generously butter an ovenproof 1 quart pâté or loaf pan, then line it with the smoked salmon slices, leaving the ends overhanging. Spoon in the sole mixture and level the surface. Fold the smoked salmon over the top.

Butter a sheet of foil and cover the pan with it, sealing the edges tightly. Stand the pan in a water bath half-filled with boiling water and bake in the oven at 375°F for 30 minutes. Remove and leave to stand for 10 minutes before unmolding it.

It can be served hot or cold. Either way, drizzle over some olive oil and serve with toast.

LEFT: *Terrine of sole.*

Cauliflower à la Grecque

Cavolfiore del Pireo

olive oil
juice of 2 large lemons
2 bay leaves
2 garlic cloves
3–4 black peppercorns
salt and pepper
1½ lb cauliflower

SERVES 4–6

PREPARATION AND COOKING TIME:
ABOUT 1 HOUR, PLUS CHILLING

Bring about 1 quart of cold water to the boil, and add ½ cup of olive oil, the lemon juice, bay leaves, halved garlic cloves, peppercorns and salt.

Meanwhile, wash the cauliflower and separate it into florets without breaking them. Cook in the boiling liquid, covered, and over low heat, for about 12 minutes.

Remove the pan from the heat and, keeping it covered, let the florets cool. Only at this point remove the garlic and peppercorns (leave the bay leaves), then pour the preparation into a salad bowl. Cover with plastic wrap and keep in the refrigerator for at least 1½ hours before serving. This dish keeps well in the refrigerator for up to a week.

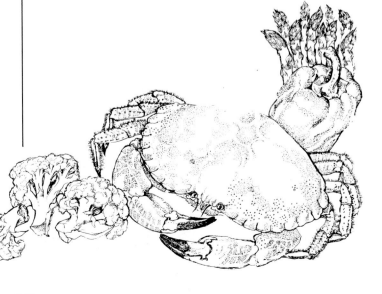

Fish Mousses

Spumette di pesce

---

8 oz small squid
1 medium onion
2 tablespoons olive oil
⅔ cup tomato passata (sieved tomatoes)
salt and pepper
1 lb sole fillets, roughly chopped
2 eggs
scant ⅔ cup whipping cream
butter for greasing

SERVES 6

PREPARATION AND COOKING TIME:
ABOUT 45 MINUTES

Preheat the oven to 400°F. Clean the squid, rinse them under cold running water, drain and dry them with kitchen paper. Then finely dice the body sacs.

Slice the onion very thinly, then sweat in a small saucepan with the olive oil. Add the diced squid and cook for 3–4 minutes, then add the tomato passata. Season with salt and pepper and cook the squid, uncovered, for about 15 minutes.

Meanwhile, purée the sole in a food processor or blender. Transfer to a bowl and break in the eggs. Using a wooden spoon, mix the purée, adding the cream to soften it. Season to taste and mix thoroughly.

Grease six ramekins or small molds with butter and place a tablespoon or two of sole mixture in each, spreading it out and making a hollow in the center of each one with the back of a spoon.

Fill these small cavities with the prepared squid mixture, then fill up the ramekins with the remaining sole purée. Finally, smooth over the surface, then stand the ramekins in a Pyrex dish or on a baking sheet and cook in the oven for about 20 minutes.

Remove the fish mousses from the oven as soon as they are cooked, and leave them to rest for about 5 minutes. Finally, unmold them onto a large, warmed plate. Decorate the fish mousses if you wish with mâche and radish slices.

Creamed Smoked Salmon Tartlets

Tartellette all crema d'uovo e salmone

2 oz smoked salmon
a small bunch of fresh parsley
5 eggs
⅔ cup whipping cream
tomato ketchup

1¾ cups all-purpose flour, plus extra for dusting
4 oz butter, diced and softened, plus extra for greasing
1 egg
paprika

SERVES 4–6

PREPARATION AND COOKING TIME:
ABOUT 1½ HOURS

To make the pastry, sift the flour onto a work surface, make a well in the center and put in a pinch of salt and the softened butter. Work quickly until the ingredients are just amalgamated, then make a well again and put the egg and 3 tablespoons of cold water into the center. Add a pinch of paprika, then work quickly into a smooth dough. Roll it into a ball, cover with plastic wrap and leave to rest in the refrigerator for about 30 minutes.

Meanwhile, preheat the oven to 400°F. Butter and flour sixteen 2 inch round tartlet pans with fluted edges. Roll out the dough to a thickness of ⅛ inch, prick with a fork then, using a plain round 2½ inch pastry cutter, cut out 16 circles (re-roll and cut the trimmings). Line the tartlet pans with the dough circles, pressing them in firmly at the edges. Add foil and beans, place all the pans on a baking sheet and bake blind in the oven for 20 minutes.

Meanwhile, chop the smoked salmon and separately chop the parsley. In a saucepan, beat the eggs, stir in the cream and season with salt. Place the saucepan either over another saucepan of simmering water on the heat or over very low heat and, stirring continuously with a wire whisk, beat the eggs until almost set and very creamy. Take the pan off the heat and mix in the chopped smoked salmon and parsley.

Take the tartlets out of the oven, unmold them and fill with the salmon cream. Decorate with a drop of ketchup in the center of each one. If you wish, garnish with parsley leaves, place the tartlets on a serving dish and serve tepid, so that the pastry does not become too soggy.

Shrimp in Aspic

Aspic di gamberetti

12 oz fresh uncooked small shrimp
lemon juice
1 ½ tablespoons of powdered gelatin
a small bunch of parsley
salt and pepper
pieces of red pimiento in vinegar
4 hard-boiled egg yolks
⅓ cup mayonnaise
Worcestershire sauce

SERVES 6

PREPARATION AND COOKING TIME:
ABOUT 40 MINUTES, PLUS SETTING

Shell the shrimp and cook in a pan of salted water, acidulated with a little lemon juice. Drain and leave to cool. Meanwhile, prepare the gelatin according to the instructions on the packet. Gently heat it and spoon a little into the bottom of six ramekins then, using a toothpick, arrange a shrimp, a parsley twig and a small triangle of red pimiento in each ramekin.

Rub the egg yolks through a strainer into a bowl. Add the mayonnaise and 4 drops of Worcestershire sauce and mix well.

Chop all the remaining shrimp and mix them into the egg mixture. Wash and finely chop the remaining parsley leaves and add to the mixture, with a pinch of salt and pepper. Put the mixture into a piping bag and pipe it into the ramekins.

Fill the ramekins almost to the top with the remaining gelatin and place in the refrigerator for at least 6 hours before serving. Remove from the refrigerator, unmold the aspics onto a plate and decorate as you wish.

Crabmeat Salad

Insalata di polpa di granchio

7 oz mixed salad leaves: e.g. lettuce heart, escarole,
radicchio, mâche
11 oz canned crabmeat
2 eggs
a small bunch of parsley, finely chopped
½ teaspoon capers
salt and pepper
juice of 1 lemon, strained
extra virgin olive oil
nutmeg

SERVES 6

PREPARATION AND COOKING TIME:
ABOUT 20 MINUTES

Trim and wash the salad leaves, dry well and place in a salad bowl. Flake the crabmeat and remove any cartilage. Arrange the crabmeat on the salad leaves.

Place the eggs in a pan of cold water, bring to the boil and hard-boil them for 8 minutes. Keep the whites for another use and rub the yolks through a strainer. Sprinkle them over the salad, together with the chopped parsley and the well-drained capers.

Now prepare the dressing. In a bowl, mix ½ teaspoon salt with the lemon juice, then incorporate about 6 tablespoons olive oil. Season with pepper and a pinch of nutmeg and pour the dressing over the salad. Toss just before serving.

You could also serve this starter on individual plates: arrange the crabmeat in the center and surround it with the salad leaves.

Egg with Tuna and Peas

Uova al tonno e piselli

---

1 ¼ cups frozen young peas
1 small onion
olive oil
about 6 oz canned tuna fish
4 eggs
salt and pepper

SERVES 4

PREPARATION AND COOKING TIME:
ABOUT 25 MINUTES

Boil the peas, still frozen, in salted water for 5 minutes, then drain them. Peel and finely slice the onion, then fry in 2 tablespoons of olive oil over low heat until transparent. Add the peas and leave. Drain the tuna of oil and mash it coarsely. Add it to the peas and leave over the heat for 7–8 minutes.

Meanwhile heat 2 tablespoons of olive oil in a large frying pan and break in the eggs, which should be at room temperature, taking care not to break the yolks. Add a little salt and pepper, and turn the heat down low. Cook until the whites are opaque. Remove the eggs one at a time with a spatula and drain off any excess oil.

Place each egg on a warm plate and surround with the tuna and pea mixture. Serve at once.

Tuna Delight

Delizia di tonno

---

an envelope of gelatin to make 2½ cups
2 tablespoons lemon juice
1 egg
12 oz canned tuna
1½ tablespoons capers
4 anchovy fillets in oil
Worcestershire sauce
a little oil
1 red pepper, cut into strips
a few leaves of frisée

SERVES 6

PREPARATION AND COOKING TIME:
ABOUT 1 HOUR

Dissolve the gelatin in 2 cups of hot water and add the lemon juice. Hard-boil the egg, shell and chop it and blend with the well-drained tuna, the drained capers, the anchovy fillets, a dash of Worcestershire sauce and the gelatin. Blend gently for a couple of minutes.

Oil a 1 quart fluted mold and pour in the tuna mixture. Place the mold in the refrigerator and allow the mixture to set. Turn out the mold, slice it and arrange on a large plate.

Garnish with strips of red pepper and sprigs of frisée.

Three-flavored Pie

Torta ai tre gusti

---

8 oz frozen puff pastry
4 tablespoons butter
4 oz frisée, boiled and drained
8 oz spinach, boiled and drained
1 medium onion
olive oil
½ chicken or vegetable bouillion cube
6 oz very fresh ricotta cheese
1 thick slice ham, finely chopped
3 eggs
salt and pepper
¼ cup grated Parmesan cheese
nutmeg
1 tablespoon breadcrumbs

SERVES 8
PREPARATION AND COOKING TIME:
ABOUT 1 HOUR, PLUS ANY DEFROSTING TIME

Thaw the pastry if necessary. Butter a 10 inch pie dish. Finely chop the frisée and spinach and put in a bowl. Finely chop the onion and sauté in 2 tablespoons of the butter and the olive oil, taking care not to let it brown. Crumble in the bouillion cube and keep the pan over the heat until it has dissolved, then combine the onion with the frisée and spinach, mixing thoroughly.

Rub the ricotta through a strainer, letting it fall on to the mixture in the bowl, then add the ham. Beat the eggs with a pinch of salt and a little freshly ground pepper, the Parmesan cheese and a little grated nutmeg. Pour this into the bowl with the other ingredients, stirring vigorously after the addition of each new ingredient until smooth. Taste and adjust the seasoning.

Preheat the oven to 375°F. Roll out the pastry to a thickness of about ⅛ inch, then line the pie dish and trim the edges. Prick the pastry with a fork and sprinkle with breadcrumbs. Spread the filling mixture evenly in the dish, then tap the dish lightly to eliminate air bubbles. Decorate the top with the pastry trimmings and bake for about 30 minutes in the bottom of the oven. Serve piping hot.

Spicy Eggs

Uova piccante

---

6 eggs
6 oz canned tuna in oil
a handful of parsley
2 tablespoons capers in oil
1 gherkin
4 anchovy fillets in oil
⅓ cup thick mayonnaise
1 tablespoon mustard
Worcestershire sauce
6 stuffed olives
1 head of frisée
salt and pepper
white wine vinegar
olive oil

SERVES 4–6
PREPARATION AND COOKING TIME:
ABOUT 40 MINUTES

Hard-boil the eggs and cool thoroughly under running water. Shell and halve the eggs lengthwise. Remove the yolks and rub them through a strainer into a bowl. Drain the oil from the tuna, purée it and add to the egg yolks. Finely chop the parsley with the capers, gherkin and anchovy fillets and add the mixture to the other ingredients. Mix with the mayonnaise, mustard and a generous dash of Worcestershire sauce to a smooth paste. Taste and adjust the seasoning.

Put the mixture into a piping bag with a star tip and fill the 12 egg halves. Arrange on a serving dish. Cut the olives in half and press them into the filling. Place the frisée leaves in the center of the dish, seasoned simply with salt, pepper, vinegar and olive oil and serve at once.

RIGHT: *Three-flavored pie* (top);
Spicy eggs (bottom).

32

Chicken and Tuna Pâté

Pâté di pollo e tonno

---

1 lb chicken breast
olive oil
1 small onion, finely chopped
dry white wine
salt and pepper
5 oz canned tuna in oil
½ tablespoon capers, soaked
and drained
7 oz butter, softened
anchovy paste
arugula leaves, to accompany
FOR THE SAUCE
¼ cup extra virgin olive oil
capers
fresh basil

SERVES 10

PREPARATION AND COOKING TIME:
ABOUT 1 HOUR, PLUS CHILLING

Remove the chicken skin and bones, and trim the fillets. Cut into bite-sized pieces and sauté in 3 tablespoons olive oil, together with the chopped onion. Moisten with quarter of a glass of wine and season with salt and pepper. When the wine has evaporated, add the drained tuna and the soaked capers. Cook for a further 5–6 minutes, then take off the heat and leave to cool.

Purée the mixture very finely in a food processor and transfer to a bowl. Mix in the softened butter and half a teaspoon of anchovy paste, beating the mixture with a small whisk until it is light and fluffy. Correct the seasoning, then pour the mixture on to a sheet of baking parchment and form it into a salami shape. Roll it in the parchment and chill in the refrigerator for at least 3 hours.

To serve, remove the parchment and cut the pâté into even slices. Arrange these on a bed of arugula. Make a sauce by whisking together the olive oil with a tablespoon of capers and about 10 basil leaves, torn and chopped, and dress the pâté with this. Garnish the serving platter with rounds of radish and hard-boiled egg.

Filled Focaccia

Focaccia farcita

---

5 oz zucchini

olive oil

1½ lb bread dough

7 oz mozzarella cheese, sliced

salt and pepper

fresh rosemary

coarse salt

5 oz tomatoes

SERVES 6–8

PREPARATION AND COOKING TIME:
ABOUT 40 MINUTES, PLUS RISING TIME

Trim the zucchini and cut into thin slices. Season with salt and moisten with a trickle of olive oil, then brown under a hot broiler.

Generously oil a round 12 inch pizza pan. Lightly roll out the dough without compressing it too much, and cover the pizza pan with about half the dough. Arrange the sliced zucchini and mozzarella on top. Season with salt and pepper, then cover with the remaining dough, pressing the edges together to seal the two pieces. Brush the top of the focaccia with olive oil and sprinkle with rosemary leaves and a pinch of coarse salt, then arrange the tomato slices around the edge. Leave the focaccia to rise in a warm place for about 45 minutes.

Preheat the oven to 475°F, then bake the focaccia for 20–25 minutes or until it is puffed and brown. Sprinkle with more fresh rosemary. Serve hot.

Chicken and Vegetables in Aspic

Aspic di pollo e verdure

---

5 tablespoons of powdered aspic
1 egg
1 lb chicken breast
olive oil
salt and pepper
8 oz carrots
1 lb zucchini
8 oz red pepper
5 oz celery
4 oz sliced cooked ham

SERVES 12
PREPARATION AND COOKING TIME:
ABOUT 1 HOUR, PLUS CHILLING

Dissolve the aspic according to the instructions on the packet, using the given amount of water, then leave to cool. Hard-boil the egg by placing it in cold water, bringing it to the boil, and cooking for precisely 10 minutes from the time the water boils. Cool and shell. Remove the chicken skin and bones and trim the fillets. Flatten with a meat mallet and sauté in 2 tablespoons of hot olive oil. Season the chicken with salt and pepper and cut into thin strips.

Peel and trim the carrots and slice them thinly lengthways, using a mandoline, then cut into thin strips. Do the same with the zucchini. Remove the stem, core, seeds and membrane from the pepper and cut the flesh into thin strips. Trim the celery and slice thinly. Cut out four diamond shapes from the ham to use as decoration, and cut the rest into thin strips.

When the aspic is cold enough to coat the back of a spoon, pour a ladleful into 9 inch jelly mold. Decorate the bottom with quarters of hard-boiled egg, arranging them like a rosette, and place the ham diamonds between them. Cover with a little more aspic, then place the mold in the refrigerator to set. As soon as the aspic has set, layer half the zucchini, carrots, ham, pepper, celery and chicken into the mold, then continue to make layers, arranging them in the same order as before, ending with a layer of chicken. Level this well, and pour in the remaining aspic until all the layers are covered.

Chill in the refrigerator at least 4 hours, Unmold on to a plate (this is easiest if you hold the mold briefly over boiling water). Serve immediately.

LEFT: *Stuffed and glazed eggs* (top);
Chicken and vegetables in aspic (bottom).

Stuffed and Glazed Eggs

Uova farcite e glassate

---

8 eggs
4 oz zucchini
1 small carrot
3 gherkins
fresh parsley
½ cup mayonnaise, plus ½ tablespoon salt
1½ oz ricotta cheese
2 oz cooked ham, diced

FOR THE GLAZE
1 tablespoon gelatin
1 tablespoon flour
1½ tablespoons butter
scant 1 cup hot milk
1½ oz spinach, cooked and squeezed dry
¼ cup whipping cream

SERVES 8
PREPARATION AND COOKING TIME:
ABOUT 1 HOUR, PLUS CHILLING

Hard-boil the eggs, cool under running water and drain. Halve four of the eggs lengthways and scoop out the yolks into a bowl. Cut the zucchini, carrot and gherkins into tiny dice and mix them with the egg yolks, together with a handful of finely chopped parsley and the mayonnaise. Mix to blend thoroughly, season with salt and fill the egg whites with the mixture. Arrange on a plate, cover with plastic wrap and place in the refrigerator.

Halve the four remaining eggs lengthways, scoop out the yolks and rub through a strainer set over a bowl. Add the ricotta, ham, ½ tablespoon of mayonnaise and a pinch of salt. Fill the egg whites, place on a wire rack and put in the refrigerator.

Soften the gelatin in a little cold water. Meanwhile, make a roux by mixing the flour and butter over medium heat, then pour on the hot milk in a thin stream. Place the pan over the heat and simmer the sauce for 5 minutes, stirring continuously. Chop the spinach in a food processor, then rub through a strainer, and add it and the gelatin to the sauce, which should be perfectly smooth. Stir in the cream. Leave to cool until it coats the back of a spoon.

Take the ricotta-stuffed eggs out of the refrigerator, still on the wire rack, and place the rack over a tray. Coat the eggs repeatedly with the glaze (the tray will catch the excess glaze), then return them to the refrigerator (still on the rack) and leave for at least 1 hour. Arrange on a serving plate and garnish.

Pink Grapefruit Salad

Insalata di polpelmo rosa

———

12 oz asparagus
4 oz shrimp, shelled
2 pink grapefruit
4 oz mâche
extra virgin olive oil
salt and pepper

SERVES 4

PREPARATION TIME: ABOUT 30 MINUTES

Trim the asparagus, discarding the woody part of the stalks. Wash thoroughly, then tie in a bundle with kitchen twine, stand upright in a saucepan and cook until tender in two fingers of boiling, salted water. In a separate pan, cook the shrimp. Halve the grapefruit horizontally and scoop out the flesh. Discard the seeds and the white pith, then dice finely (do all this over a bowl, so as to catch all the grapefruit juice).

Trim the mâche, cutting off the roots, and wash thoroughly in several changes of water. Drain and arrange in the grapefruit shells. Mix the diced grapefruit pulp with the shrimp and asparagus (use only the tips) and pile the mixture into the shells. Thoroughly whisk 8 tablespoons of olive oil into the grapefruit juice until emulsified. Season with a pinch of salt and pepper. Place the filled grapefruit on individual serving plates and serve the dressing separately in a bowl for everyone to help themselves.

Lettuce "Cigars"

'Sigari' di lattuga

———

1 fresh leafy lettuce
5 oz fresh ricotta cheese
2 oz Gorgonzola cheese
1 tablespoon juniper-flavored
grappa or brandy
salt and pepper
dried tarragon

MAKES 24 "CIGARS"

PREPARATION TIME: ABOUT 25 MINUTES

Pull out the leaves of the heart of the lettuce and wash and dry them gently. Using a sharp knife, remove the central stalks and divide each leaf in half.

Drain and mash the ricotta and place it in a bowl. Finely dice the Gorgonzola cheese and beat it with the ricotta to form a smooth creamy mixture. Stir in the *grappa*, a pinch of salt and pepper and a generous pinch of tarragon.

Blend thoroughly, then place a teaspoon of the mixture on each piece of lettuce. Fold up to form cigar-shaped rolls, making sure that the filling does not ooze out.

Arrange the "cigars" around the edge of a plate and garnish the center as desired. This dish makes an excellent light hors d'oeuvre, or it can be served with aperitifs before the meal.

Smoked Salmon with Tuna

Salmone tonnata

———

10 capers
10 gherkins
4 oz canned tuna in oil
2 tablespoons mayonnaise
¼ teaspoon mustard
6 large slices smoked salmon
2 slices wholewheat bread
anchovy paste
a little white wine vinegar
Worcestershire sauce
lettuce leaves for garnish

SERVES 6

PREPARATION AND COOKING TIME:
ABOUT 40 MINUTES

Drain the capers and gherkins thoroughly and chop them finely, together with the well-drained tuna. Add 1 tablespoon of mayonnaise and the mustard and mix thoroughly. Spread this on the salmon slices, taking care not to go over the edges. Using the blade of a knife, roll up the salmon into six roulades and put them in the warmest part of the refrigerator for a few minutes.

Meanwhile, toast the bread and cut each slice into three fingers. Squeeze about 1¼ inches anchovy paste into a bowl and add 2 drops of vinegar, a dash of Worcestershire sauce and the remaining mayonnaise. Spread on one side only of the toast fingers. Press a smoked salmon roulade firmly onto each piece of toast. Arrange on a dish and serve immediately.

Savoy Cabbage with Smoked Salmon

Antipasto pazzerello

---

*2 leaves savoy cabbage
4 oz smoked salmon
3 oz Fiorello cheese
juice of ½ lemon
1 tablespoon tomato ketchup
1 tablespoon mustard
salt and pepper
Worcestershire sauce
a little stock (or use vegetable bouillion cube)*

SERVES 4
PREPARATION TIME: ABOUT 30 MINUTES

Cut the cabbage and salmon into long strips. To prepare the dressing, pour the Fiorello cheese into a bowl and whisk until slightly stiff. Add the lemon juice, the tomato ketchup and the mustard. Blend carefully and season with a pinch of salt and pepper and a generous splash of Worcestershire sauce. Stir in 2 tablespoons of stock and blend until smooth and creamy.

Arrange the strips of salmon and cabbage on a serving dish and dress with the sauce at the table. This is an unusual combination of ingredients, but the result is delicious and the dressing enhances the flavor of both the cabbage and the salmon.

Savory Canapés

Tartine dolcipiccanti

---

*4 tablespoons butter, cut into small pieces
salt and pepper
4 oz soft Gorgonzola cheese
1 teaspoon lemon juice
1 tablespoon chopped parsley
4 slices white bread
1 red pimiento
1 lettuce leaf, cut into strips*

SERVES 4
PREPARATION TIME: ABOUT 30 MINUTES

Beat the butter with a pinch of salt and pepper until creamy. Add the sieved and mashed Gorgonzola cheese and a teaspoon of lemon juice. Stir vigorously for a few minutes and then blend in the chopped parsley. Check and adjust the seasoning according to taste.

Spread the mixture over the slices of bread. Cut each slice in half diagonally to form two triangles and arrange on a plate. Cut the pimiento into eight small strips and use to decorate the canapés. Garnish the center of the plate with the strips of lettuce and serve immediately.

Soups

Italian soups can be light meals in themselves, including
pasta, rice, eggs, meat, fish and vegetables, or they can be
less substantial versions served as an alternative to the
pasta course. Two of the best-known types of soup
featured here are fish soups, a speciality of the Adriatic
coast, and variations on minestrone, the rich vegetable
soup with dried beans or pasta.

Rich Fish Soup

Zuppa di pesce, ricca

———

6½ lb mixed fish (scorpion fish, gurnard, mullet, John
Dory and skate)
1 lb squid and small octopus
1 lb shrimp
2½ cups dry white wine
salt
olive oil
3 garlic cloves
6 anchovy fillets
1 small piece red chilli pepper
2 bunches of parsley
6 basil leaves
1 lb ripe tomatoes,
chopped and seeded
12 mussels
6 razor-shell clams
oregano
6 slices toast

SERVES 6

PREPARATION AND COOKING TIME:
ABOUT 2 HOURS

Gut and wash the fish thoroughly, cut off the heads
and fillet the larger ones. Cut the others into
similar-sized pieces, wash again and leave to drain.
Clean the squid and octopus, removing the heads, the
hard beaks and the viscera, then wash several times in
plenty of water. Wash the shrimp.

Heat the white wine, 1 quart of water and all the
fish heads and bones in a large saucepan. Salt lightly
and simmer over very low heat for about 1 hour.

Meanwhile, brown the crushed garlic cloves in ½
cup of olive oil in a small saucepan, and mash the
anchovy fillets in the oil. Add the shrimp, salt lightly,
pepper and leave to brown for about 10 minutes,
turning them often. Pour the mixture into the pan
containing the fish heads, add the pieces of chilli
pepper and continue to cook over very low heat.

Wash the parsley and basil and chop them finely.
Heat about ½ cup of oil in a very large saucepan. As
soon as it is hot add the puréed tomatoes, salt lightly
and cook until the sauce is thick. Place the squid and
octopus in the pan and, after about 20 minutes, add
the fish. Cover and cook over high heat without
stirring.

Strain the prepared stock through a fine cloth,
discarding the heads; if you wish you can keep the
shrimp and add the shelled meat to the soup. Pour

the stock into the pan containing the fish and cook for
another 10 minutes. Five minutes before removing
the soup from the heat, add the washed mussels and
razor-shell clams and season with the mixture of
chopped parsley and basil and a pinch of oregano.
Serve the soup with slices of toast.

Baked Fish Soup

Zuppa di pesce, in forno

———

4½ lb mixed fish (red mullet, skate, shark, John Dory,
gurnard and hake)
5–6 sprigs of parsley
1 medium onion
2 bay leaves
1 celery heart and a few leaves
2 garlic cloves
1 lb ripe tomatoes
olive oil
salt and pepper
⅔ cup dry white wine
4 slices bread

SERVES 4

PREPARATION AND COOKING TIME:
ABOUT 1½ HOURS

Gut and wash the fish; leave the smaller ones whole
and cut the others into pieces, removing as many
of the bones as possible and cutting off the heads.
Place the heads in a saucepan with the bones and
scraps, cover them with water, salt lightly, add a sprig
of parsley, a quarter of the onion cut in slices and a
bay leaf. Put the saucepan on the heat and allow the
stock to simmer for about 30 minutes, covered.

Preheat the oven to 400°F. In an ovenproof dish
with a lid, place the rest of the sliced onion, the celery
heart, the rest of the finely chopped parsley sprigs, a
whole garlic clove, a bay leaf and the chopped and
puréed tomatoes. Arrange the fish on top of the
vegetables, pour in ½ cup of olive oil, salt and pepper
lightly and then moisten with the white wine and the
fish stock strained carefully through a fine cloth.
Cover the dish and bake for about 30 minutes.

Toast the bread in the oven; when golden brown
rub the slices with the remaining garlic clove and
place them in four soup plates. Pour over the soup,
sprinkle each portion with a few finely chopped
celery leaves and a few drops of olive oil, then serve.

RIGHT: *Shellfish soup* (top left, recipe on page 44); *Fish soup
with anchovy* (center left, recipe on page 44); *Rich fish soup* (top
right); *Baked fish soup* (bottom right).

Shellfish Soup

Zuppa di molluschi

4½ lb mixed shellfish (mussels, clams, razor-shell clams
and cherry stone clams)
8 slices bread
olive oil
3 garlic cloves
a small piece red chilli pepper
2 tablespoons tomato sauce
3 cups good fish stock
a few celery leaves

SERVES 4

PREPARATION AND COOKING TIME:
ABOUT 40 MINUTES, PLUS 2 HOURS SOAKING

Scrape the shells of the shellfish, holding them under cold running water, place them all in a large bowl, cover with cold water and leave them undisturbed for about 2 hours. Then leave them to drain for a while to remove any sand.

Fry the slices of bread on both sides in ½ cup of oil; while still hot brush them with a large halved garlic clove and arrange them in four soup bowls. Fry the remaining large lightly crushed garlic cloves and the chilli pepper in oil until browned, then discard them. Place the shellfish in the pan, cover and keep on the heat until all the shells have opened. Remove them from the pan one by one, detaching one half-shell and placing the other one containing the mussel or clam in a clean saucepan.

Strain through 2 layers of cheesecloth the liquid which the shellfish gave out during cooking and add it to the saucepan. Add 2 tablespoons of ready-made tomato sauce blended with the hot fish stock, shake the saucepan slightly and keep it on the heat for a few moments, then pour the soup over the bread slices. Sprinkle each portion with chopped celery leaves and a few drops of olive oil. Serve immediately.

Fish Soup with Anchovy

Zuppa 'marechiaro'

---

4 small striped mullet
4 small scorpion fish
12 oz cleaned skate
8 crayfish
12 cleaned baby cuttlefish
3 garlic cloves
4 anchovy fillets
olive oil
1 small onion
1 carrot
a few sprigs of parsley
1 lb ripe tomatoes
salt and pepper
1 bay leaf
white wine
¾ cup good fish stock
4 slices bread

SERVES 4

PREPARATION AND COOKING TIME:
ABOUT 1½ HOURS

Clean and scale the mullet and scorpion fish, cut off the fins, then wash and drain them well.

Chop the skate and wash the crayfish and cuttlefish. Slightly crush 2 large garlic cloves and place them in a large saucepan with the anchovy fillets and ½ cup of oil. Fry gently and mash the anchovies. Discard the garlic and add the onion and carrot, finely chopped with a sprig of parsley; soften for a few minutes, then add the cuttlefish and cook for about 10 minutes.

Meanwhile, peel and purée the tomatoes and add them to the pan. Season with salt, pepper, and a small bay leaf. Simmer for about 20 minutes with the pan covered, then add the mullet, the scorpion fish and the pieces of skate in a single layer. Moisten with the white wine and pour in the fish stock.

Shake the saucepan gently and cook for 15 minutes, then add the crayfish and keep on the heat for a further 5 minutes before serving.

Rice, Potato and Mushroom Soup

Minestra di riso, patate e funghi

---

1 oz dried cep mushroom caps (or porcini)
1½ quarts light vegetable stock
1 medium onion
1 garlic clove
1 celery stalk
4 tablespoons butter
olive oil
14 oz potatoes
½ cup rice
¼ cup grated Parmesan cheese
ground nutmeg
a little chopped parsley

SERVES 4–6
PREPARATION AND COOKING TIME:
ABOUT 2 HOURS INCLUDING SOAKING

Soak the dried mushrooms in warm water for about 1 hour. Drain them well and slice thinly. Heat the stock. Finely chop the onion with the garlic and celery. Place the mixture in a saucepan, add half the butter and 2 tablespoons of olive oil, then sauté without browning, stirring occasionally.

Peel the potatoes, wash, and cut them into cubes of about ¾ inch. Add them to the lightly fried mixture together with the mushroom slices and leave for a few moments, then pour in the hot stock. Stir and slowly bring to the boil, then reduce the heat, cover the pan and simmer for 15 minutes.

Mash a few of the potato cubes, pressing them with a wooden spoon against the sides of the pan, then add the rice to the boiling soup, stirring with a wooden spoon. Cook over a rather high heat until the rice is *al dente*. Remove the pan from the heat and stir in the rest of the butter, cut into small pieces with the Parmesan cheese and the ground nutmeg. If you like, sprinkle the soup with chopped parsley.

Tapioca and Egg Soup

Pavese di tapioca

---

6 tablespoons butter
8 slices white bread, 1 day old
1 quart good meat stock
4 oz tapioca
4 eggs
¼ cup grated Parmesan cheese
a little chopped parsley

SERVES 4
PREPARATION AND COOKING TIME: 30 MINUTES

In each of two separate frying pans melt 2 tablespoons of butter. Fry the bread slices until they are golden brown, then place them in four soup plates. Keep them warm in the oven. Heat the stock in a saucepan and gradually bring to the boil. As soon as it starts boiling, sprinkle in the tapioca and whisk. Simmer gently for about 10 minutes, stirring occasionally.

Meanwhile heat the rest of the butter in the second frying pan. When it has melted, break the eggs into the pan and fry over low heat so that the white cooks but does not harden. Cut the eggs out with a 4 inch pastry cutter and place them on top of the bread. Sprinkle the Parmesan cheese over the eggs and pour in the boiling tapioca soup. Garnish with a little parsley and serve.

Farmhouse Soup with Egg

Zuppa contadina all'uovo

2 vegetable bouillion cubes
4 oz butter
4 slices white bread
4 very fresh eggs
½ cup grated Parmesan cheese

SERVES 4

PREPARATION AND COOKING TIME:
ABOUT 20 MINUTES

Heat about 1 quart of water in a saucepan, dissolve the bouillion cubes and bring to the boil. Melt half the butter in a large frying pan and fry the bread lightly browning on both sides. Place on a baking tray or plate and keep hot.

As soon as the stock begins to boil, reheat the frying pan in which the bread was fried and melt the remaining butter. When it is bubbling hot, break in the eggs, which have been kept at room temperature until this point, very carefully so as not to break the yolks, and fry. Do not let the whites become brown and dry. Cook until the yolks are done on the outside but still almost raw inside.

Place a slice of fried bread in each soup plate and sprinkle with a tablespoon of grated Parmesan cheese. Remove the eggs from the frying pan, draining off as much fat as possible. Place an egg on each square of fried bread and, using a ladle, pour in the soup very carefully at the side of the plate so as not to break the egg.

Valpelline Soup

Zuppa di valpelline

4 tablespoons cooking fat
about 1 lb cabbage
bread
5 oz rindless Fontina cheese
juices from a roast
4 tablespoons butter
4 oz raw ham
about 1 quart good chicken stock

SERVES 4

PREPARATION AND COOKING TIME:
ABOUT 2 HOURS

Preheat the oven to 325°F. Heat the blade of a sharp knife and finely chop the fat on a chopping board. Melt it in a large frying pan over low heat. Trim the cabbage, removing the outer leaves and the thick ribs. Wash the rest, drain well and fry in the fat until tender and slightly browned.

Meanwhile slice the bread and toast, either in the oven or under the broiler. Cut the Fontina cheese into very thin slices. Place a slice of toast in each of four soup bowls and pour over a little of the juices from the roast. Make a layer of cabbage and sprinkle with freshly ground pepper, then a layer of raw ham followed by Fontina. Cover with another layer of bread and continue alternating the ingredients until they are all used up. Finish with a layer of Fontina and add slivers of butter.

Put enough stock into each bowl to cover the layers of bread. Place in the oven for about 1 hour until the surface is golden brown. Serve piping hot straight from the oven.

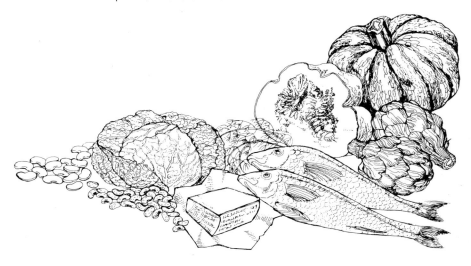

LEFT: *Valpelline soup.*

Cabbage and Cheese Soup

Zuppa di verza e fontina

2–3 slices bacon
4 tablespoons butter
savoy cabbage heart, ribs removed
2 quarts meat stock
small French loaf
6 oz Fontina cheese

SERVES 4–6
PREPARATION AND COOKING TIME:
ABOUT 1¾ HOURS

Pound the bacon and fry it gently in half the butter. Add the cabbage and sauté it slowly, then add 1 cup of the stock, put a lid on and leave it on a moderate heat for about 40 minutes or until tender.

Preheat the oven to 375°F. Cut the bread into slices about ¾ inch thick, melt the rest of the butter and let the bread soak it up, then toast the slices in the oven. Increase the oven temperature to 400°F.

Slice the Fontina thinly. In a wide soup tureen arrange layers of toast, cabbage and cheese, finishing with the cheese. Bring the remaining stock to the boil and pour it over the other ingredients. Cook for 15 minutes in the oven, then serve.

Minestrone with Semolina

Minestrone di verdure con semolino

½ small onion
1 large garlic clove
2 slices bacon, diced
2 tablespoons butter
olive oil
14 oz frozen mixed vegetables
1 tablespoon tomato paste
2 vegetable bouillion cubes
1½ tablespoons semolina
grated Parmesan cheese
black pepper
olive oil

SERVES 4
PREPARATION AND COOKING TIME:
ABOUT 1 HOUR

Finely chop the onion and garlic and fry gently in a saucepan with the bacon, butter and 2 tablespoons of olive oil until transparent. Add the mixed vegetables, cover the pan and cook for a few minutes over low heat.

Stir in the tomato paste and pour on 2 quarts of boiling water. Season with the crumbled bouillion cubes, cover the pan and cook for 30 minutes. Slowly add the semolina, stirring constantly. Cook for a further 10 minutes and serve with grated Parmesan cheese, black pepper and olive oil.

ABOVE RIGHT: *Chestnut and mushroom soup.*

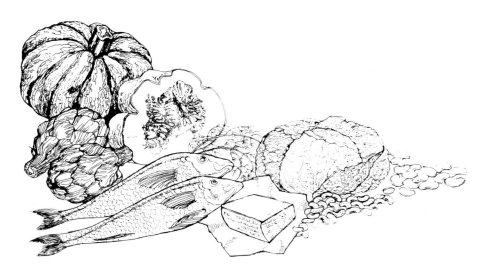

Chestnut and Mushroom Soup

Zuppa di castagne e funghi

1 medium onion
4–5 tablespoons olive oil
3 tablespoons butter
2 small cep mushrooms, trimmed (or fresh porcini)
2 tablespoons Marsala wine
10 chestnuts, boiled and puréed
1¼ quarts good meat stock
2 teaspoons cornstarch
½ cup whipping cream
4 thick slices white bread

SERVES 4

PREPARATION AND COOKING TIME: ABOUT 1 HOUR

Chop the onion and process in a blender with 2–3 tablespoons of the oil. Put the purée in a saucepan over low heat. Add 2 tablespoons butter, cut into small pieces. Fry without letting the onion brown.

Wash the mushrooms and cut into small pieces. Add to the onion and fry for a few minutes, stirring all the time. Pour in the Marsala and, when it has evaporated, add the chestnuts. After 4–5 minutes, gradually add the boiling stock and mix with a small whisk. Bring to the boil, stirring occasionally. Lower the heat and simmer gently.

Put the cornstarch in a bowl with the cream and mix until it has completely dissolved. After 20 minutes, add this to the soup. Bring the soup back to the boil and simmer for another 5 minutes. Cut the bread into small squares and fry in the rest of the butter and olive oil. When the soup is ready, taste and adjust the seasoning. Serve with the hot croûtons.

Parmesan Strands ("Passatelli") in Lemon-flavored Broth

Pasatelli al limone

---

juice and grated zest of 1 lemon
1½ quarts chicken broth, degreased
2 cups breadcrumbs
1¾ cups grated Parmesan cheese
salt
nutmeg
fresh parsley
fresh chervil
4 eggs

SERVES 5–6

PREPARATION AND COOKING TIME:
ABOUT 40 MINUTES

Add 1 tablespoon lemon juice to the cold chicken broth, then bring to the boil.

Meanwhile, prepare the 'passatelli'. In a bowl, combine the breadcrumbs, Parmesan cheese, a pinch of salt, a grating of nutmeg, the lemon zest and 1 tablespoon parsley chopped with a few chervil leaves. Bind the mixture with the eggs and amalgamate thoroughly (it must be completely blended). Pass the mixture through the largest holes of a potato ricer to make large strands about ¼ inch wide and 1½ inches long. Tip these into the boiling broth and, as soon as they rise to the surface, turn off the heat.

Divide the lemon-flavored soup and "passatelli" between six soup bowls or plates. Garnish each bowl with a few parsley or chervil leaves, and serve immediately, while it is piping hot.

Cream of Artichoke Soup

Crema di carciofi

---

4 globe artichokes
juice of ½ lemon
1 medium leek
½ small onion
olive oil
flour
1¼ cups milk
1½ quarts hot stock (or use a vegetable bouillion cube)
1 bay leaf
salt
½ cup whipping cream

TO ACCOMPANY:
croûtons of toast topped with grilled cheese

SERVES 6

PREPARATION AND COOKING TIME:
ABOUT 1 HOUR 20 MINUTES

Trim the artichokes: cut off the spiny leaf tips and discard the hardest outer leaves and the fibrous parts of the base; halve the artichokes lengthwise and remove the hairy chokes, then cut the rest into thin slivers and toss them into a bowl filled with water acidulated with the lemon juice.

Trim and chop together the leek and onion, then sweat them in 4 tablespoons olive oil. Thoroughly drain the artichoke slivers, add them to the softened vegetables and brown over very high heat for 2–3 minutes. Sprinkle with 2 tablespoons flour, stir in the milk, taking care that no lumps form, then add the hot stock. Stir in the bay leaf, adjust the seasoning with salt, cover and cook for about 1 hour over medium heat.

When the soup is ready, transfer everything to a food mill fitted with a medium disc and purée the soup back into the original saucepan. Return the pan to the heat, stir and bind the soup with the cream. As soon as the soup comes back to the boil, pour it into individual bowls and serve with hot croûtons.

Cream of Chick Pea Soup Au Gratin

Crema di ceci gratinata

10 oz dried chick peas
1 medium onion
fresh sage
2 garlic cloves
¼ cup olive oil
fresh rosemary
salt and pepper
8 slices white bread
4 oz Emmental cheese

SERVES 8

PREPARATION AND COOKING TIME: ABOUT
1½ HOURS, PLUS SOAKING THE CHICK PEAS

Soak the chick peas for 12 hours. To prepare the soup, drain off the soaking water and place the chick peas in a saucepan with 2 quarts cold water. Add the onion, halved, and 3 sage leaves. Place the pan on the heat and bring to the boil, then cover and cook the chick peas over medium heat for about 1¼ hours. When the chick peas are tender, transfer them with their cooking liquid to a blender. Blend on maximum speed for 2 minutes to obtain a cream (given the quantity of chick peas and liquid, it is best to do this in two batches). Lightly crush the garlic cloves, leaving them whole, and heat them with the oil and a sprig of rosemary. Strain the oil and add it to the soup, to give it a good flavor. Season with salt and pepper.

Divide the soup between eight ovenproof bowls or soup plates. Using a pastry cutter, cut out eight rounds of bread and toast them in the oven. Place one on each bowl, grate the Emmental and sprinkle it over the toast rounds. Place the soup bowls in a very hot oven or, better still, under the broiler, until the cheese melts and forms a golden crust. Serve straight from the oven, piping hot.

Pumpkin Soup

Minestra di zucca

1 medium onion
olive oil
1 × 1¼ lb slice of pumpkin
2½ quarts hot stock (or use a vegetable bouillion cube)
6 oz dried egg pasta
salt
3 tablespoons butter
3 tablespoons grated Parmesan cheese
1 tablespoon chopped parsley

SERVES 6

PREPARATION AND COOKING TIME:
ABOUT 1¼ HOURS

Chop the onion, place in a large saucepan and sweat with 2 tablespoons oil.

Meanwhile, discard the pumpkin skin and seeds, dice the flesh and add it to the softened onion. Brown the diced pumpkin, stirring frequently with a wooden spoon, then pour the hot stock into the saucepan. Cover and cook the soup over medium heat for about 50 minutes.

When the soup is ready, add the pasta, stir, salt to taste and cook the pasta for about 5 minutes. Take the pan off the heat and whisk in the butter, Parmesan cheese and parsley. Pour into a soup tureen and serve.

LEFT: *Cream of chick pea soup au gratin* (top);
Pumpkin soup (bottom).

Cream of Lettuce and Green Bean Soup

Crema di lattuga e fagiolini

---

4 oz butter
½ cup rice flour
1½ quarts meat stock (can be made with a bouillion cube)
2 heads of lettuce, washed and separated into leaves
4 oz green beans
salt and pepper
2 egg yolks
grated Parmesan cheese
⅔ cup whipping cream
croûtons

SERVES 6

PREPARATION AND COOKING TIME: ABOUT 1½ HOURS

Melt half the butter in a large saucepan and stir in the rice flour. Gradually stir in the boiling stock and bring to the boil, stirring constantly. Add the lettuce leaves, cover the pan and cook over moderate heat for about 1 hour, stirring frequently.

Meanwhile, top and tail the beans and cook them in salted boiling water for about 8 minutes or until just tender. Drain the beans thoroughly and chop them coarsely. Mix the egg yolks, the remaining butter, melted, and a tablespoon of grated Parmesan cheese in a bowl, and stir in the cream.

Strain the lettuce soup into a clean saucepan, season with pepper and stir in the cooked and chopped green beans. Bring to the boil and gradually blend in the egg and cream mixture, stirring constantly with a whisk. Serve the soup while piping hot with hot croûtons and grated Parmesan cheese.

Shrimp Soup under a Pastry Lid

Zuppette di gamberi in crosta

---

10 oz uncooked shrimp,
in the shell
2 medium shallots
½ medium leek
2 tablespoons olive oil
1 bay leaf
salt and pepper
brandy
dry white wine
2 tablespoons butter, softened
¾ cup flour
⅔ cup whipping cream

FOR THE LIDS:
7 oz frozen puff pastry, thawed
1 egg

SERVES 2
PREPARATION AND COOKING TIME:
ABOUT 1 HOUR 15 MINUTES

Thoroughly wash the shrimp under cold running water. Finely chop the shallots and leek and sweat in a saucepan with the olive oil and bay leaf until tender. Add the shrimp, season to taste and cook for 2–3 minutes until they turn pink. Pour on a small glass of brandy and flame it, or, if you prefer, evaporate the liquid over very fierce heat. Sprinkle a little white wine over the shrimp, then pour over 1½ cups cold water and boil for about 20 minutes.

Meanwhile, preheat the oven to 350°F.
Take the soup off the heat and take out the shrimp. Remove the heads, if any, and shells and set aside the flesh. Return the soup to the heat and add the shrimp heads and shells. Mash together the softened butter and flour, mix into the soup and cook for another 10 minutes. Pass the soup through a food mill, using the finest disc, or a fine-mesh strainer. Cut up the shrimp flesh and add this to the soup, together with the whipping cream. Cook for another 10 minutes, until the soup thickens to the consistency of double cream. Divide the mixture between two ovenproof soup bowls.

Roll out the thawed pastry to a thin rectangle. Cut out two circles slightly larger than the diameter of the two ovenproof soup bowls. Brush the edges with a little beaten egg, then cover the filled bowls with the pastry circles, pressing the edges lightly against the sides of the bowls. Brush the lids with a little egg, then bake in the oven for about 20 minutes. Serve the soup straight from the oven.

Swordfish and Sweet Pepper Soup

Zuppetta di spada e peperoni

---

2 light fish bouillion cubes
1 medium onion
3 tablespoons olive oil
1 garlic clove
1 each small red and yellow pepper
fresh basil leaves
12 oz swordfish steaks, diced
salt and pepper

SERVES 6
PREPARATION AND COOKING TIME:
ABOUT 30 MINUTES

Bring about 1 quart water to the boil with the bouillion cubes. Chop the onion and sweat in a saucepan with the olive oil and garlic. Peel and dice the peppers and add them to the onions, together with 3 or 4 basil leaves.

After about 10 minutes, add the diced swordfish. Increase the heat to high and cook for 2 minutes, then pour on the boiling stock. Remove the basil leaves, lower the heat and simmer for 5 more minutes.

Taste the soup, correct the seasoning and remove the pan from the heat. Leave to rest for 2–3 minutes before serving. If you like, place a round of toasted French bread or a few croûtons in the bottom of each serving bowl before ladling on the soup.

FAR LEFT: *Cream of lettuce and French bean soup.*

Classic Spelt Soup

Zuppa di farro all'antica

---

8 oz spelt (a grain)
1 medium stalk celery
2 medium onions
1 medium carrot
olive oil
5 oz smoked pancetta (Italian bacon)
8 oz beef
1¼ quarts hot chicken stock (or use a bouillion cube)
12 oz potatoes
salt and pepper
chopped parsley
SERVES 6

PREPARATION AND COOKING TIME:
ABOUT 1 HOUR PLUS SOAKING THE SPELT

Soak the spelt in cold water for about 2 hours. When you are ready to make the soup, peel the celery, onion and carrot, chop them and soften in 4 tablespoons oil. Add the finely chopped pancetta and the beef, cut into small, thin slices. Brown over high heat, then add the spelt, hot stock and potatoes, cut into small pieces. Adjust the seasoning with salt and pepper, then reduce the heat, cover and cook the spelt soup for about 50 minutes.

Sprinkle with parsley and serve, accompanied by triangles of white bread toasted in the oven, if you like them.

Minestrone with Pesto

Minestrone al pesto

---

1 small onion
2 garlic cloves
butter
olive oil
1 lb frozen mixed vegetables
3 bouillion cubes
1 large potato
15 fresh basil leaves
1 tablespoon pine nuts
¼ cup grated Parmesan cheese
pinch of salt
a little chopped parsley
SERVES 4

PREPARATION AND COOKING TIME:
ABOUT 1 HOUR

Finely chop the onion and 1 garlic clove, then soften in a pan in a large knob of melted butter and 2 tablespoons of oil; make sure they don't brown. Add the frozen vegetables and fry for a few moments, stirring with a wooden spoon. Pour in 1½ quarts of boiling water and crumble in the bouillion cubes. Peel the potato, chop into 2–3 pieces and add to the *minestrone*; cook covered over medium heat for about 45 minutes, stirring two or three times as it simmers.

Meanwhile, place the basil leaves, half a large garlic clove, the pine nuts, a tablespoon of Parmesan cheese and a pinch of salt in a mortar. Pound with a wooden pestle, adding, in a trickle, 5 tablespoons of olive oil, until you have obtained a smooth *pesto*.

Remove the pieces of potato from the soup with a slotted spoon, mash them and return them to the pan. Add the *pesto*, stir, pour the *minestrone* into four soup bowls and sprinkle with chopped parsley. Serve with more Parmesan cheese.

Barley and Sorrel Soup

'Maritata' di orzo e acetosa

---

2 shallots, peeled
olive oil
1⅓ cups pearl barley
1½ quarts hot stock (or use a vegetable bouillion cube)
1 egg
2 tablespoons grated Parmesan cheese
1 tablespoon dried breadcrumbs
salt
2 slices white bread, made into crumbs
12 sorrel leaves

SERVES 6
PREPARATION AND COOKING TIME:
ABOUT 1 HOUR

Chop the shallots and sweat in a large saucepan with the oil. Add the barley and toast it over high heat, then pour in the hot stock. Cover, lower the heat and cook the soup for about 40 minutes.

Meanwhile, in a bowl, mix the egg with the Parmesan cheese, dried breadcrumbs, a pinch of salt and the fresh breadcrumbs. When the soup is ready, wash and chop the sorrel leaves and put them into the soup. Tip in all the egg mixture at once. Stir (it will form strands) and cook for 1 minute from when the soup comes back to the boil. Then take the pan off the heat and serve the soup immediately, piping hot.

Quick Minestrone

Minestrone rapido con i ditaloni

---

1 small onion
1 garlic clove
olive oil
½ celery heart
3 small carrots
1 medium zucchini
1 small turnip
2 small potatoes
1 cup shelled peas
6 oz canned kidney beans
4 oz peeled, puréed tomatoes
1½ quarts stock (or use a vegetable bouillion cube)
4 oz fluted pasta
freshly ground pepper
¼ cup grated Parmesan cheese

SERVES 4–6
PREPARATION AND COOKING TIME: 1¼ HOURS

Finely chop the onion with the garlic and fry in 4 tablespoons of olive oil in a large saucepan, taking care not to let the vegetables brown.

Meanwhile clean and dice the celery, carrots, zucchini, turnip and potatoes into ¾ inch cubes. Add to the onion and leave for a few moments. Add the peas, the beans with their liquid and the tomatoes. Stir with a wooden spoon and simmer for about 10 minutes.

Boil the stock and pour into the mixture. Stir, cover and simmer for about 45 minutes over moderate heat. Add the pasta and stir. Simmer until the pasta is cooked *al dente* and remove from the heat. Add a little freshly ground pepper, 3 tablespoons of olive oil and the grated Parmesan cheese. Serve at once.

Pearl Barley and Vegetable Soup

Zuppa d'orzo con verdure

---

1 medium onion
1 oz pancetta, thinly sliced (Italian bacon)
olive oil
1 bay leaf
12 oz savoy cabbage
5 oz fresh spinach, trimmed
2½ quarts hot stock (or use a vegetable bouillion cube)
1 cup pearl barley
salt
3 tablespoons grated Parmesan cheese

SERVES 6
PREPARATION AND COOKING TIME:
ABOUT 1¼ HOURS

Finely chop the onion and pancetta, place in a large saucepan and sweat with 3 tablespoons oil and the bay leaf. Meanwhile, trim the cabbage, wash the leaves thoroughly under running water and drain well. Shred the cabbage leaves and spinach, and add them to the saucepan. Leave the vegetables to soften for several minutes, then pour in the hot stock, cover and cook over medium heat for about 15 minutes.

Add the barley, stir, taste and add salt if necessary. Cover the pan again and cook for a further 40 minutes or so. Take the pan off the heat and whisk the Parmesan cheese into the soup. Pour into a soup tureen and serve.

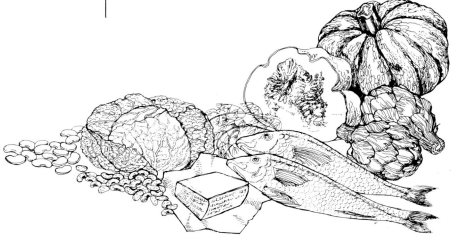

Pasta, Risottos & Gnocchi

The *primo piatto*, as it is called in Italy, is the most *Italian* part of the meal, consisting as it does of pasta, rice (always the short-grain variety grown in the northern part of the country), or gnocchi, small balls or parcels made from grains or potatoes and usually served with a sauce. Here we offer a whole selection of traditional and new classics to continue the meal in style.

Fish Ravioli

Ravioli di pesce

FOR THE PASTA

1¾ cups all-purpose flour
2 eggs
olive oil
salt

FOR THE FILLING

3 slices white bread
¼ cup whipping cream
1 shallot
olive oil
½ medium leek, trimmed and sliced
7 oz sole fillets
7 oz raw shrimp, peeled
salt and pepper
dry white wine

FOR THE SAUCE

2 shallots
1 cup dry white wine
scant 1 cup whipping cream
chopped fresh herbs (parsley, thyme, marjoram)

SERVES 6–8

PREPARATION AND COOKING TIME:
ABOUT 2 HOURS

Sift the flour on to a work surface and make a well. Break in the eggs and mix them into the flour, together with the olive oil and a pinch of salt. Begin mixing with a fork, then use your hands to make a firm but elastic dough. Wrap it in plastic wrap and refrigerate for about 30 minutes.

To prepare the filling soften the bread in the cream. Chop the shallot and sweat it and the leek in 2 tablespoons oil. Add the fish and shrimp. Season with salt and pepper, and moisten with about one-third of a glass of wine. Evaporate the liquid over high heat. Purée the mixture in a food processor and transfer to a bowl. Add the bread without squeezing it out. Mix to make a smooth paste.

Roll out the dough into two thin sheets. Put little heaps of the filling on half the dough, spacing them about 2 inches apart. Cover with the other sheet of dough and press down around each heap of filling with your fingers to seal completely. Cut around each heap to make square ravioli. Re-roll the trimmings and continue to make more ravioli until all the ingredients are used up; you should have about 54 ravioli. Cook until *al dente* in plenty of boiling salted water; they are ready when they rise to the surface of the water.

While they are cooking, make the sauce. Chop the shallots, add the wine and reduce by three-quarters, then add the cream, ravioli and a pinch of chopped mixed herbs. Toss the pasta over high heat to flavor with the sauce, and serve.

Chestnut Tagliatelle

Tagliatelle di castagne

FOR THE TAGLIATELLE

2½ cups all-purpose flour
1¾ cups chestnut flour
4 eggs
salt

FOR THE SAUCE

2 shallots
2 small carrots
3 tablespoons butter
6 oz calves' liver
1 cup whipping cream
salt
½ teaspoon truffle paste

SERVES 10–12

PREPARATION AND COOKING TIME:
ABOUT 1 HOUR

To prepare the tagliatelle (you can do this a day in advance), mix the two flours and sift them onto a work surface. Make a well and put the eggs and a pinch of salt in the middle. Mix with a fork, adding a few drops of water if the dough seems too dry, then work with your hands to make a smooth dough, firm but elastic. Wrap in plastic wrap and leave to rest in the refrigerator for about 30 minutes.

Roll out the dough into thin sheets. Leave to dry, but take care not to let it dry out too much. If you are using a pasta maker, use the appropriate blade to cut it into tagliatelle, if not, carefully cut the thin sheets into long strips. Just before serving, cook the tagliatelle *al dente* in plenty of boiling salted water.

Prepare the sauce. Chop the shallots and peel and finely dice the carrot. Sweat the vegetables in the butter. Finely dice the liver and add it and the cream to the pan. Season with salt and the truffle paste, then put the tagliatelle into the sauce and sauté over high heat to flavor the pasta. Drain and transfer the tagliatelle to a serving dish and serve immediately.

RIGHT: *Chestnut tagliatelle* (top);
Fish ravioli (bottom).

Lasagne with Wild Boar Sauce

Lasagne al ragù di cinghiale

FOR THE PASTA
1¼ cups all-purpose flour
1½ oz cooked spinach, drained and squeezed dry
1 egg
salt
oil
FOR THE BECHAMEL SAUCE
½ cup all-purpose flour
4 tablespoons butter
1 quart hot milk
salt
nutmeg
FOR THE SAUCE AND FINISHING THE DISH
1 lb wild boar fillet
1¾ cups robust red wine
2 large carrots, chopped
2 medium onions, chopped
1 celery stalk, chopped
2 bay leaves
1 teaspoon peppercorns
olive oil
salt and pepper
white flour
1 tablespoon tomato paste
1 cup grated Parmesan cheese
butter for glazing
SERVES 6

PREPARATION AND COOKING TIME:
ABOUT 3 HOURS, PLUS MARINATING

Cut the wild boar fillet into pieces and marinate overnight in the wine, vegetables, bay leaves and peppercorns. Next day, strain off the marinade, reserving separately the wine, vegetables and meat. Remove and discard the peppercorns.

Brown the vegetables from the marinade in 3 tablespoons olive oil, then add the meat and brown well. Season with salt and pepper, and sprinkle on a heaped tablespoon of flour. Add the wine from the marinade and immediately afterwards, stir in the tomato paste. Cover the pan and cook over medium heat for about 2 hours. (This sauce can be prepared a day in advance.)

LEFT: *Lasagne with wild boar sauce*

Now prepare the pasta. Put the flour on a work surface and make a well. Put in the spinach and break in an egg, mixing them into the flour with a pinch of salt and a tablespoon of olive oil. Begin by mixing with a fork, then use your hands to make a firm but elastic dough. Wrap it in plastic wrap and place in the refrigerator for about 30 minutes. Roll out the dough through a pasta machine into lasagne sheets and spread out to dry on a tea towel.

While the pasta is drying, make the béchamel. Make a roux with the flour and butter, then gradually whisk in the hot milk. Season with salt and nutmeg and cook for 5 minutes, stirring constantly.

Preheat the oven to 475°F. Chop the wild boar with its cooking liquid in a food processor. Pour a ladleful of bechamel into an ovenproof dish, then fill the dish with alternating layers of pasta, meat, bechamel and Parmesan cheese, until all the ingredients are used up. Dot the surface with flakes of butter and bake the lasagne in the hot oven for about 25 minutes.

Pasta with Zucchini

Pasta con zucchini

---

1 lb zucchini
1 medium onion
a little parsley
1 large garlic clove
olive oil
½ vegetable bouillion cube
salt and pepper
12 oz fresh pasta
a little grated Parmesan cheese
SERVES 3–4

PREPARATION AND COOKING TIME: 45 MINUTES

Clean the zucchini and trim them. Wash and dry well, and cut into rounds about ¼ inch thick. Finely chop the onion, parsley and garlic and fry in 5 tablespoons of olive oil without browning. Then add the zucchini and crumble in the bouillion cube with a little freshly ground pepper. Cover with boiling water and stir well.

Cover the pan and cook over moderate heat for about 10 minutes, until the zucchini are tender and the liquid has been absorbed. Season to taste.

Cook the pasta until *al dente* in plenty of salted boiling water, drain and stir in 2 tablespoons of olive oil. Mix in the sauce and serve at once with the Parmesan cheese.

Agnolotti with Cep Mushroom Sauce

Agnolotti con sugo di porcini

---

2 cabbage leaves
2 small onions
4 tablespoons butter
olive oil
2 oz sausagemeat
6 oz cooked beef
4 oz roast pork
1/2 cup grated Parmesan cheese
salt and pepper
nutmeg
5 small eggs
3 cups flour
8 oz cep mushrooms (or fresh porcini)
1 garlic clove
2–3 sprigs fresh parsley
4 tablespoons Marsala wine
1/2 beef or chicken bouillion cube
ground thyme
1 1/4 cups milk
3 tablespoons whipping cream
1 teaspoon cornstarch

SERVES 4–5

PREPARATION AND COOKING TIME:
ABOUT 2 HOURS

Wash the cabbage leaves thoroughly, then cook in boiling salted water for about 15 minutes. Drain, and when the cabbage has cooled, squeeze out all the moisture. Finely slice 1 onion and fry in 2 tablespoons butter and 1 tablespoon of olive oil. Add the cabbage leaves and crumble the sausagemeat before adding that too. Cook for about 10 minutes, then mince finely with the beef and the pork. Collect the mixture in a bowl and add 4 tablespoons of grated Parmesan cheese, a little salt, pepper and grated nutmeg. Bind with 2 small eggs to a smooth consistency. Taste and adjust the seasoning if necessary.

To prepare the pasta put the flour on a work surface and make a well. Break in the remaining eggs and mix them into the flour together with a pinch of salt and a tablespoon of olive oil. Begin by mixing with a fork, then use your hands to make a firm but elastic dough. Wrap it in plastic wrap and store in the refrigerator for about 30 minutes. Roll out the dough into thin sheets, a little at a time, keeping the rest beneath an upturned earthenware dish. Cut out rounds about 2 inches in diameter. Place a little of the stuffing on one half of each round, then fold over to make semicircular *agnolotti*, pressing down the edges well to seal in the filling. Cover with a clean tea towel and leave in a cool place.

Trim the mushrooms, wash rapidly under running water and drain carefully. Finely chop the remaining onion together with the garlic clove and a handful of parsley and fry in the remaining butter and 2 tablespoons of olive oil, taking care not to brown them. Finely slice the mushrooms and add to the other ingredients. Cook for 3–4 minutes over fairly high heat, stirring with a wooden spoon. Pour in the Marsala and crumble in the bouillion cube. Add a pinch of thyme, stir and, when two thirds of the Marsala has evaporated, pour in the boiling milk. Dissolve the cornstarch in the cold cream and stir that in too. Mix thoroughly and simmer for a further few minutes until the sauce has thickened.

Cook the *agnolotti* until *al dente* in plenty of salted boiling water and when they are cooked, after a few minutes, remove with a slotted spoon. Pour over the sauce and remaining Parmesan cheese. Mix carefully and serve.

Tagliatelle with Spicy Liver Sauce

Salsa peverada per tagliatelle

---

4 oz chicken livers
4 oz calves' liver
1 onion
4–5 sprigs fresh parsley
4 oz smoked bacon
2 oz capers
zest of 1/2 lemon
olive oil
6 anchovy fillets
2 garlic cloves
1/2 cup red wine
freshly ground pepper
1 lb tagliatelle

SERVES 4

PREPARATION AND COOKING TIME:
ABOUT 20 MINUTES

Mince or chop the livers and reserve them. Chop the onion, parsley, bacon, capers and lemon zest and mix together.

Heat 3 tablespoons of olive oil in a pan and add the chopped anchovies and garlic. When the garlic is golden, remove and discard it. Add the chopped onion and bacon mixture to the pan and as soon as it is browned, pour in the red wine and add the livers. Cook over high heat for 5 minutes and season with freshly ground black pepper.

Cook the pasta until *al dente* in plenty of salted boiling water, drain and serve with the sauce.

Fettucine with Pink Sauce

Sugo rosa per fettucine

---

1 sprig fresh rosemary
1 large garlic clove
²/₃ cup meat gravy, skimmed
²/₃ cup light cream
1 tablespoon tomato ketchup
brandy
1 × 14 oz can of tomatoes
14 oz fettucine
salt
¼ cup grated Parmesan cheese
¼ cup grated Gruyère cheese
fresh parsley
ground paprika

SERVES 4
PREPARATION AND COOKING TIME:
ABOUT 25 MINUTES

Chop the rosemary leaves finely with the garlic. Place them in a pan large enough to hold all the pasta, add the gravy and cream and simmer for 5 minutes, stirring frequently. Add the ketchup, a dash of brandy and the tomatoes, finely chopped. Simmer for about 10 minutes.

Cook the pasta in plenty of salted, boiling water until *al dente*, drain and tip it into the sauce. Bind with the two cheeses and sprinkle with chopped parsley and a pinch of paprika.

Fusilli with Asparagus Sauce

Fusilli con asparagi

---

butter
5–6 green asparagus tips, boiled and cooled
flour
½ cup hot milk
¼ vegetable bouillion cube
grated nutmeg
4 oz fusilli
salt and pepper
2 tablespoons whipping cream

SERVES 1
PREPARATION AND COOKING TIME:
ABOUT 30 MINUTES

Melt 2 tablespoons butter in a small saucepan, add the asparagus tips and sauté gently, making sure that they do not brown. Sprinkle with a little sifted flour, stir and, after a few moments, pour in the hot milk in a trickle. Crumble in the bouillion cube and add a pinch of nutmeg. Stirring constantly, bring the sauce to the boil, then remove it from the heat and purée it.

Cook the pasta until *al dente* in plenty of salted boiling water. Meanwhile place the asparagus mixture on a very low heat in the saucepan and reheat gently. Stirring constantly, mix in the cream. Adjust the seasoning to taste.

Drain the pasta, but not too thoroughly, pour over the creamy asparagus sauce and garnish, if you like, with more asparagus tips tossed in a little butter. Serve at once.

Noodles with Bolognese Sauce

Paglia e fieno con ragú pasquale

---

1 medium onion
1 large garlic clove
1/2 sprig rosemary
1 small bunch of parsley
1 celery stalk
2 small carrots
butter
olive oil
4 oz beef
4 oz lamb
4 oz sausagemeat
2 slices bacon
1/2 cup dry white wine
1/4 cup flour
12 oz tomatoes
1 chicken bouillion cube
salt and freshly ground black pepper
1 cup young peas
1 lb green and white tagliatelle
1/4 cup grated Parmesan cheese

SERVES 6

PREPARATION AND COOKING TIME:
ABOUT 2 HOURS

Finely chop the onion with the garlic clove, the rosemary leaves and a small bunch of parsley. Dice the celery and carrots. Put these ingredients into a saucepan with 2 tablespoons of butter and 3 tablespoons of oil. Soften but do not allow to brown.

Meanwhile, mince the beef, lamb and sausagemeat and dice the bacon. Add to the vegetables in the pan, stir and brown slightly. Pour in the white wine and allow to evaporate almost completely. Then sprinkle in a level tablespoon of flour, stirring thoroughly to prevent any lumps from forming.

Purée the tomatoes and add them immediately after the flour, together with 2 1/2 cups of cold water, the crumbled bouillion cube and some freshly ground black pepper. Stir and bring to the boil, turn the heat down to simmer, cover the pan and cook for about 1 1/2 hours. Stir occasionally and dilute with a little boiling water if necessary. Parboil the peas and add them 15 minutes before cooking is completed.

Cook the pasta until *al dente* in plenty of salted boiling water. Drain and mix in 2 tablespoons of olive oil, then serve with the sauce and the grated Parmesan cheese.

Rigatoni with Crabmeat

Rigatoni al granchio

---

1 small shallot
1 small piece celery heart
butter
olive oil
2 oz crabmeat
2 tablespoons sparkling white wine
1 tablespoon tomato paste
2–3 tablespoons concentrated fish stock
salt and white pepper
4 oz large fluted rigatoni

SERVES 1

PREPARATION AND COOKING TIME:
ABOUT 30 MINUTES

Finely chop the shallot and the celery heart and sauté, without browning, in 2 tablespoons of butter and a teaspoon of olive oil. Meanwhile, drain the crabmeat, removing any cartilage, and shred finely before adding to the pan. Cook for a few minutes, stirring.

Next, moisten the crabmeat with a sprinkling of sparkling wine and let it evaporate almost completely, keeping the heat low and stirring often. Add the tomato paste and fish stock. Stir once more and leave the sauce to simmer for 5–7 minutes. If it dries out too much, moisten with another tablespoon of fish stock. Season with salt and white pepper.

Cook the pasta until *al dente* in plenty of salted boiling water. Drain, remove to a warmed plate and pour the hot crab sauce over it. Garnish, if you like, with celery leaves. Serve at once.

RIGHT: *Noodles with Bolognese sauce.*

66

Seafood Fusilli

Fusilli 'marechiaro'

1 ¼ lb firm, ripe tomatoes
1 medium onion
1 garlic clove
1 small green pepper
olive oil
4 oz cooked mussels
6 fresh basil leaves
salt and pepper
a little sugar
1 ¼ lb fusilli
1 sprig fresh parsley

SERVES 6

PREPARATION AND COOKING TIME: ABOUT 1 HOUR

Purée the tomatoes. Finely chop the onion, garlic and pepper and sauté the mixture gently in olive oil, taking care not to let it brown. Add the drained mussels, giving them a few moments to absorb the flavors, then add the puréed tomatoes and the torn-up basil leaves. Salt lightly, then add the pepper and a good pinch of sugar. Stir and simmer for 30 minutes over a moderate heat with the lid half on the pan.

Cook the pasta until *al dente* in plenty of salted boiling water. Drain, and add the prepared sauce plus 3 tablespoons of olive oil and a little more pepper. Stir carefully, pour into a heated tureen, sprinkle with chopped parsley and serve.

Cannelloni in Cream Sauce

Cannelloni ripieni in bianco

salt and pepper
1 small onion
1 carrot
1 celery stalk
1 bay leaf
half a chicken, weighing about 1¼ lb
4 chicken livers
1 stale bread roll
4 oz ham
5 oz butter
about 3 tablespoons Marsala wine
8 tablespoons grated Parmesan cheese
6 eggs
3½ cups all-purpose flour
olive oil
scant 1 cup single cream

SERVES 10
PREPARATION AND COOKING TIME:
ABOUT 3½ HOURS

Bring about 1 quart of water to the boil in a saucepan and add a little salt, half the onion, the carrot, celery, bay leaf and chicken. Cover the pan and cook over moderate heat for about 1 hour.

Trim and wash the livers. Crumble the roll and soften it with some of the cooking liquid from the chicken. Finely chop the fat of the ham and the remaining half onion.

Place the chopped onion and ham fat in a small frying pan with a large knob of butter, and cook over very low heat for a few minutes. Add the chicken livers and cook for a further 10 minutes, occasionally pouring on a little Marsala. Remove from the heat.

Remove the chicken with a slotted spoon and allow it to cool slightly. Strain the stock. Bone the chicken and mince the meat finely in a food processor with the chicken livers and ham. Place the mixture in a bowl and stir in 4 tablespoons of grated Parmesan cheese, the drained bread and 3 of the eggs. Season to taste.

Prepare the pasta: put the flour on a work surface and make a well in the center. Break in 3 eggs and add a tablespoon of olive oil. Begin by mixing with a fork, then use your hands to make a firm but elastic dough. Wrap it in plastic wrap and place in the refrigerator for about 30 minutes. Roll out thinly.

Heat plenty of water in a large saucepan. Coat the rolled-out dough in flour, roll it up and cut it into pieces about 4 inches wide. Unroll the strips and cut them into 4 inch lengths. Once the water has come to the boil, add salt and a tablespoon of olive oil. Put the squares of pasta in the water, one at a time. As soon as the water comes back to the boil, drain the pasta and spread it out on a tea-towel to dry.

Place some of the prepared filling on each square of pasta and then roll them up and put them in a greased baking dish.

Preheat the oven to 400°F. Melt 4 tablespoons of butter in a saucepan and blend in ½ cup of flour to form a smooth *roux*. Pour in 2½ cups of the strained chicken stock, stirring constantly. Bring to the boil, blend in the cream and then season to taste.

Cover the cannelloni with the prepared sauce and dot with about 4 tablespoons of butter, cut into small pieces. Sprinkle with the rest of the grated Parmesan cheese and bake in the oven for about 15 minutes. Serve hot.

Linguine with Clams

Linguine alle vongole

1 garlic clove
olive oil
1 small onion, finely chopped
8 oz frozen clams
12 oz clam sauce
4 oz frozen peas
1 vegetable bouillon cube
12 oz linguine

SERVES 4
PREPARATION AND COOKING TIME:
ABOUT 20 MINUTES

Sauté the garlic cloves in 4 tablespoons of olive oil. Discard the garlic and add the finely chopped onion to the pan. Fry gently. Add the clams to the pan and allow to defrost over low heat. Stir in the clam sauce, peas and crumbled bouillion cube, and simmer over moderate heat.

Cook the pasta until *al dente* in plenty of salted boiling water, drain and pour into a warmed tureen. Dress with the prepared sauce and serve immediately.

FAR LEFT: *Seafood fusilli.*

Farfalle with Langostinos

Farfalle ai gamberoni

---

salt and pepper
4 oz farfalle
1 cup shelled peas
8 raw langostinos
1 shallot
olive oil
white wine
3 tablespoons butter
chopped parsley

SERVES 4

PREPARATION AND COOKING TIME:
ABOUT 40 MINUTES

Bring a large pan of salted water to the boil and cook the pasta until *al dente*. Drain.

Cook the peas and shell the langostinos, removing the black thread-like intestines. Chop the shallot and soften in 2 tablespoons olive oil. Add the langostinos and cooked peas, and brown them, then moisten with half a glass of wine. As soon as it has evaporated, add the butter and farfalle. Stir vigorously to flavor them, and season with salt and pepper and a bunch of chopped parsley.

Tagliolini with Asparagus

Tagliolini alle verdure

FOR THE PASTA
1 ¾ cups all-purpose flour
2 eggs
salt
1 tablespoon olive oil

FOR THE SAUCE
12 oz asparagus
5 oz button mushrooms
1 shallot
olive oil
1 cup whipping cream
salt and pepper
chopped parsley

SERVES 4

PREPARATION AND COOKING TIME:
ABOUT 40 MINUTES, PLUS RESTING THE PASTA

To prepare the pasta, sift the flour onto a work surface and make a well in the center. Break in the eggs, then add a pinch of salt and the oil. Begin by mixing with a fork, then use your hands to make a firm but elastic dough. Wrap in plastic wrap and leave to rest in the refrigerator for 30 minutes.

Meanwhile, make the sauce. Trim the asparagus and scrape the stalks, then cook them in two fingers of salted water until tender but still crisp. Drain and cut into short lengths, leaving the tips whole. Trim, wash and drain the mushrooms. Roll out the dough into very thin sheets, then (if you have a pasta machine) pass it through the appropriate cutter to make tagliolini; if you haven't, cut the sheets into long thin shreds. Cook in plenty of boiling salted water until *al dente*, then drain.

To finish the sauce, peel and chop the shallot and slice the mushrooms. Soften them in 2 tablespoons of oil, together with the asparagus lengths. Brown well, then add the cream and tagliolini. Toss well to flavor the pasta, season with salt, pepper and a pinch of chopped parsley. Serve, topped with the asparagus tips.

Tortelloni with Goat's Cheese and Potatoes

Tortelloni con caciottina e patate

FOR THE PASTA
1 ¾ cups all-purpose flour
2 eggs
salt
1 tablespoon olive oil
½ tablespoon chopped parsley

FOR THE FILLING
14 oz spinach beet
10 oz unpeeled boiled potatoes
1 egg
salt
3 tablespoons grated Parmesan cheese
8 oz fresh goat's cheese

FOR THE SAUCE
1 shallot
2 tablespoons butter
fresh thyme

RIGHT: *Tortelloni with goat's cheese and potatoes* (top left); *Tagliolini with asparagus* (right); *Farfalle with langostinos* (bottom).

SERVES 6

PREPARATION AND COOKING TIME:
ABOUT 1½ HOURS

To prepare the pasta, sift the flour onto a work surface and make a well. Put the eggs, a pinch of salt, the oil and parsley in the center. Begin by mixing with a fork then use your hands to make a firm but elastic dough. Wrap in plastic wrap and leave to rest in the refrigerator for at least 30 minutes.

Meanwhile, make the filling. Wash the spinach beet in several changes of water, then cook it in just the water clinging to the leaves. Drain, squeeze dry and chop coarsely. Peel the potatoes and mash them through a potato ricer set over a bowl. Add the egg, a pinch of salt, the chopped spinach beet, Parmesan cheese and sieved goat's cheese. Mix well to make a smooth paste.

Roll out the dough into thin sheets. Brush with cold water, then arrange little heaps of filling about 2½ inches apart in a single row on each sheet of pasta. Fold the other half of the pasta over the filling to cover it. Press down around the filling with your hands, then cut out around each heap to make securely closed 2 inch squares (tortelloni). Cook the tortelloni in plenty of boiling salted water until *al dente*, then drain.

Peel and chop the shallot and soften in the butter. Add the tortelloni and sauté over high heat to flavor them. Season with a generous pinch of fresh thyme, transfer to a serving dish and serve immediately while still piping hot.

Trenette with Basil Sauce

Trenette al pesto

---

2 garlic cloves
2 teaspoons pine nuts
about 18 fresh basil leaves
2 tablespoons grated Pecorino cheese
2 tablespoons grated Parmesan cheese
olive oil
2 oz French green beans
1 potato
12 oz trenette or other thin noodles

SERVES 4
PREPARATION AND COOKING TIME:
ABOUT 45 MINUTES

Preheat the oven to 350°F.
Chop the garlic and place in a mortar with a little salt. Lightly toast the pine nuts in the oven for 3–4 minutes and leave to cool. Wash and dry the basil leaves and add them one at a time to the mortar, alternating them with a few pine nuts. Pound with a pestle, gradually adding the grated cheeses. Continue pounding until the ingredients have blended to form a green paste. Then transfer the mixture to a bowl and gradually stir in enough olive oil to form a smooth paste.

Top and tail the beans and cut them into small pieces. Dice the potato. Cook the beans for 10 minutes in plenty of boiling salted water. Add the diced potato and the pasta. Cook the pasta until *al dente* and drain it, reserving 2 tablespoons of the cooking liquid to dilute the basil sauce. Dress the pasta with the basil sauce, stir well and serve with more grated Parmesan cheese.

Penne with Mortadella and Cream

Penne 'due torri'

---

2 oz mortadella sausage
2 oz ham
1 small onion, thinly sliced
1 garlic clove
butter
olive oil
½ cup dry white wine
1 teaspoon cornstarch
2½ cups light chicken or vegetable stock
(can be made with a bouillion cube)
Worcestershire sauce
12 oz penne
½ cup light cream
2 tablespoons grated Parmesan cheese
2 tablespoons chopped fresh parsley

SERVES 4

PREPARATION AND COOKING TIME:
ABOUT 40 MINUTES

Cut the mortadella and ham into ¼ inch cubes. Gently fry the onion and a crushed garlic clove in 2 tablespoons of butter and 2 tablespoons of olive oil until transparent. Add the cubes of mortadella and ham and cook for a few minutes. Pour on the wine and allow it to evaporate almost completely. Dissolve the cornstarch in 3 tablespoons of cold water and add it to the pan, together with the boiling stock and a splash of Worcestershire sauce. Stir and simmer gently until the liquid has reduced by two-thirds to form a creamy sauce.

Cook the pasta until *al dente* in plenty of boiling salted water, drain and stir it into the prepared sauce. Blend in the cream. Remove the pan from the heat and stir in the grated Parmesan cheese and chopped parsley. Serve at once.

Pasta with Tuna and Peppers

'Sedani' al tonno e peperone

1 small onion
olive oil
2 small red peppers
4 oz canned tuna
12 oz short macaroni
scant 1 cup tomato sauce
1 vegetable bouillion cube
1 sprig fresh parsley
a little grated Pecorino cheese

SERVES 4

PREPARATION AND COOKING TIME:
ABOUT 25 MINUTES

Finely chop the onion and fry gently in 3 tablespoons of olive oil until transparent. Meanwhile wash the peppers and cut in half, discarding the stalks and seeds. Cut into short, thick strips and add them to the onion and cook for a few minutes. Drain the tuna, break it into pieces with a fork and add it to the pan.

Cook the pasta until *al dente* in plenty of boiling salted water and drain. Add the tomato sauce and the crumbled bouillon cube to the tuna mixture and cook for a few minutes over low heat.

Pour the pasta into a tureen and dress with the prepared sauce. Top with chopped parsley and serve immediately with the grated Pecorino cheese.

Farfalle with Chicken and Shrimp Sauce

Farfalle con pollo e gamberetti

½ small onion
butter
small chicken breast
few shelled shrimp
1 tablespoon brandy
2 tablespoons dry white wine
½ cup chicken stock
½ teaspoon cornstarch
4 tablespoons light cream
salt and pepper
4 oz farfalle

SERVES 1

PREPARATION AND COOKING TIME:
ABOUT 40 MINUTES

Finely chop the onion and soften it gently, without browning, in 2 tablespoons butter. Meanwhile, finely mince the trimmed chicken breast and shrimp. Add them to the onion and let them cook over low heat, stirring frequently with a wooden spoon. Moisten with the brandy and, when it has evaporated almost entirely, pour in the white wine.

When the wine has been absorbed, pour in the cold chicken stock, in which you have dissolved the cornstarch, and the cream. Stir and simmer gently over very low heat for a few minutes, then process in a blender to obtain a smooth and creamy sauce. Season with pepper, adjust the salt to taste and keep it warm.

Cook the pasta in plenty of boiling salted water until *al dente*. Drain and pour over the chicken and shrimp sauce and serve at once.

Orecchiette with Tomato and Sausage Ragout

Orecchiette con pomodoro e salsiccia

1 small onion
1 celery stalk
1 small carrot
2 oz bacon
4 tablespoons butter
1 garlic clove
1 sprig basil
3–4 sprigs parsley
4 oz skinned sausages
½ cup dry white wine
flour
1 lb ripe tomatoes
salt and pepper
14 oz orecchiette pasta
olive oil
4 tablespoons grated mild Pecorino cheese

SERVES 4–5
PREPARATION AND COOKING TIME:
ABOUT 2 HOURS

Finely chop the onion, celery and carrot and fry with the diced bacon in the butter until they are soft but not browned. Add the garlic clove (to be removed and thrown away later) the sprig of basil and the parsley, tied in a small bunch. Add the sausages, mashed with a fork. Moisten with the wine and let it evaporate almost completely, then sprinkle with a teaspoon of flour. Skin and purée the tomatoes then add them to the pan. Stir, season lightly and cook over very low heat for about 1½ hours, moistening with a small amount of hot water or stock when the sauce becomes too thick.

About 10–20 minutes (check cooking instructions on packet) before the ragout is ready (check cooking instructions on packet), cook the pasta until *al dente* in plenty of boiling salted water. Drain the orecchiette and mix immediately with 3 tablespoons of olive oil. Add the ragout, discarding the garlic and the small bunch of seasoning herbs. Sprinkle with the Pecorino cheese, mix once more and serve at once.

Tagliolini with Mascarpone Sauce

Sugo al mascarpone per tagliolini

4 oz prosciutto
5 oz Mascarpone cheese
1 tablespoon Worcestershire sauce
12 oz tagliolini or other thin pasta
¼ cup grated Parmesan cheese
¼ cup grated Gruyère cheese

SERVES 4
PREPARATION AND COOKING TIME:
ABOUT 15 MINUTES

Cut the ham into fine strips. Warm the Mascarpone in a wide saucepan with the Worcestershire sauce and the ham over a low heat, stirring with a wooden spoon.

Cook the pasta until *al dente*, in plenty of boiling salted water, drain and tip into the sauce. Add the grated cheeses, stir and serve at once.

Fettucine with Mushrooms

Fettuccine riccia ai funghi

---

1 thick slice onion
few fresh sprigs parsley
1 garlic clove
butter
1 cep mushroom (or fresh porcini)
1 tablespoon of Marsala wine
¼ vegetable bouillon cube
½ teaspoon cornstarch
milk
4 oz fettucine
salt
a little chopped parsley

SERVES 1

PREPARATION AND COOKING TIME:
ABOUT 30 MINUTES

Finely chop the onion, a few parsley sprigs and the garlic clove. Fry them in 2 tablespoons of butter, until soft but do not allow to brown.

Meanwhile, scrape the dirt from the mushroom stalk and wash or wipe the cap. Slice thinly and add the slices to the onion mixture. Sauté for a few minutes, stirring gently.

Next, moisten with the Marsala and season with the bouillion cube. Dissolve the cornstarch in 2 tablespoons of cold milk and add it to the slices of mushroom, stirring gently. Leave the sauce on a very low heat for 4–5 minutes.

Cook the pasta until *al dente* in plenty of boiling salted water. Drain and pour over the mushroom sauce, to which you have added, at the very last moment, a little chopped parsley.

Pasta with Lentils

Pasta e lenticche

1½ cups dried lentils
5 oz potatoes
2 sage leaves
1 large garlic clove
a little parsley
4 oz peeled tomatoes
olive oil
2 vegetable bouillon cubes
8 oz pasta shells
3 tablespoons grated Parmesan cheese
chopped parsley

SERVES 6

PREPARATION AND COOKING TIME: 2½ HOURS

Pick over the lentils to make sure there are no impurities or grit. Wash under warm running water and place in a saucepan. Peel and dice the potatoes and put these in too. Chop the sage, garlic and parsley and add to the pan. Purée the tomatoes and add these together with 3 tablespoons of olive oil. Stir and pour in 2 quarts of cold water and bring to the boil. Turn the heat down to the minimum as soon as the mixture starts to boil, crumble in the bouillion cubes, cover and simmer for about 2 hours, stirring from time to time.

When the cooking is completed, purée a ladleful of the mixture and return the purée to the pan. Stir in and bring back to the boil, then add the pasta. Stir and cook until the pasta is *al dente*. Remove from the heat, add a little freshly ground pepper, 3 tablespoons of olive oil and the Parmesan cheese. Serve, sprinkling each portion with a little chopped parsley to garnish.

RIGHT: *Spinach beet and ham rolls.*

Spinach Beet and Ham Rolls

Rotolo di erbette e prosciutto

FOR THE PASTA
1 ¾ *cups all-purpose flour*
2 eggs
salt

FOR THE FILLING
1 ½ *lb spinach beet*
salt
8 oz cooked ham, thinly sliced
1 cup grated Parmesan cheese

FOR THE SAUCE
1 shallot
2 tablespoons butter
scant 1 cup whipping cream
salt and pepper
Parmesan cheese

SERVES 8–10
PREPARATION AND COOKING TIME:
ABOUT 1 HOUR

Sift the flour on to a work surface and make a well. Break in the eggs and mix them into the flour with a pinch of salt. Begin with a fork, then use your hands to make a firm but elastic dough. Wrap in plastic wrap. Refrigerate for 30 minutes.

Meanwhile, trim the spinach beet and boil it with a pinch of salt. Drain, squeeze dry and chop coarsely.

Roll out the dough into thin sheets. Cut these into 6 inch squares and cook them, a few at a time, in plenty of boiling salted water. Drain, refresh in a bowl of cold water, then lay the squares side by side on a tea towel, overlapping slightly, to make a regular 16 × 11 inch rectangle. With the given quantity of ingredients, you should be able to make two rectangles. Spread over the spinach beet, ham and Parmesan cheese, then roll up. Cut the rolls into thickish slices and arrange them in an oven-to-table dish. Preheat the oven to 475°F.

Shortly before serving, chop the shallot and brown it in the butter. Add the cream and salt and pepper to taste. Thicken the sauce slightly, then coat the rolls with it, sprinkling them with Parmesan. Cover the dish with foil and cook in the hot oven for about 10 minutes. Uncover and place under the grill to form a golden crust. (Our photo, below, shows the rolls before cooking in the oven.)

Tortelloni with Zucchini

Tortelloni di zucchini

---

1 lb zucchini
4 oz button mushrooms
olive oil
garlic
1 cup grated Parmesan cheese
5 eggs
a little marjoram
¼ cup all-purpose flour
nutmeg
salt and pepper
12 oz tomatoes
4 tablespoons butter
fresh basil

SERVES 6

PREPARATION AND COOKING TIME:
ABOUT 2 HOURS

Clean and dice the zucchini and mushrooms. Heat ⅔ cup of olive oil in a large frying pan and add a garlic clove (to be removed before blending). Add the mushrooms and zucchini and cook for 10 minutes, then remove from the heat and allow to cool. Blend the mixture in a food processor then stir in the Parmesan cheese, 2 egg yolks, a sprinkle of marjoram, a level tablespoon of flour, a sprinkle of nutmeg and salt and pepper to taste.

Prepare the pasta, sift the flour onto a work surface and make a well. Break in the three remaining eggs and mix them into the flour, together with a pinch of salt. Begin by mixing with a fork, then use your hands to make a firm but elastic dough. Wrap it in plastic wrap and place in the refrigerator for about 30 minutes.

Roll out the dough into thin sheets and cut into 2 inch strips; now cut the strips into 2 inch squares. Put a teaspoon of zucchini mixture on to the center of one half of the square, then fold over to make a triangle, sealing the edges firmly with your fingertips.

To make the sauce, peel and dice the tomatoes. Melt the butter in a large frying pan, add the tomatoes, salt to taste and seven chopped basil leaves and cook the sauce for about 5 minutes or until all the ingredients are thoroughly combined and hot.

Meanwhile, cook the tortelloni in a large pan of boiling salted water until *al dente*. Drain (remove from the pan with a slotted spoon) and add to the sauce. Cook together for a few minutes, then transfer to a serving bowl and serve while still hot.

Fusilli with Squid

Fusilli calamari

---

12 small squid (about 1 lb)
a small bunch of fresh parsley
1 garlic clove
3 slices white bread
⅓ cup grated Parmesan cheese
olive oil
salt and pepper
2 medium onions
scant 1 cup dry white wine
1 lb fusilli

SERVES 6

PREPARATION AND COOKING TIME:
ABOUT 1 HOUR

Preheat the oven to 375°F. Clean the squid; separate the heads from the body sacs and remove the cartilage and intestines from the sacs. Wash the sacs, taking care not to tear them. Chop a good bunch of parsley with the squid heads and garlic and place in a bowl. Add the bread, finely crumbled, the Parmesan, a tablespoon of olive oil and salt and pepper to taste. Mix this stuffing thoroughly, then fill the squid with it, closing the openings with wooden cocktail sticks or thread.

Slice the onions very thinly. Heat 4 tablespoons of oil in a flameproof baking dish, then put in the onions and sweat until transparent. Immediately add the squid and cook over high heat for several minutes, then pour in the white wine and a little water and season. Cover the dish with foil, transfer to the oven and cook for about 40 minutes.

When the squid are ready, cook the fusilli until they are *al dente* in plenty of boiling salted water. Take the squid out of the baking dish and remove the cocktail sticks. Drain the pasta and tip it into the dish with the sauce.

Transfer to a serving dish, toss the squid into the pasta, sprinkle with chopped parsley if you wish, and serve.

RIGHT: *Tortelloni with zucchini.*

Fish Ravioli with Cream and Basil

Ravioli di pesce con panna e basilico

FOR THE PASTA
1 ¾ cups all-purpose white flour
2 eggs
olive oil
salt

FOR THE FILLING
10 oz sole fillets
4 oz uncooked shrimp, shelled
2 egg yolks
3 tablespoons cream
a bunch of fresh parsley, finely chopped
salt and pepper

FOR THE SAUCE
a bunch of fresh basil
3 tablespoons butter
1 cup whipping cream

SERVES 4–6

PREPARATION AND COOKING TIME:
ABOUT 1 ½ HOURS

Sift the flour onto a work surface and make a well. Break in the eggs and mix them into the flour with a pinch of salt and the oil. Begin mixing with a fork, then use your hands to make a firm but elastic dough. Wrap it in plastic wrap and refrigerate for 30 minutes.

Meanwhile, prepare the filling. Mince the sole fillets and shrimp and place in a bowl. Add the egg yolks, cream, the finely chopped parsley leaves, a few grindings of pepper and a small pinch of salt.

Roll out the dough into thin sheets, about ¼ inch thick and about 24 inches square. Spoon little heaps of the stuffing on to the lower half of each sheet, spacing them at regular intervals. Fold over the top half of each pasta sheet to cover the filling, pressing well to seal. Using a fluted pasta cutter or sharp knife, cut out individual ravioli about 2 inches square.

Cook the ravioli in plenty of boiling salted water until they are *al dente*. Chop the basil leaves and sweat in a shallow pan with the butter. Add the cream and bring to the boil. Drain the ravioli, pour on the sauce, mix and serve at once.

Spiral Pasta with Seafood Sauce

Trofie al sugo di mare

---

14 oz langostinos
4 oz jumbo shrimp
1 large onion, peeled
a small bunch of fresh parsley
olive oil
²⁄₃ cup dry white wine
²⁄₃ cup tomato passata (sieved tomatoes)
2 shallots
4 tablespoons butter
1 lb spiral pasta
salt

SERVES 6
PREPARATION AND COOKING TIME:
ABOUT 1 HOUR

Carefully wash the langostinos and shrimp, then shell them, reserving the shells. Using poultry shears, cut up the shells into tiny pieces. Slice the onion very thinly and finely chop half the parsley. Put 3 tablespoons of olive oil in a saucepan, add the onion, parsley and crustacean shells and color over high heat for 3–4 minutes, stirring continuously with a wooden spoon. Pour in half the white wine, let it evaporate, then add the tomato passata and 2½ cups of cold water. Mix again, bring to the boil, lower the heat and simmer gently for 40 minutes. Check the sauce from time to time, and if it starts to dry out, add another glass of water. When the sauce is ready, tip it into a strainer, and press down hard on the shells.

Finely chop the shallots and sweat in a shallow pan with a tablespoon of oil; add the shrimp and langostinos and color lightly, stirring with a wooden spoon, then add the remaining wine and evaporate it. Season the strained sauce with salt and mix it with the shellfish, bring to the boil and cook for 5 minutes. Pour the mixture into a blender and process on full power for 1 or 2 minutes.

Meanwhile, cook the pasta in plenty of boiling salted water until it is *al dente*. One minute before draining it, melt the butter in a shallow pan, add the remaining finely chopped parsley and soften it, then pour in the blended sauce and finally the drained pasta. Mix well so that the sauce goes right into the spirals and serve immediately.

LEFT: *Fish ravioli with cream and basil.*

Pasta Shells "Sailor-style"

Conchiglie marinare

---

8 oz jumbo shrimp
8 oz shark steak
olive oil
2 garlic cloves, lightly crushed
salt and pepper
a small bunch of fresh parsley, chopped
½ cup dry white wine
scant 1 cup tomato passata (sieved tomatoes)
1 lb pasta shells (conchiglie)

SERVES 6
PREPARATION AND COOKING TIME:
ABOUT 40 MINUTES

Remove and discard the shrimp shells. Cut the shark into ½ inch slices.

In a large frying pan, heat 4 tablespoons of olive oil, add the lightly crushed garlic and cook until well colored. Remove the garlic and put the shrimp and shark slices into the pan. Season and, over high heat, let the fish absorb the flavors for a few minutes. Add a tablespoon of chopped parsley, pour in the wine and allow it to evaporate.

As soon as the wine has evaporated from the sauce, add the tomato passata and half a glass of water, mix and simmer over low heat for 15 minutes.

Meanwhile, cook the pasta in plenty of boiling salted water until it is *al dente*. Drain and add it to the pan with the sauce. Toss well and transfer to a serving dish.

Tortelli with Broccoli and Butter Sauce

Tortelli di broccoletti al burro fuso

FOR THE PASTA
2 cups all-purpose flour
1 tablespoon tomato paste
1 tablespoon olive oil
salt
2 eggs
FOR THE FILLING
1 ¾ lb broccoli
1 ½ tablespoons butter
2 shallots, chopped
4 slices white bread soaked in milk
1 cup grated Parmesan cheese
salt and pepper
nutmeg
FOR THE SAUCE
6 tablespoons butter
grated Parmesan cheese
SERVES 6
PREPARATION AND COOKING TIME:
ABOUT 1 ¼ HOURS

First prepare the pasta. Sift the flour onto a work surface and make a well. Put the tomato paste, oil, a pinch of salt and the eggs in the middle. Begin by mixing with a fork, then use your hands to make a firm but elastic dough. Wrap the dough in plastic wrap and place in the refrigerator for about 30 minutes.

Meanwhile, prepare the filling. Carefully trim the broccoli, dividing it into florets and cutting off the hardest and most fibrous parts of the stalks. Cook in plenty of boiling salted water.

Brown the butter and flavor it with the chopped shallots. As soon as the broccoli is cooked, drain it and toss it immediately in the butter. Place in a food processor with the squeezed-out bread and mix to a paste. Transfer to a bowl, mix in the Parmesan cheese and season with a pinch of salt and pepper and a little nutmeg.

Roll out the dough into thin sheets. Pile the filling in small heaps, 2 ¼ inches apart, on half the sheets. Cover with the other pasta sheets, then press down all round and cut out the tortelli with a fluted 2 inch pastry cutter. Cook the tortelli in plenty of boiling salted water until *al dente* and dress them with the butter, heated until nutty brown. Sprinkle the cooked tortelli generously with Parmesan cheese.

Tagliatelle with Seafood Sauce

Tagliatelle alla marinara

---

1 ¾ cups all-purpose plain flour
2 eggs
olive oil
salt

FOR THE SAUCE
1 medium onion
olive oil
9 oz whiting fillets, cut into bite-sized pieces
4 oz peeled shrimp
¼ cup white wine
1 tablespoon tomato paste
1 × 14 oz can chopped tomatoes
salt and pepper
1 tablespoon finely chopped parsley

SERVES 4
PREPARATION AND COOKING TIME:
ABOUT 1 ¼ HOURS

First prepare the pasta. Sift the flour onto a work surface and make a well. Break in the eggs and mix them into the flour with a tablespoon of olive oil and a pinch of salt. Begin by mixing with a fork, then use your hands to make a firm but elastic dough. Wrap it in plastic wrap and place in the refrigerator for 30 minutes.

Meanwhile, finely chop the onion, then sweat it gently in a saucepan with 2 tablespoons of oil. As soon as the onion is soft, add the whiting fillets and the shrimp. Seal the fish on both sides for a couple of minutes, then sprinkle with white wine. When the wine has evaporated, add the tomato paste and the chopped tomatoes. Season to taste, then cover the pan and simmer for about 35 minutes.

Roll out the dough into thin sheets, then cut into thin strips. Cook in plenty of boiling salted water until *al dente*. Drain and place in a serving dish. Pour over all the sauce, sprinkle with chopped parsley and serve at once.

RIGHT: *Tortelli with broccoli and butter sauce.*

Garlic, Oil and Hot Pepper Sauce for Macaroni

Aglio, olio e peperoncino per fusilli lunghi bucati

---

6 garlic cloves
2 hot chilli peppers
1 lb macaroni
¾ cup good olive oil
½ cup grated Parmesan cheese
½ cup grated Pecorino cheese

SERVES 6
PREPARATION AND COOKING TIME:
ABOUT 35 MINUTES

Chop the garlic and chilli peppers coarsely and purée them in a blender with ½ cup of cold water. Add this to a panful of salted hot water, bring to the boil and simmer for 15 minutes, then sieve the liquid into a second pan. Boil the pasta in this and, when it is cooked *al dente*, drain it and add the olive oil and the two cheeses, stirring well.

Pasta Shells with Four Cheeses

Lumaconi ai quattro

---

2 oz Parmesan cheese
1 oz Sbrinz cheese
1 oz Emmental cheese
1 oz Fontina cheese
1½ tablespoons butter
¼ cup milk (not skimmed)
nutmeg
1 egg yolk
4 oz pasta shells
a little chopped parsley for garnish

SERVES 1
PREPARATION AND COOKING TIME:
ABOUT 30 MINUTES

Grate the Parmesan and Sbrinz cheeses and cut the Emmental and Fontina cheeses into small cubes; mix all the cheeses together well.

In a saucepan melt the butter without browning. Remove the saucepan from the heat and add the four cheeses, stirring vigorously with a small wooden spoon. Place the saucepan again over a very low heat and, stirring constantly, melt the cheeses slightly. Add the warm milk in a trickle, mixing constantly until thoroughly smooth and blended, then season it with a grinding of nutmeg. Take off the heat, and add a fresh egg yolk. Keep the sauce warm, stirring often.

Cook the pasta in plenty of boiling salted water until *al dente*. Drain, pour the cheese 'fondue' over it and sprinkle with a pinch of finely chopped parsley. Serve at once before the cheese mixture becomes firm.

Green Tortelloni with Duck

Tortelloni verdi all-anatra

FOR THE PASTA
2 cups all-purpose flour
2 eggs
1 oz spinach, cooked, squeezed dry and finely chopped
salt

FOR THE FILLING
2 duck legs, boned
5 oz pork fillet
olive oil
2 shallots, chopped
1 bay leaf
nutmeg
dry white wine
2 oz prosciutto
½ cup grated Parmesan cheese
salt and pepper

FOR THE SAUCE
4 oz butter
⅓ cup grated Parmesan cheese

SERVES 6
PREPARATION AND COOKING TIME:
ABOUT 1¾ HOURS

To prepare the pasta, sift the flour onto a work surface and make a well. Break in the eggs and mix them into the flour with the finely chopped spinach and a pinch of salt. Begin by mixing with a fork, then use your hands to make a firm but elastic dough. Wrap in plastic wrap and place in the refrigerator for 30 minutes.

Meanwhile, cut the duck meat and pork into bite-sized pieces and brown in 4 tablespoons oil, together with the chopped shallots, bay leaf and a grating of nutmeg. When the meat is browned, sprinkle on half a glass of wine and, when this has evaporated, add a small ladleful of hot water. Reduce the heat, cover and cook the meat for about 35 minutes. Remove from the pan and chop it finely in a food processor with the cooking liquid and ham. Transfer to a bowl. Mix the filling with the Parmesan cheese and season with salt, pepper and nutmeg.

Roll out the pasta into very thin sheets and cut into 2 inch squares. Put a teaspoon of filling in the middle of each square, then fold the pasta into a triangle, sealing the edges well and forming it into a ring. When all the tortelloni are ready, cook them in plenty of boiling salted water until *al dente*.

Toss in melted butter, sprinkle with grated Parmesan cheese and serve immediately, piping hot.

Tagliatelle with Clams and Zucchini

Tagliatelle con vongole e zucchine

---

14 oz clams
1 garlic clove
olive oil
12 oz tagliatelle
salt
8 oz zucchini
fresh basil
fresh sage

SERVES 4

PREPARATION AND COOKING TIME:
ABOUT 20 MINUTES

Rinse the clams in several changes of water, then leave them to soak in fresh water for at least 2 hours to remove all traces of sand. Split the garlic clove and lightly crush it, using the flat edge of a knife. Place in a large shallow pan with 1 tablespoon of olive oil, heat, then add the clams. Trim the zucchini and cut them into rounds.

In another shallow pan, heat 3 tablespoons of olive oil, flavor with a few basil and sage leaves, then add the zucchini. Season and sauté over very high heat. Transfer the open clams still in their shells from the other pan (discard any that are not open) and strain over all their cooking juices.

Leave to simmer while you cook the tagliatelle in plenty of boiling salted water until it is *al dente* then drain it. Pour the pasta into the sauce, shake the pan vigorously to spread the flavor, then transfer to a serving dish and serve at once.

Penne with Shellfish

Penne ai frutti di mare

---

1 lb cockles (or clams)
8 oz bay scallops
14 oz mussels
olive oil
1 garlic clove
1 shallot
½ leek
3 tablespoons butter
salt and pepper
1 tablespoon chopped fresh herbs (parsley, sage, thyme, rosemary, marjoram)
4 tablespoons dry white wine
14 oz penne

SERVES 4

PREPARATION AND COOKING TIME:
ABOUT 1 HOUR

Scrub the shellfish and wash in cold water to remove all traces of sand or beard. Discard any mussels that are open. Heat 2 tablespoons of oil with the garlic in a saucepan, then add the mussels and cook them until they open. (Discard any that do not open.) Set aside. Strain the mussel cooking juice and reserve it.

Meanwhile, chop the shallot and leek and sweat in the butter for 2 minutes. Add the scallops and cook for 1 minute, then add the mussels and season with a pinch each of salt and pepper and the chopped herbs. Sprinkle over the white wine and evaporate it over high heat, then add half a glass of the mussel juice. Reduce by about half.

Cook the pasta until *al dente* in plenty of boiling salted water. Drain it, then add immediately to the sauce and, still over high heat, toss the pasta to flavor it well. Transfer to a serving dish and serve immediately.

Crown of Rice with Chicken

Corona di riso con pollo

FOR THE CROWN
1 1/2 cups arborio rice
1 small onion
olive oil
dry white wine
3 1/2 cups hot chicken stock (or use a bouillion cube)
1 pinch of saffron
1 egg
2 tablespoons grated Parmesan cheese
FOR THE FILLING
1 1/4 cups shelled peas
8 oz chicken breast
1 small onion
olive oil
dry white wine
1 1/4 cups chicken stock (or use a bouillion cube)
1/2 tablespoon cornstarch
2 egg yolks
1/2 cup whipping cream
fresh parsley and fresh basil

SERVES 8
PREPARATION AND COOKING TIME:
ABOUT 1 HOUR

Preheat the oven to 400°F. Soften the onion in the oil. Add the rice and toast it over high heat, then moisten with half a glass of wine. When this has evaporated, add the hot stock, a little at a time, until the rice is cooked *al dente* (about 20 minutes). Add the saffron diluted in half a ladleful of stock. Take the risotto off the heat and beat in the egg and cheese. Transfer the risotto to a well-buttered 9 inch diameter ring mold. Stand in a roasting pan filled with two fingers of hot water and for about 30 minutes.

Trim the skin and bones from the chicken breast and cut the flesh into bite-sized pieces. Soften the onion in the oil, then add the chicken pieces and brown them. Season with salt and pepper, then add the peas and one-third of a glass of wine. When this has evaporated, add the stock and the cornstarch, diluted in a very little cold water. Cook for about 15 minutes, then stir in the eggs mixed with the cream. Cook for another 2 minutes, until the mixture has thickened slightly, sprinkle on a few drops of lemon juice and the parsley and basil, finely chopped together. Unmold the rice crown on to a plate, fill with the chicken mixture and serve.

Stuffed Rice Croquettes

Suppli di riso

1/2 medium onion
olive oil
1 cup arborio rice
dry white wine
3 cups hot chicken or vegetable stock
(can be made from a bouillion cube)
1/4 cup grated Parmesan cheese
2 eggs, beaten, plus 2 yolks
5 oz button mushrooms
1 shallot, chopped
4 oz cooked ham, chopped
flour
breadcrumbs

SERVES 6
PREPARATION AND COOKING TIME:
ABOUT 1 HOUR

Sweat the onion in 1 tablespoon oil. Add the rice and toast it over high heat. Sprinkle on the wine. As soon as this has evaporated, add the hot stock, a little at a time, until the rice is cooked (20–25 minutes). Finally, beat in 2 tablespoons cheese and the egg yolks. Spread the risotto on a tray to cool.

Chop the mushrooms coarsely and brown them in 2 tablespoons of oil flavored with the shallot, doing this quickly so that they do not give off any water. When they are still *al dente* add the ham, a spoonful of cheese and a pinch of salt. Turn off the heat.

Form the cold risotto into walnut-sized balls. Make a cavity in each and spoon in a small quantity of the mushroom mixture. Coat the croquettes first in a little flour, then in beaten egg, and finally in breadcrumbs. Fry them, a few at a time, in plenty of oil. Take them out as soon as they are golden. Drain them on paper towels and keep hot. Serve as soon as they are all fried.

RIGHT: *Crown of rice* (top left); *Stuffed rice croquettes* (top right); *Barley and sorrel soup* (bottom, recipe on page 56).

Rice Croquettes with Spinach and Cheese

Crocchette di riso con spinaci e fontina

---

1 lb fresh spinach
1 small onion
olive oil
1³⁄₄ cups arborio rice
¹⁄₃ cup dry white wine
1 quart hot vegetable stock (or use a bouillion cube)
4 tablespoons butter
¹⁄₃ cup grated Parmesan cheese
salt
4 oz Fontina cheese, finely diced
flour
3 eggs, beaten
breadcrumbs

SERVES 6
PREPARATION AND COOKING TIME:
ABOUT 1 HOUR 20 MINUTES

Trim the spinach and wash in several changes of water to eliminate any dirt. Cook briefly in just the water clinging to the leaves after washing. Drain, squeeze thoroughly and chop coarsely.

Chop the onion and soften in 3 tablespoons olive oil. Add the rice, toast it over high heat, then sprinkle on the wine. As soon as this has evaporated, start adding the hot stock, a little at a time, until the risotto is cooked (about 20–25 minutes). Take the pan off the heat and beat in the chopped spinach, butter, Parmesan cheese and a pinch of salt. Leave until cold, then stir in the diced Fontina.

Divide the risotto into 12 equal parts and form each one into a long croquette. Roll the croquettes first in a little flour, then in the beaten eggs and finally in the breadcrumbs. Coat the croquettes twice. Fry in deep hot oil, drain on a double thickness of paper towels, and serve, decorating the plate as you wish.

Risotto with Salmon Trout

Risotto saporito

---

1 shallot
olive oil
1¹⁄₂ cups Italian rice, such as arborio
¹⁄₃ cup dry Martini
3³⁄₄ cups hot vegetable or fish stock
(can be made from a bouillion cube)
5 oz salmon trout fillet
¹⁄₄ cup light cream
salt
1 tablespoon chopped fresh herbs (parsley, sage,
rosemary, marjoram)

SERVES 4
PREPARATION AND COOKING TIME:
ABOUT 30 MINUTES

Peel and chop the shallot and sweat it in a saucepan with 2 tablespoons of olive oil. Add the rice and toast it over high heat, then sprinkle on the Martini. As soon as it has evaporated, start adding the hot stock, a little at a time.

Remove any bones or skin from the salmon trout and cut the fish into small pieces. Add these to the half-cooked rice. Finish cooking the rice until it is *al dente*, but still moist (about 20–25 minutes), then remove from the heat and stir in the cream to give it a rich texture. Season with salt and the chopped herbs.

Cover the pan and leave the risotto to cool for 2–3 minutes. Transfer it to a serving dish and decorate as you wish.

LEFT: *Classic spelt soup* (top left, recipe on page 56);
Rice croquettes with spinach and cheese (top right);
Green tortelloni with duck (bottom, recipe on page 84).

Risotto with Quails

Risotto con le quaglie

---

4 quails, cleaned and prepared
olive oil
1 medium stalk celery, 1 small carrot and 1 small onion
1½ cups arborio rice
1 teaspoon tomato paste
chopped fresh herbs (parsley, sage, rosemary)
1¼ quarts hot chicken stock (or use a bouillion cube)
salt and pepper
1 small onion (for the risotto)
dry white wine
6 tablespoons butter
1 tablespoon grated Parmesan cheese

SERVES 4

PREPARATION AND COOKING TIME: ABOUT 1 HOUR

Brown the quails in 3 tablespoons oil.
Meanwhile, finely dice the celery, carrot and onion. As soon as the quails are well browned, add the vegetable mixture and soften over low heat, then add the tomato paste, a pinch of herbs and half the stock. Season with salt and pepper, cover and braise over medium heat for about 30 minutes.

When you are ready to cook the risotto, finely chop the small onion and soften in 3 tablespoons oil. Add the rice, toast it over high heat, then sprinkle with half a glass of wine. As soon as this has evaporated, lower the heat and continue to cook, adding the sauce from the quails and the hot stock, a little at a time. Stop cooking when the rice is still *al dente* and slightly soupy (about 20 minutes). Season with salt and beat in the butter and a spoonful of Parmesan. Cover and leave the risotto to rest for a few minutes before serving it with the quails.

Seafood Risotto

Risotto alla marinara

FOR THE RISOTTO
1 medium onion, chopped
olive oil
1¼ cups Italian rice, such as arborio
2½ cups, more if necessary, light fish or vegetable stock
(can be made with a bouillion cube)
butter for the mold

FOR THE GARNISH
14 oz mussels
olive oil
2 garlic cloves
8 oz small squid
5 oz uncooked shrimp
oregano
1 tomato, peeled and chopped

SERVES 6
PREPARATION AND COOKING TIME:
ABOUT 1 HOUR

Soften the onion in 3 tablespoons of olive oil. Add the rice, toast it over high heat, then sprinkle on a little stock. As soon as this has evaporated, start adding the rest of the stock, a little at a time, until the risotto is just cooked (about 20 minutes). Preheat oven to 400°F.

Meanwhile, scrub the mussels, removing the beards and any that are open. Put them in a saucepan with 2 tablespoons of olive oil and a lightly crushed clove of garlic. Set over high heat and, as soon as they open, take them out of their shells and strain and reserve the cooking juices. Discard any that do not open. Clean the squid, removing the cartilage and eyes. Then separate the tentacles and bodies and cut into pieces. Shell the shrimp and chop them.

Heat 3 tablespoons of olive oil and half a chopped garlic clove in a saucepan, add a grinding of pepper, oregano to taste and the squid tentacles and bodies. Add the tomato and, when the sauce is almost boiling, add the shrimp and mussels. Thin the sauce with the mussel juices, season with salt and boil for 3 minutes. Pour the sauce over the prepared risotto.

Butter a fish-shaped (or any other suitable shape) mold and fill with the seafood risotto. Stand the 'fish' in a water bath and cook in the preheated oven for about 20 minutes. Leave to stand for a moment before unmolding onto a serving dish. Decorate as you wish, and serve immediately.

Mussel Stew with Rice

Zuppetta di cozze al riso

olive oil
1 cup arborio rice
2 cups light fish or vegetable stock (or use a bouillion cube)
a small bunch of fresh parsley
½ garlic clove, crushed
about 1¾ lb mussels
8 oz chopped tomato pulp
1 medium onion, chopped
salt
oregano
¼ cup dry white wine

SERVES 4
PREPARATION AND COOKING TIME:
ABOUT 40 MINUTES

Preheat the oven to 400°F. Heat 2 tablespoons of olive oil in a saucepan, add it to the rice and toast it over high heat. Sprinkle over a little of the stock then, as soon as it has evaporated, start adding the rest of the stock, a little at a time, until the risotto is just cooked (about 20 minutes). Transfer to a large bowl. Wash, drain and finely chop the parsley leaves. Season the rice with a trickle of olive oil, chopped parsley and the crushed garlic.

Thoroughly wash the mussels and scrub them to remove the beards and any impurities. Discard any that are open. Using a sharp knife, open them raw, leaving the mussel in place and the two halves of the shell still joined. Place a spoonful of the prepared rice in each shell, close and tie with kitchen thread so that the mussels do not open during cooking.

In a baking dish, make a bed of tomato pulp. Scatter over the chopped onion and a pinch each of salt and oregano. Arrange the mussels neatly on this bed, sprinkle over the white wine and a trickle of olive oil, then cook in the preheated oven for about 20 minutes. Serve the mussels piping hot, either straight from the baking dish, or in a serving bowl.

FAR LEFT: *Risotto with quails.*

Rice and Artichoke Timbale

Timballo di riso ai carciofi

1 small onion
1 sprig fresh sage
1 garlic clove
4 tablespoons butter
olive oil for frying
1 slice smoked bacon
4 oz boned breast of chicken
flour
1 tablespoon brandy
4 tablespoons dry white wine
²/₃ cup milk
¼ chicken bouillion cube, crumbled
grated nutmeg
1 sprig fresh parsley
2 fresh artichokes
3¾ cups good meat stock
1 tablespoon dry sherry
1½ cups rice
1 pinch saffron

SERVES 4

PREPARATION AND COOKING TIME:
ABOUT 1¼ HOURS

Fry a third of the onion, a sage leaf and half the garlic gently in half of the butter and a tablespoon of olive oil. Coat the chicken cubes in flour and fry the bacon and chicken gently for a few minutes, then add the brandy and wine. As soon as the wine has evaporated, pour on the boiling milk, blended with the bouillion cube and the nutmeg. Stir, cover and allow to reduce slowly.

Fry another third of the onion, the remaining garlic and the parsley gently in 3 tablespoons of oil. Top and tail the artichokes and remove the tough outer leaves. Add them to the pan. Cook for a few minutes and then add half the boiling stock and the sherry. Stir, cover and cook over low heat for 15 minutes or until the artichokes are tender. Drain them, retaining the stock. Preheat the oven to 400°F.

Heat the remaining stock with the stock from the artichokes. Sauté the rest of the onion in the remaining butter in a deep ovenproof pan. Add the rice and cook for a few minutes. Add the saffron, then the stock, stir and bring back to the boil. Cover with foil and bake for 15 minutes or until the rice has absorbed the stock. Remove from the oven and use three-quarters of the rice to line a 1 quart oiled baking mold. Add the chicken mixture and cover with the remaining rice. Cook in the oven a further 5 minutes. Unmold on to a warmed dish and garnish with the artichokes. Serve at once.

Rice with Tomatoes and Mushrooms

Riso al pomodoro con funghi

---

12 oz wild mushrooms (preferably ceps)
butter
olive oil
1 garlic clove
2–3 sprigs fresh parsley
1½ cups rice
1 cup tomato sauce
grated Parmesan cheese

SERVES 4

PREPARATION AND COOKING TIME:
ABOUT 1 HOUR 10 MINUTES

Clean the mushrooms carefully, scraping any earth from the stalks and wiping the caps. Rinse quickly, dry carefully and then slice them. Melt the butter with the oil and the garlic clove. Add the mushrooms and cook for about 10 minutes, then add some pepper and the parsley.

Cook the rice in plenty of boiling water until just tender. Drain, turn onto a heated deep serving dish and combine with the boiling tomato sauce. Add the mushrooms, which should also be hot.

Serve immediately, with grated Parmesan cheese.

Country-style Risotto

Risotto alla rusticana

6 leaves savoy cabbage
3–4 shallots
4 tablespoons butter
olive oil
1½ cups arborio rice
3 tablespoons dry white wine
1 quart vegetable stock
2 oz Italian sausage
3 oz canned chick peas
3 oz canned borlotti beans
salt
½ cup grated Parmesan cheese

SERVES 4

PREPARATION AND COOKING TIME:
ABOUT 40 MINUTES

Remove the central rib from the cabbage leaves, wash the leaves and cook in boiling salted water for about 10 minutes. Remove them from the water with a slotted spoon and lay them on a sloping plate to drain. Meanwhile heat the stock.

Chop the shallots and soften half of the butter and a tablespoon of oil. Add the rice, toast it over high heat, then sprinkle on the wine. As soon as this has evaporated, add the hot stock a little at a time.

When the rice is half-cooked, mix in the coarsely chopped cabbage leaves, the skinned sliced sausage, and the drained chick peas and beans, a third of them pureéd. Taste and add salt if necessary. Once the rice is cooked but still a little firm, remove the pan from the heat and mix in the remaining butter, soften and cut into pieces. Then stir in the grated Parmesan cheese and then serve.

Gnocchi with Egg Sauce

Gnocchetti sardi in salsa d'uova

2 eggs
4 oz cooked ham
4 oz mushrooms
2 oz capers
12 green olives, pitted
5 gherkins, finely sliced
1–1¼ lb small dumplings (gnocchi)
2 tablespoons vinegar
salt and pepper
¼ cup olive oil
3 oz cheese

SERVES 8
PREPARATION AND COOKING TIME:
ABOUT 30 MINUTES

Hard-boil the eggs and cool them under running water. Cut the ham into tiny cubes, discarding any fat. Place the mushrooms, capers, olives and gherkins in a large salad bowl.

Cook the gnocchi in plenty of boiling salted water until *al dente*, drain well and spread on a tray to cool. Shell the eggs then finely crumble the yolks into a bowl. Moisten with the vinegar and season with a little salt and pepper. Gradually blend in the olive oil.

Place the gnocchi and the diced ham in the salad bowl with the other ingredients. Dress with the prepared sauce and stir well. Dice the cheese and stir it into the salad. Serve at once.

LEFT: *Country-style risotto.*

Gnocchi with Cheese Sauce

Gnocchi alla bava

1½ lb potatoes
1 cup flour
2 egg yolks
salt and pepper
nutmeg
2 oz Parmesan cheese (in a block)
4 tablespoons butter
¼ cup light cream

SERVES 4
PREPARATION AND COOKING TIME:
ABOUT 30 MINUTES

Boil the potatoes in salted water, drain, peel and mash them. Add the flour, 1 egg yolk, a little salt and some grated nutmeg. Knead together and divide the dough into small balls. Give the dough balls an interesting texture by rolling them on the back of a cheese grater.

Remove the rind from the cheese and dice it. Put it in a pan with the melted butter and the cream. Place over low heat and stir with a wooden spoon until the cheese has melted. Add the other egg yolk and a generous grinding of pepper, and stir briskly.

Cook the gnocchi in plenty of boiling salted water until *al dente* and they rise to the surface. Drain. Pour the cheese sauce over the boiled gnocchi and serve them at once.

Timbale of Spinach-flavored Gnocchi

Timballo di gnocchi agli spinaci

FOR THE GNOCCHI
2¼ lb potatoes
2½ cups all-purpose flour, plus extra for dusting
1 egg
4 oz spinach, cooked, squeezed dry and finely chopped
salt
2 tablespoons grated Parmesan cheese

FOR THE SAUCE
7 oz cep mushrooms (or fresh porcini)
olive oil
1 garlic clove, chopped
chopped parsley
salt and pepper
3 oz canned chopped tomatoes

FOR THE BECHAMEL
3 tablespoons butter
6 tablespoons flour
2¼ cups hot milk
salt

FOR THE TIMBALE
2 cups all-purpose flour, plus extra for dusting
4 oz butter, plus extra for greasing
salt
4 tablespoons grated Parmesan cheese

SERVES 6

PREPARATION AND COOKING TIME:
ABOUT 1¼ HOURS

Peel and boil the potatoes, then press them through a potato ricer, letting the pulp fall onto a floured work surface. Add the flour and egg, then the chopped spinach, salt and Parmesan cheese. Combine into a dough, then divide the dough into cylinders and cut into small pieces ('gnocchi'). Cook in salted water, drain well and refresh.

To prepare the timbale, quickly make a dough with the flour, butter, a pinch of salt and ⅓ cup water. Leave to rest in the refrigerator for 30 minutes. Preheat the oven to 375°F. On a well-floured surface, pull the dough into a 10 inch diameter circle and use it to line a buttered and floured round mold. Line the dough with baking parchment and fill with baking beans, to prevent it from puffing up as it cooks. Bake in the oven for 25 minutes, then remove the parchment and beans and bake for a further 5 minutes.

To make the sauce, slice the ceps, then stew them in 3 tablespoons oil with the garlic and a pinch of chopped parsley. Season with salt and pepper and add the tomatoes. Cook for 5 minutes until the ingredients are combined and heated through.

Finally, prepare the béchamel. Melt the butter in a saucepan, remove from the heat and stir in the flour to make a smooth paste. Pour in the hot milk and a pinch of salt, return to the heat and, stirring constantly, cook for 2–3 minutes or until the sauce thickens. Remove from the heat.

Fill the timbale with alternating layers of gnocchi, tomato sauce and béchamel. Top with 4 tablespoons Parmesan cheese, dot with butter and bake at 475°F for 10 minutes. Remove from the oven and carefully remove the timbale from the mold onto a serving dish. Serve at once.

LEFT: Timbale of spinach-flavored gnocchi.

Little Fish Gnocchi

Gnocchetti di pesce

1 small onion
olive oil
1 garlic clove
1 bay leaf
1¼ lb whiting fillets
¼ cup dry white wine
a small bunch of fresh parsley
nutmeg
FOR THE SAUCE
1 shallot, finely chopped
olive oil
fresh sage and rosemary
1 anchovy fillet
1½ cups tomato passata (sieved tomatoes)
1 cup whipping cream
FOR THE GNOCCHI
2 lb potatoes
2 cups all-purpose flour, plus extra for dusting
2 eggs

SERVES 8

PREPARATION AND COOKING TIME:
ABOUT 1 HOUR 10 MINUTES

Soften the onion in a shallow pan with 3 tablespoons of olive oil, the garlic and bay leaf. Add the fish to the pan. Pour in the wine, season and cook over high heat until tender.

Make the gnocchi. Cook the potatoes in salted water for about 20 minutes or until tender. Peel and push through a potato ricer or sieve onto a lightly floured work surface.

Remove the garlic clove and bay leaf from the fish, break up the fish with a fork and add it to the potatoes, together with the finely chopped parsley. Season with salt, pepper and a grating of nutmeg. Add the flour and eggs, and mix to a smooth dough.

Divide the dough into several pieces and roll them along the work surface into long cylinders. Cut each cylinder into short pieces and press them against the back of a fork to create ridges. Cook them, a few at a time, in boiling salted water until they rise to the surface. Remove with a slotted spoon and keep warm.

Soften the shallot in olive oil, adding a few sage and rosemary leaves and the anchovy. Stir in the passata and thicken with the cream. Simmer for a minute or two.

Pour the sauce over the gnocchi and serve at once.

Polenta with Mushrooms

Polenta delicata ai funghi

3 cups milk
1½ cups corn meal
½ cup semolina
salt and pepper
12 oz small mushrooms (preferably ceps)
6 tablespoons butter
2½ teaspoons flour
grated nutmeg
1 cup grated Emmental cheese
2 egg yolks
1 garlic clove
a handful of parsley
2 tablespoons olive oil
ground thyme

SERVES 4

PREPARATION AND COOKING TIME:
ABOUT 1 HOUR

Pour 2½ cups each of water and milk into a large saucepan and slowly bring to the boil. Mix the corn meal with the semolina. As soon as the liquid boils add the salt and, after a few moments, gradually sprinkle in the mixed corn meal and semolina. At the beginning stir with a small whisk, then use a wooden spoon. Cook over medium heat for about 40 minutes, stirring frequently.

Clean the mushrooms, trim the stems and wipe the mushrooms with a damp cloth. Slice them thinly. In a small saucepan melt 2 tablespoons of butter, add the flour and stir with a wooden spoon. Moisten with the remaining boiling milk poured in a trickle and, stirring constantly, bring to the boil. Remove from the heat, season with salt and nutmeg, then add the cheese and egg yolks, stirring hard after each addition. Keep the sauce warm, stirring occasionally.

Finely chop the garlic clove with the parsley and soften the mixture in 2 tablespoons of butter and 2 tablespoons of oil, without browning. Add the mushrooms and leave for not more than 5 minutes, seasoning with salt and pepper and a pinch of thyme.

Remove the polenta from the heat and fold in the remaining butter, softened and cut into small pieces, then pour it on to a round serving plate and make a hollow in the center. Pour in the cheese sauce, spread over the mushroom slices and sprinkle with a little chopped parsley. Serve at once.

RIGHT: *Polenta with mushrooms.*

Polenta and Cheese Pudding

'Budino' di polenta al formaggio

---

2 cups milk
salt
1½ vegetable bouillion cubes
3 cups quick-cooking polenta
4 tablespoons butter
olive oil
1 cup grated Parmesan cheese
¼ cup all-purpose flour
2 egg yolks
4 oz Fontina cheese
celery leaves

SERVES 6–8

PREPARATION AND COOKING TIME:
ABOUT 40 MINUTES

Heat 1½ quarts of water and ⅔ cup of milk together. Add a little salt and crumble in a bouillion cube. As soon as the mixture begins to boil, sprinkle in the polenta, stirring first with a whisk and then a wooden spoon. Cook for about 20 minutes, then remove from the heat. Mix in 2 tablespoons of butter in small knobs and half the Parmesan cheese, stirring constantly. Put the polenta into a greased mold with fluted sides. Cover with a cloth while you prepare the sauce.

Melt the remaining butter in a saucepan. Remove from the heat and stir in the flour to make a smooth roux. Boil the remaining milk and add to the roux, a little at a time. Return to the heat and, stirring constantly, bringing the sauce to the boil and flavor with half a bouillion cube.

Remove from the heat and add the 2 egg yolks, the remaining Parmesan cheese and the Fontina cheese cut into small pieces. Mix well, then pour the boiling sauce over the polenta which has been turned out onto a deep dish.

Place chopped celery leaves in the center of the polenta pudding and serve immediately.

LEFT: *White polenta with smoked cheese and spinach.*

White Polenta with Smoked Cheese and Spinach

Polenta bianca alla provola e spinaci

---

1 cup white cornmeal
salt and pepper
1 shallot
4 tablespoons olive oil
8 oz spinach, cooked and squeezed dry
4 tablespoons butter
12 oz smoked provola cheese

SERVES 6

PREPARATION AND COOKING TIME:
ABOUT 1¼ HOURS

Pour a generous cup of water into a saucepan and bring to the boil. Add a small handful of salt, then scatter in the cornmeal, mixing hard so that no lumps form. As soon as the mixture comes to the boil, lower the heat and cook for about 45 minutes, stirring frequently.

Meanwhile, preheat the oven to 475°F. Peel and finely chop the shallot and soften in the olive oil. Add the spinach, leave to absorb the flavor for a few minutes, then season with salt and pepper. Butter an ovenproof dish and pour in the cooked polenta. Dot over the remaining butter, and cover with the spinach and thin slices of cheese. Cook in the hot oven for about 15 minutes.

Remove from the oven and allow to cool for about 10 minutes, then serve the polenta straight from the dish. This makes an excellent complete meal served with a slice or two of cooked ham.

102

Fish & Seafood

Fish and seafood have pride of place in a country largely surrounded by water, and the way in which they are cooked is second to none anywhere in the world. In these pages, you'll find a wonderful selection of marine delicacies that have an authentically Italian style and simplicity. Try baked stuffed seabass, swordfish *en papillote, or trout in green jackets.*

Taranto-style Mussels

Cozze tarantine

---

1 lb tomatoes
2¼ lb mussels
1 garlic clove
olive oil
12 oz potatoes
8 oz zucchini
12 oz onions
salt and pepper
2 tablespoons grated Pecorino cheese
a few sprigs fresh parsley

SERVES 4
PREPARATION AND COOKING TIME:
ABOUT 1¾ HOURS

Parboil the tomatoes and then skin and slice them thinly, discarding the seeds. Scrape and rinse the mussels and place them in a frying pan with the sliced garlic clove and 2 tablespoons of olive oil. Cover the pan and heat briskly to open the shells. Discard any mussels that don't open, then discard the empty half of each shell and place the half containing the mussel on a plate. Strain the cooking juices into a bowl. Peel and wash the potatoes and slice them, not too thinly. Top and tail the zucchini and cut them into slices about ⅛ inch thick. Slice the onions very finely.

Preheat the oven to 325°F. Grease a large ovenproof pan or dish with plenty of olive oil and line the bottom of it with a quarter of the onion rings. Arrange all the potato slices on top in one layer. Add another layer of onion rings and sprinkle with salt. Arrange half the mussels on top of the onion rings. Add half the tomatoes and season with pepper and a tablespoon of grated Pecorino cheese. Add another layer of onion rings, then all the zucchini slices and then the rest of the onions. Sprinkle with salt. Add another layer of mussels and top with the remaining tomato and a little pepper.

Sprinkle with the remaining grated Pecorino cheese and pour on all the strained mussel juices and 5–6 tablespoons of oil. Add a few sprigs of parsley and cover the pan with a lid or with foil. Bake in the oven for about 1 hour or until the potatoes and zucchini are tender.

Stuffed Bream

Pagellini alla ghiotta

---

8 small fresh bream, gutted and cleaned
1–2 sprigs fresh parsley
2–3 leaves fresh basil
2 tablespoons capers
2 anchovy fillets in oil
a little oregano
7 tablespoons fresh white breadcrumbs
1 egg
salt and pepper
1 egg, hard-boiled
olive oil
¼ cup dry white wine

SERVES 4
PREPARATION AND COOKING TIME: 1¼ HOURS

Rinse the bream under running water and dry thoroughly. Finely chop 1 sprig of the parsley, the basil, capers and drained anchovy fillets. Stir in a little oregano and 4 tablespoons of the breadcrumbs and bind the mixture with beaten egg. Season with salt and pepper. Stuff the bream with the prepared mixture and sew up with kitchen string.

Preheat the oven to 375°F. Mix the remaining breadcrumbs with the crumbled yolk of the hard-boiled egg and a tablespoon of olive oil. Arrange the bream in a well-greased ovenproof serving dish. Brush them with olive oil and sprinkle with a little salt. Top with the breadcrumbs and egg mixture and a little finely chopped parsley. Sprinkle with olive oil and cook in the oven for 25–30 minutes. Pour on the white wine and cover with foil. Return to the oven for about 10 minutes to finish cooking, then serve immediately.

RIGHT: *Octopus with tomatoes and olives* (top, recipe on page 107); *Taranto-style mussels* (bottom).

Stuffed Squid

Calamari ripieni di magro

8 medium squid
3 handfuls of fresh parsley
3 garlic cloves
4 oz shrimp
1 cup breadcrumbs
2 tablespoons grated Pecorino cheese
2 eggs
olive oil
salt and pepper
1 small onion
½ cup dry white wine
⅔ cup fish stock
1 teaspoon cornstarch

SERVES 4
PREPARATION AND COOKING TIME:
ABOUT 1½ HOURS

Separate the tentacles from the body of each squid. Empty the body pouches and discard the dark outer skins. Discard the eyes and 'beaks' and wash and drain both the tentacles and pouches.

Finely chop a handful of parsley and 2 large garlic cloves and place in a bowl. Peel and chop the shrimp and add to the bowl. Stir in the breadcrumbs, cheese, eggs and 3 tablespoons of olive oil. Season with salt and pepper and blend thoroughly. Stuff the pouches of the squid with the mixture and stitch up the opening.

Finely chop the onion, the remaining garlic clove and a small handful of parsley, and fry gently in 4 tablespoons of olive oil. Add the stuffed squid and their tentacles and fry gently for a few minutes, turning once. Pour over the wine and allow it to evaporate rapidly over a brisk heat. Dissolve the cornstarch in the fish stock and add to the pan.

Shake the pan to make sure that nothing is sticking and then cover it. Lower the heat and simmer for about 40 minutes, shaking the pan occasionally and adding a little more fish stock if necessary. By the end of the cooking, the squid should be fairly dry and the sauce well reduced.

Transfer to a warmed dish and serve sprinkled with a little extra chopped parsley.

Octopus with Tomatoes and Olives

Moscardini, Pomodori e Olive

2¼ lb small octopuses
1 celery stalk
1 small onion
1 sprig fresh parsley
2 small garlic cloves
olive oil
1 lb tomatoes
1 piece lemon rind
salt and pepper
8 pitted green olives
celery leaves

SERVES 4–6

PREPARATION AND COOKING TIME:
ABOUT 2½ HOURS

Remove the 'beak', eyes and viscera from the octopuses' body pouches and discard them. Wash and drain the octopuses. Trim the celery and chop it finely with the onion, parsley and garlic. Heat 4 tablespoons of olive oil in a saucepan and lightly fry the chopped vegetables. Wash and chop the tomatoes and purée them. Add them to the pan, stir the mixture and bring it slowly to the boil.

Beat the octopus tentacles with a wooden meat mallet, slice tentacles and bodies, and stir them into the boiling sauce. Add a piece of lemon rind. Season with a little salt and pepper and bring the mixture back to the boil. Lower the heat, cover the pan and cook for about 1¾ hours, stirring occasionally. If the sauce reduces too much, pour on a little boiling water.

Stir in the olives and cook for 15 minutes more. Test and adjust the seasoning according to taste. Serve topped with a few finely chopped celery leaves.

Red Mullet and Hake with Anchovies

Triglie e merluzzetti all'acciuga

---

5 small red mullet, together weighing about 12 oz, gutted
and cleaned
5 baby hake, together weighing about 12 oz
olive oil
1 garlic clove
1 sprig parsley
2 anchovy fillets
2 tablespoons breadcrumbs
oregano
salt and pepper
1 tablespoon lemon juice
1 lemon, sliced
a little dry white wine

SERVES 5

PREPARATION AND COOKING TIME:
ABOUT 45 MINUTES

Rinse the fish well under running water and dry. Oil an ovenproof dish which is large enough to hold all the fish without any overlap. Preheat the oven to 375°F.

Finely chop a large garlic clove, the parsley and well-drained anchovy fillets, and place them in a shallow bowl. Add the breadcrumbs, a little oregano and a generous pinch of salt and pepper. Mix to blend.

In another shallow bowl, beat the lemon juice with 3 tablespoons of olive oil and a large pinch of salt to form a smooth sauce. Dip the fish one by one in the sauce and then sprinkle them with the breadcrumb mixture. Arrange the fish on the ovenproof dish, alternating the two different types of fish.

Place half-slices of lemon between the heads of the fish and sprinkle with a little olive oil. Cook in the oven for about 15 minutes, pouring on a little white wine halfway through cooking. Serve hot.

LEFT: *Stuffed squid.*

Swordfish Skewers

Spiedini di pesce spada

---

*1 red and 1 yellow bell pepper, each weighing
about 10 oz*
2 thick slices of swordfish, together weighing 1 ¼ lb
flour
olive oil
1 garlic clove
½ cup dry white wine
Worcestershire sauce

SERVES 4

PREPARATION AND COOKING TIME:
ABOUT 1 HOUR

Broil the peppers, turning them often, to scorch the skins. Wrap them individually in paper towels and set them aside for a few minutes. Peel away the skins, cut them in half, remove the seeds and stem, then cut them into 1½ inch squares.

Remove the skin from the swordfish and cut each slice into 16 small pieces of similar size. Thread eight pieces on a long wooden skewer, alternating with the pepper squares, and beginning and ending with a pepper square. Make four skewers. Roll each skewer in the flour until well covered, shaking off the excess.

Heat 5 tablespoons of hot oil flavored with a slightly crushed garlic clove in a large frying pan and arrange the skewers side by side in the pan. Let the skewers of fish brown well, then sprinkle with the white wine and season with a generous dash of Worcestershire sauce and some salt. Let the wine evaporate almost completely and serve on a heated plate.

Hake with Tomato Sauce

Filetti di nasello infuocati

---

3 hake, each weighing about 12 oz
salt and pepper
milk
flour
olive oil
8 oz firm ripe tomatoes
¾ cup fish stock
2 basil leaves
granulated sugar
1 garlic clove
½ green pepper, scorched and peeled
salt and pepper
1 teaspoon cornstarch

SERVES 6

PREPARATION AND COOKING TIME:
ABOUT 1 HOUR

Gut, clean and fillet the hake. Dip the fillets first in lightly salted cold milk, then roll them in flour. Heat 5 tablespoons of olive oil in a pan large enough to hold all the fish in one layer. When the oil is hot, add the fillets and brown, adding salt and pepper to taste. As soon as they are cooked, remove from the pan and arrange them in a fan on a heatproof dish, without overlapping them. Cover with foil and keep them warm.

Chop and purée the tomatoes, then whisk them together with the fish stock. Strain the mixture through a fine strainer into the pan used to fry the fillets. Add the basil leaves, a pinch of sugar, a slightly crushed garlic clove, salt, pepper, and finely chopped pepper. Simmer for about 10 minutes, then thicken the sauce with a teaspoon of cornstarch dissolved in 5 tablespoons of cold water; stir and simmer for a few more minutes. Discard the garlic and basil. Pour the sauce over the fish fillets and serve at once, garnishing as you wish.

RIGHT: *Hake with tomato sauce* (top);
Swordfish skewers (bottom).

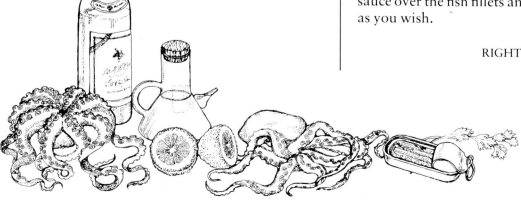

Golden Langostinos

Gamberoni dorati

---

12 fresh langostinos
1 small leek
1 small celery stalk
1 small carrot
1 garlic clove
a few sprigs fresh parsley
4 tablespoons dry white wine
salt
flour
1 large egg
breadcrumbs
oil for frying
1 bay leaf
1 lemon

SERVES 4

PREPARATION AND COOKING TIME:
ABOUT 40 MINUTES, PLUS 1 HOUR MARINATING

Peel the langostinos and lay them in a shallow bowl. Finely slice the leek, celery and carrot and arrange on top of the langostinos. Coarsely chop the garlic with the parsley and add these to the mixture. Pour over the wine and lightly sprinkle with salt. Cover the dish with plastic wrap and leave to marinate for 1 hour in a cool place or the warmest part of the refrigerator.

Remove the langostinos from the marinade, shaking off the other ingredients without wiping them, then dip them first in the flour, next in the beaten egg and finally in the breadcrumbs. Ensure that they are coated all over with these ingredients. Heat the oil with a bay leaf in a large pan and, when it is hot, add the langostinos and fry until they are golden brown all over. Use two forks to turn them over carefully while cooking.

Drain the langostinos from the oil and put them on a plate covered with a double layer of paper towels to absorb any excess oil. Then arrange on a serving dish, sprinkle lightly with salt and garnish with slices of lemon.

Bream San Marco

Orata 'San Marco'

---

1 large bream, weighing about 3¼ lb, gutted and cleaned
1 small onion, thinly sliced
1 small carrot, thinly sliced
1 small celery stalk, thinly sliced
3 tablespoons butter
1 garlic clove
1 small bay leaf
½ cup dry white wine
½ cup fish stock
2–3 whole black peppercorns
salt
olive oil
a handful of fresh parsley
3 anchovy fillets in oil
Worcestershire sauce
1 tablespoon mustard
juice of ½ lemon

SERVES 6

PREPARATION AND COOKING TIME:
ABOUT 1 HOUR

Rinse and dry the bream. Sauté the onion, carrot and celery in 1 tablespoon of the butter. Add the lightly crushed garlic clove and the bay leaf and pour over the white wine and fish stock. Add the whole peppercorns, half-cover the pan and simmer gently until almost all the liquid has been absorbed.

Preheat the oven to 400°F. Arrange half the vegetables on a large sheet of buttered aluminum foil. Lay the fish on top and cover with the remaining vegetables. Season with a pinch of salt and a little olive oil. Wrap the foil around the fish, place on a shallow baking dish and cook in the oven for about 30 minutes or until it is cooked through.

Meanwhile, finely chop the parsley and anchovy fillets and place them in a bowl. Add a generous dash of Worcestershire sauce, the mustard, lemon juice and 4 tablespoons of olive oil. Mix carefully and adjust the seasoning to taste.

Take the fish out of the oven, unwrap it and cut off the head and tail. Discard the vegetables. Divide the fish in half and remove all the bones. Arrange the two halves on a warmed dish, cover with the prepared sauce, garnish and serve hot.

Savory Anchovies

Acciughe 'in savore'

---

1 ½ lb very fresh anchovies
flour
frying oil
salt
2 large onions
2 large garlic cloves
1 sprig fresh rosemary
1 bay leaf
3–4 peppercorns
a piece of cinnamon stick
olive oil
²/₃ cup white wine vinegar
2 cups white wine
salt
1 vegetable bouillion cube
1 leek, green part only

SERVES 4–6

PREPARATION AND COOKING TIME:
ABOUT 1 ½ HOURS, PLUS 36 HOURS MARINATING

Clean and gut the fish if necessary. Wash them rapidly under running water and drain carefully. Flour them, a few at a time, and shake off any excess flour. Heat plenty of oil in a deep-frying pan and fry the anchovies until they are browned all over. Drain from the oil and lay on a plate covered with a double layer of paper towels to absorb the excess oil. Lightly sprinkle with salt.

Meanwhile, finely slice the onions. Make a small cheesecloth bag and place inside the lightly crushed garlic, rosemary, bay leaf, peppercorns and cinnamon. Secure the bag firmly. Heat 3 tablespoons of olive oil in a frying pan and put in first the bag of herbs and then the onion. Fry gently, stirring with a wooden spoon. As soon as the onions begin to brown, pour in the vinegar and the wine. Mix and bring slowly to the boil, then turn down the heat and cover the pan. Leave to simmer for about 15 minutes. Add salt 5 minutes before removing pan from heat.

Crumble in the bouillion cube. Remove the bag of herbs and squeeze it out well.

Place the anchovies and the boiling marinade in a deep dish and leave to cool, first at room temperature and then in the warmest compartment of the refrigerator for at least 36 hours. Be sure to cover the dish. Before serving, slice the leek into thin rings and use for garnish.

Fried Mixed Seafood

Frittura 'misto mare'

---

²/₃ cup mayonnaise
juice of ½ lemon
Worcestershire sauce
1 teaspoon mustard
paprika
1 sprig parsley, finely chopped
2 gherkins, finely chopped
1 tablespoon capers, finely chopped
oil for frying
12 oz mixed seafood
8 oz squid rings

SERVES 4

PREPARATION AND COOKING TIME:
ABOUT 30 MINUTES

Mix the mayonnaise and lemon juice and season with a splash of Worcestershire sauce, the mustard and a pinch of paprika. Add the chopped parsley, gherkins and capers to the mayonnaise. Blend to make a smooth sauce. Check and adjust the seasoning to taste. Pour into a serving bowl or jug.

Heat plenty of oil in a deep-frying pan and fry the mixed seafood and squid briskly until crisp and golden (2–3 minutes should be enough). Drain well on paper towels and arrange on a warm plate. Garnish and serve with the prepared sauce.

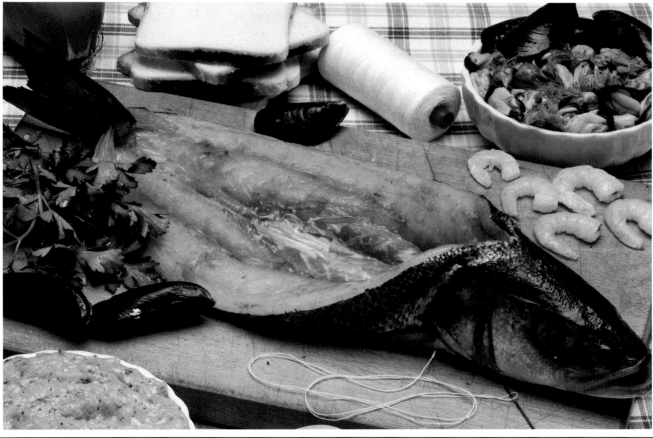

Baked Stuffed Sea Bass

Spigola farcita, al forno

---

1 small onion
2 garlic cloves
a few sprigs parsley
¼ cup olive oil
4 oz cod fillet
1 slice white bread soaked in milk
1 egg
salt and pepper
10 shrimp
15 mussels
breadcrumbs
1 sea bass, weighing about 2¾ lb
2–3 bay leaves
3–4 tablespoons dry white wine

SERVES 8
PREPARATION AND COOKING TIME:
ABOUT 1½ HOURS

Chop the onion, 1 garlic clove and parsley, and sauté in half the oil. Leave to cool. Cut the cod fillet into small pieces, drain the milk from the bread and then place the sautéed mixture, the cod, bread, egg and a pinch of salt and pepper in the blender. Blend briskly for a couple of minutes. Shell the shrimp, dice them and add to the blended mixture.

Scrape and wash the mussel shells and place them in a pan with a tablespoon of oil, the remaining garlic clove and a few leaves of parsley. Cover the pan and place over high heat to open the shells; discard any that do not open. Shell the mussels and add to the blended mixture. Strain the mussels' cooking juices through cheesecloth and reserve. If the stuffing seems too liquid, add some breadcrumbs and leave to stand in a cool place. Preheat the oven to 400°F.

Clean and gut the bass if necessary, then rinse under running water and dry it. Stuff the bass with the prepared mixture and sew up the opening. Brush the fish with olive oil and coat it thoroughly in breadcrumbs.

Place the bay leaves in the bottom of a well-oiled ovenproof pan, put the fish in the pan and bake in the oven for about 30 minutes, turning the fish once or twice during cooking and being careful not to damage it. Sprinkle it with 3–4 tablespoons each of white wine and the cooking liquid from the mussels. Serve the fish cut into large slices.

Aromatic Stewed Clams

Telline in umido aromatico

2¼ lb clams
salt and pepper
a handful of fresh parsley
1 garlic clove
4 fresh basil leaves
¼ cup olive oil
¾–1 lb firm ripe tomatoes
extra basil leaves for garnish

SERVES 4
PREPARATION AND COOKING TIME:
ABOUT 40 MINUTES, PLUS 1 HOUR SOAKING

Wash the clams well under cold running water then soak them in a bowl of cold salted water for about 1 hour to release any sand. Meanwhile, finely chop the parsley with the garlic and the basil. Put the herbs in a large pan with the olive oil and cook over moderate heat. Do not allow to brown.

Blanch the tomatoes in boiling water, peel and chop them. Add them to the pan and stir with a wooden spoon. Cook for about 10 minutes, then drain the clams thoroughly and put these in too. Stir, and cover the pan for a few minutes until the clams have opened (discard any that do not open). Then remove the lid and simmer gently, stirring from time to time. After 5–6 minutes, season with freshly ground pepper, taste and correct the seasoning if necessary. Serve in a warmed bowl or serving dish, garnished with fresh basil.

FAR LEFT: *Aromatic stewed clams* (top);
Baked stuffed sea bass (bottom).

Mussels with a Sea Tang

Cozze al Sapore di Mare

---

6 lb mussels
salt and pepper
4–6 shallots
½ celery heart
10 oz mushrooms
a handful of fresh parsley
1 tablespoon chopped chives
3 tablespoons butter
⅔ cup dry white wine
nutmeg
1 teaspoon cornstarch
a few drops lemon juice

SERVES 6
PREPARATION AND COOKING TIME:
ABOUT 1½ HOURS

Scrape the mussels with a small knife under running water, then leave them in a bowl of salted cold water for at least 30 minutes. Discard any that open.

Meanwhile, finely chop the shallots with the celery, mushrooms and parsley. Add the finely chopped chives and fry in 2 tablespoons of butter, taking care not to let the ingredients brown. Put the mussels into the pan, pour in the wine, season generously with freshly ground black pepper and a little grated nutmeg. Cover the pan and allow the mussels to open over a high heat, shaking the pan from time to time.

Remove from the heat as soon as the mussels have opened (discard any that do not open). Take the mussels from their shells and place on a serving dish. Filter the liquid from the pan through a piece of cheesecloth, then heat the liquid until it has reduced by half. Add the rest of the butter, softened, in small pieces. Dissolve the cornstarch in 2 or 3 tablespoons of cold water and a few drops of lemon juice and add this too. Simmer gently for a few seconds then pour over the mussels and sprinkle generously with chopped parsley. Serve immediately.

Mixed Shellfish

'Capriccio' marino

---

12 sea scallops
8 oz shrimp
1–1 1/4 lb mussels
1/4 cup olive oil
3 garlic cloves
a little lemon juice
1 small onion
a small bunch of fresh parsley
2 tablespoons butter
1/4 cup brandy
1/3 cup dry white wine
1/2 fish bouillion cube
Worcestershire sauce

SERVES 4

PREPARATION AND COOKING TIME:
ABOUT 45 MINUTES

If the scallops are still in their shells, open them using an oyster knife and remove them from their shells. Carefully separate the membranes that surround the scallops and rinse them under running water to remove any sand.

Carefully peel the shrimp. Scrub the mussel shells and rinse under running water; discard any that open. Place the mussels in a pan with 2 tablespoons of olive oil, 2 cloves of garlic and a few drops of lemon juice. Cover the pan and heat briskly to open the shells (discard any that do not open). Remove the mussels from their shells and place on a plate. Strain the cooking juices.

Finely chop the onion, the remaining garlic and a small handful of parsley and fry gently in the butter, and remaining olive oil. Add the scallops, shrimp and mussels, and cook for a few minutes. Pour over the brandy and dry white wine. Season with the crumbled cube and a generous dash of Worcestershire sauce. Add 3–4 tablespoons of the strained mussel cooking juices and simmer until a light sauce has formed. Stir in a little chopped parsley and serve.

Mackerel with Piquant Sauce

Sgombro in salsa forte

---

6 whole mackerel, gutted and cleaned
plain flour
1 garlic clove
olive oil
10 black peppercorns, coarsely crushed
dry white wine
1 onion, finely chopped
1 yellow pepper, seeded and sliced
2½ oz black olives
scant 1 cup tomato passata (sieved tomatoes)

SERVES 6

PREPARATION AND COOKING TIME:
ABOUT 30 MINUTES

Wash the mackerel inside and out, dry then roll in flour, shaking off any excess.

Crush the garlic, using the flat edge of a knife. In a shallow pan, heat 4 tablespoons of oil, add the garlic and coarsely crushed peppercorns and cook for about a minute. Brown the mackerel on both sides, then season to taste and moisten with a very little wine (approximately 2 or 3 tablespoons).

Remove the fish from the pan and keep warm. Add the onion and yellow pepper to the pan with the whole olives. Mix and sweat until the vegetables are tender, then add the tomato passata. Bring to the boil, add the mackerel again and cook over medium heat for 10 minutes.

Transfer the fish to a serving platter, surround with the olives, spoon over some of the sauce and serve the rest separately, in a sauceboat.

Swordfish "En Papillotte"

Pesce spada al cartoccio

---

3 large ripe tomatoes, peeled
1 garlic clove
a small bunch of fresh parsley
4 swordfish steaks or fillets
olive oil
10 oz mussels
7 oz clams
4 oz shelled shrimp
2 basil leaves
1 sprig thyme
1 egg white

SERVES 4

PREPARATION AND COOKING TIME:
ABOUT 1 HOUR

Preheat the oven to 375°F.
Fold a 20 × 28 inch rectangle of baking parchment in half and draw a half heart shape on one side. Cut out the parchment into a heart shape. Prepare three more hearts in the same way.

Wash the tomatoes and cut into small pieces. Place in a bowl with the finely chopped garlic and parsley. Rinse the swordfish slices and flour lightly. Heat 3 tablespoons of oil in a frying pan and add the fish. Brown for 2 minutes on each side.

Scrub and wash the mussels and wash the clams, removing beards and sand, and discarding any that are open. Put them in a saucepan and set over high heat until they open. Discard any that do not open. Heat 2 tablespoons of oil in a frying pan, put in the shrimp and herbs then, after 2–3 minutes, add the mussels and clams with their strained juices, and the tomatoes. Cook for 5 minutes.

Lay one parchment heart on a flat plate, and on it arrange a piece of fish. Season and add some of the mussel and shrimp sauce. Brush the edges of the parchment heart with egg white.

Close the heart-shaped *papillotte* and place it on a lightly oiled baking sheet. Make three more hearts in the same way, place them on the baking sheet and trickle over a little oil. Bake in the preheated oven for about 20–25 minutes, until well puffed up. Transfer to warmed plates and serve immediately.

RIGHT: *Swordfish "en papillotte".*

Monkfish with an Aromatic Sauce

Pescatrice in salsa aromatica

---

1 small onion
1 small celery stalk
1 small carrot
2 tablespoons butter
3 tablespoons olive oil
2 garlic cloves
2 bay leaves
4 oz shrimp, unpeeled
1 cup dry white wine
1 teaspoon tomato paste
1 teaspoon cornstarch
½ fish bouillon cube
salt
1 monkfish weighing about 1¾ lb, head removed
1 sprig rosemary
2 or 3 sage leaves
Worcestershire sauce
celery leaves for garnish

SERVES 6
PREPARATION AND COOKING TIME:
ABOUT 1¼ HOURS

Preheat the oven to 400°F. Finely slice the onion, celery and carrot. Heat in a saucepan with the butter and 2 tablespoons of olive oil. Add a lightly crushed garlic clove and a small bay leaf. Fry gently but do not brown. Then put in the shrimp and sauté for a few minutes. Pour in half the wine and simmer until the wine has almost evaporated. Dissolve the tomato paste and the cornstarch in about ⅔ cup of cold water, pour into the pan and stir. Crumble in the bouillon cube and simmer until the liquid has reduced by half.

Remove the bay leaf and blend the mixture at maximum speed for a couple of minutes. Filter the mixture through a fine strainer, taste and add salt if required. Keep the sauce hot over a double boiler.

Clean, skin and gut the fish (the fishmonger will do this for you), then brush all over with olive oil, sprinkle with salt and place in a dish large enough to hold the whole fish. Surround with a sprig of rosemary, sage leaves, the remaining garlic and bay leaf. Put in the oven for about 30 minutes, moistening from time to time with the remaining white wine.

Towards the end of cooking, add a dash of Worcestershire sauce. Place the fish on a preheated serving dish and pour over some of the sauce. Serve the rest in a sauceboat. If you like, sprinkle chopped celery leaves over the fish for garnish.

Marine-style Clams

Cappe chione alla marinara

---

24 fresh clams
salt
1 bay leaf
8 white peppercorns
2–3 sprigs fresh parsley
1 small onion
1 garlic clove
3 tablespoons olive oil
2 egg yolks
¼ cup whipping cream

SERVES 6
PREPARATION AND COOKING TIME: ABOUT
40 MINUTES, PLUS AT LEAST 2 HOURS SOAKING

Soak the clams in plenty of lightly salted cold water for a long time, frequently turning them and changing the water at least twice. Finally wash them well, one by one, under running water, placing them in a saucepan as they are done.

Cover them with cold water and add the bay leaf, peppercorns and almost all the parsley. Gradually bring to the boil, keeping the lid on but stirring from time to time. Take them off the heat, lift them out, rinse again in the cooking water if there is any trace of sand, and then keep them covered in a large deep serving dish.

Chop the onion and garlic finely and fry them gently in the oil, taking care not to brown them. Pour in the white wine and half a glass of the clams' cooking water strained through a cloth. Simmer for 5 or 6 minutes, then thicken with the egg yolks beaten together with the cream. Taste the sauce (which will be fairly runny), adjust the seasoning as you wish, pour it over the clams, sprinkle with chopped parsley and serve at once.

Rolled Sole with Peas

Involtini di sogliole ai piselli

1 cup frozen peas
salt
10 sole fillets
²⁄₃ cup whipping cream
4 tablespoons butter, softened and diced
1 shallot
¼ cup dry white wine
1 small bunch fresh parsley

SERVES 4

PREPARATION AND COOKING TIME:
ABOUT 1 HOUR

Preheat the oven to 400°F.
To make the stuffing, cook the peas until tender in boiling salted water, then purée them and rub them through a strainer. Purée two of the sole fillets and add them to the peas, season to taste, add 4 tablespoons of cream and mix to a smooth paste. Put the mixture into a piping bag fitted with a small plain plastic tip.

Lightly beat out the remaining sole fillets, salt them and roll each one around a wide cork. Carefully remove the corks and fill the cavities with the pea mixture. Grease a baking dish with all the butter and arrange the filled sole rounds in the dish.

Finely chop the shallot and scatter it over the sole rolls, then add the remaining cream, the wine and some finely chopped parsley. Cover the dish with foil and cook in the preheated oven for 20 minutes.

Transfer the rolls to a serving dish and, if you wish, garnish with cooked, sliced zucchini. Serve at once.

Carpaccio of Salmon Trout

Carpaccio di trota

7 oz tender lettuce
2 salmon trout fillets, cleaned, about 1¼ lb
5 oz tomatoes
2 oz button mushroom caps
4 oz cucumber

FOR THE DRESSING
salt and pepper
4 tablespoons lemon juice
Worcestershire sauce
fresh chives
extra virgin olive oil

SERVES 4

PREPARATION TIME:
ABOUT 15 MINUTES, PLUS MARINATING

Carefully trim the lettuce and wash it in plenty of water, then drain and dry well. Make a bed of the leaves on a serving plate. Check that the trout fillets are perfectly clean then, using a very sharp knife, slice them very thinly, like smoked salmon. Arrange the slices on the bed of lettuce. Wash and dry the tomatoes and mushroom caps, and peel the cucumber. Dice all these vegetables very finely and sprinkle them over the fish.

To make the dressing, in a bowl, mix a pinch of salt with the lemon juice. Add a generous dash of Worcestershire sauce, a pinch of pepper, some snipped chives and 10 tablespoons of extra virgin olive oil. Whisk the dressing until very smooth and pour it over the carpaccio.

Cover the plate with plastic wrap, put in a cool place and leave to marinate for about 30 minutes before serving it.

Stuffed Cod

'Picaia' di merluzzo

4 fresh cod fillets, weighing about 1 ¾ lb in all
salt and pepper
3 large garlic cloves
large bunch of fresh parsley
¾ cup fine breadcrumbs
½ cup grated Parmesan cheese
2 eggs
olive oil

SERVES 6–8

PREPARATION AND COOKING TIME:
ABOUT 1¼ HOURS

Preheat the oven to 375°F.
Lightly beat the cod fillets and overlap them a little so as to form a rectangle with an even edge. Sprinkle with salt and pepper. Finely slice a large garlic clove and scatter over the cod. Wash and dry the parsley and chop it very finely together with the remaining garlic cloves. Place in a bowl. Add the breadcrumbs and Parmesan cheese, a pinch of salt and a generous sprinkling of freshly ground pepper. Mix well and add the eggs and 2 tablespoons of olive oil. Work into a smooth mixture and spread this evenly over the fish.

Using the blade of a long knife, raise the slab of fish, from the shorter edge, and roll it up tightly enough to keep the stuffing inside. Wrap the roll in a double sheet of oiled foil, sealing the ends and then the upper edges. Tie up with kitchen twine, as for a roast. Place the roll in a casserole that is just the right size and bake in the oven for about 45 minutes, carefully turning the roll from time to time.

Serve either hot by itself or cold with mayonnaise.

Gray Mullet with Shellfish

Cefali con crema di molluschi

12 oz mussels
8 oz clams
4 gray mullet, together weighing about 2 lb
2 garlic cloves
a handful of fresh parsley
1 bay leaf
olive oil
1 small onion
⅔ cup sparkling white wine
a pinch of cornstarch
¼ fish bouillion cube
breadcrumbs
salt and pepper
1 sprig rosemary

SERVES 4

PREPARATION AND COOKING TIME:
ABOUT 1 HOUR, PLUS 1 HOUR SOAKING

Scrape the mussel shells with a knife and then leave to soak in cold water for about 1 hour, together with the clams; discard any that do not open. Gut and clean the mullet if necessary, then rinse and dry thoroughly.

Place the mussels and clams in a pan with 2 lightly crushed garlic cloves, a few sprigs of parsley and a small bay leaf. Pour in 2 tablespoons of olive oil, cover the pan and heat gently to open the shells (discard any that do not open). Remove from the heat and leave to cool. Remove the molluscs from their shells and strain the juices.

Finely chop the onion and a small handful of parsley and fry gently in 4 tablespoons of olive oil. Add the molluscs and cook for a few minutes. Pour over half the sparkling wine and 4–5 tablespoons of the strained juices in which the cornstarch has been dissolved. Season with the crumbled bouillion cube and simmer for a few minutes. Place in the blender and blend vigorously. Pour the blended shellfish back into the pan and keep hot.

Coat the mullet in breadcrumbs. Heat 5 tablespoons of olive oil and a sprig of rosemary in a pan and fry the mullet until golden brown on both sides. Sprinkle with salt and pepper and pour over the remaining sparkling wine. Allow the wine to evaporate, then transfer the fish to a warmed dish. Top with the creamed shellfish and serve at once.

RIGHT: *Baked stuffed trout.*

Baked Stuffed Trout

Trotelle ripiene, in forno

---

4 trout, cleaned and gutted
butter for greasing
¼ cup white wine
FOR THE STUFFING
2 whiting, filleted
salt and pepper
¼ cup whipping cream
a small bunch of fresh parsley
1 egg
1 medium red pepper, seeded and diced
butter

SERVES 4
PREPARATION AND COOKING TIME:
ABOUT 1 HOUR 10 MINUTES

Preheat the oven to 400°F.

Slit the trout open from top to bottom along the belly and the back then, with a sharp knife, fillet the fish without removing the heads, skin or tails. Using a needle and fine white thread, sew up the two fillets of each trout following the line of the belly, and sew up a small section of the back fillets, starting from the tail end. The trout should now have a large opening along their backs. Place the prepared trout on a plate, cover with plastic wrap and chill in the refrigerator.

To make the stuffing, purée the whiting flesh in a food processor and place in a bowl. Season with salt and pepper, then stir in the cream, some finely chopped parsley leaves and the egg. Blend again until smooth. Sweat the red pepper in a frying pan with a knob of butter, then add it to the stuffing.

Take the trout out of the refrigerator and fill each one with about a quarter of the stuffing. Butter a baking dish and arrange them in one layer. Pour over the wine, cover with foil, and bake for about 35 minutes. Transfer the fish to a warm serving platter, garnish and serve.

Fish Vol au Vent

Stogliatina di pesce

10 oz frozen puff pastry dough, thawed
1 egg
12 oz turbot fillets
1 swordfish steak (about 12 oz)
7 oz peeled shrimp
flour
1 shallot
olive oil
salt
paprika
brandy
2 tomatoes, peeled and chopped
1 small bunch fresh parsley
flour for dusting, and butter for greasing

SERVES 4
PREPARATION AND COOKING TIME:
ABOUT 45 MINUTES

Preheat the oven to 400°F. Roll the dough on a floured work surface into an 11 × 4 inch rectangle, with a ¾ inch strip for a border of the same dimensions. Place the rectangle on a greased baking sheet, brush with egg, then place the border on top to make a rim. Brush again with egg, then bake for about 25 minutes.

Meanwhile, thoroughly wash the turbot then cut into bite-sized pieces. Remove the swordfish skin and cut the flesh into bite-sized pieces. Roll the fish and the washed and dried shrimp in flour, shaking off any excess. Place the shallot in a shallow pan with 5 tablespoons of oil and sweat until tender. Add the prepared fish, season with salt and paprika, and pour over a small glass of brandy (about ⅓ cup). Tilt the pan to set light to the brandy, flame for a few moments, then extinguish the flame and add the tomatoes and some finely chopped parsley leaves. Lower the heat and cook for about 6 minutes.

Reduce the oven temperature to 375°F. Take the vol au vent out of the oven and, with the point of a knife, carefully make an incision round the inside of the border, taking care not to cut right through the bottom. Push the pastry with your fingertips to make a cavity and fill this with the cooked fish mixture.

Return to the oven to heat through for 5 minutes, then serve immediately.

Casserole of Baby Squid

Umido di fragolini

2¼ lb baby squid, cleaned and gutted
olive oil
2 garlic cloves
1 tablespoon capers
dried oregano
flour
¼ cup full-bodied red wine
1 × 14 oz can chopped tomatoes
1 small bunch fresh parsley

SERVES 4
PREPARATION AND COOKING TIME:
ABOUT 1 HOUR

Wash the baby squid in cold water. Leave to drain and, in the meantime, heat 4 tablespoons of olive oil in a shallow pan. Crush the garlic and add it to the pan, together with the chopped, drained capers and a pinch of oregano. Add the well-drained fish, cook for a few minutes, stirring with a wooden spoon, then discard the garlic. Sift a tablespoon of flour over the mixture, mixing it in with a wooden spoon. Pour on the wine, let it evaporate, then add the chopped tomatoes. Bring to the boil, season and pour over a glass of boiling water.

Cover and cook over low heat for about 50 minutes. Sprinkle the dish with coarsely chopped parsley and serve piping hot.

FAR LEFT: *Trout in green jackets* (top, recipe on page 124); *Casserole of baby squid* (center); *Fish vol au vent* (bottom).

Trout in Green Jackets

Trota al cartoccio verde

---

2 trout, cleaned and gutted
salt and pepper
fresh dill
1 small bunch fresh parsley
sage leaves
1 bay leaf
large green lettuce leaves
extra virgin olive oil

SERVES 2

PREPARATION AND COOKING TIME:
ABOUT 50 MINUTES

Wash and dry the fish, then season inside and out with salt and pepper and put a sprig of dill into each fish. Finely chop the parsley, about 10 sage leaves and the bay leaf, and scatter this mixture over the fish.

Wrap the fish in large lettuce leaves, and secure them with a few turns of thread. Lay the fish on the rack of a steamer, fill the bottom with simmering water and steam for about 30 minutes.

Remove the fish from the pan, untie the lettuce and place them on a serving plate. Drizzle over a trickle of olive oil and serve at once, piping hot.

Baby Octopus in Green Sauce

Moscardini al verde

---

1 ¾ lb baby octopus
olive oil
1 garlic clove
1 medium onion
white wine (optional)
1 small bunch fresh parsley
2 pearl or pickling onions
2 oz lettuce
juice of ½ lemon
1 tablespoon green olive paste

SERVES 4

PREPARATION AND COOKING TIME:
ABOUT 45 MINUTES

Thoroughly clean the octopus then rinse them. Heat a pan of water and, when it starts to boil, toss in the octopus and cook for about 4 minutes. Lift them out with a slotted spoon and spread them out to dry on paper towels.

In a shallow pan, heat 4 tablespoons of oil. Finely chop the garlic and onion, place in the pan and add the octopus. Cover, lower the heat to moderate and cook, stirring frequently, for about 20 minutes, until the octopus are fairly dry. If the pan becomes too dry, moisten with a little water or white wine.

Meanwhile, wash, drain and finely chop the parsley leaves, the pearl onions and trimmed lettuce. Add this mixture to the octopus with the lemon juice and the olive paste. Stir and cook for about another 10 minutes. Transfer the octopus in sauce to a serving dish and serve immediately.

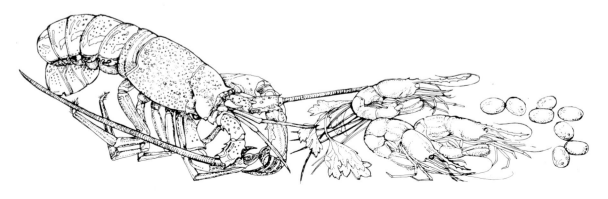

Seafood Couscous

Cuscusu

---

8 oz small cuttlefish or squid
8 oz monkfish tail
8 oz large shrimp
8 oz clams
2 garlic cloves
1 small bunch fresh parsley
1 small onion
olive oil
7 oz chopped tomatoes
salt and pepper
12 oz ready-prepared couscous

SERVES 4

PREPARATION AND COOKING TIME:
ABOUT 1 HOUR

Clean the fish and shellfish and wash carefully in cold water; chop into fairly large pieces. Chop the garlic, parsley and onion, and place in a large dish with 4 tablespoons of oil. Cook, uncovered, for 3 minutes. Add the chopped tomatoes, season and stir well. Cover and cook for 3 minutes. Add the cuttlefish or squid and cook for 12 minutes, stirring at least once. Stir, add the monkfish, clams and shrimp, and cook for 8 minutes. Discard any clams that do not open. Leave to rest, covered, for 10 minutes.

Place the couscous in a large, deep dish and pour over 1¼ cups of lightly salted hot water, to which you have added a tablespoon of oil. Stir and cook in the microwave for 2 minutes or conventionally according to packet instructions. Stir the couscous again and arrange the fish and its juices and sauce on top.

Steamed Whiting

Bianco di pesce al vapore

¼ cup dry white wine
1 shallot, peeled and halved
celery leaves
1½ lb whole whitings
1 tablespoon grated lemon rind
fresh thyme
fresh sage
lettuce leaves
salt and pepper
extra virgin olive oil

SERVES 4

PREPARATION AND COOKING TIME:
ABOUT 1 HOUR

First prepare the cooking broth: put about 1½ quarts water, the wine, shallot and a few celery leaves into a fish kettle and bring to the boil.

Wash the whitings and place on the rack of the fish kettle over the boiling liquid. Season, then scatter on the lemon rind and a few thyme and sage leaves. Cover and steam the fish for about 30 minutes.

Take the fish kettle off the heat, place the fish on a platter and remove the skin, heads and bones. Flake the flesh, following the natural grain.

On a serving platter or individual plates, make a bed of well-washed and dried lettuce leaves. Arrange the flaked fish on the lettuce, season, dress with a trickle of olive oil and serve sprinkled with a little lemon rind, some sprigs of thyme and one or two sage leaves.

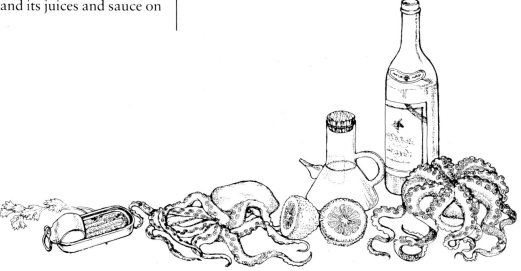

Sea Bass with Zucchini

Branzino alle zucchine

---

1 large sea bass, about 4 lb, cleaned and gutted
1 garlic clove
1 small bunch fresh parsley
fresh marjoram
fresh basil
fresh sage
fresh rosemary
salt and pepper
olive oil
¼ cup dry white wine
2 zucchini
3 slices of white bread
3 tablespoons grated Parmesan cheese
lemon slices, for decoration

SERVES 8

PREPARATION AND COOKING TIME:
ABOUT 1 HOUR

Preheat the oven to 350°F. Wash the fish well, inside and out, and place it in a greased baking dish just large enough to hold it snugly.

Crush the garlic clove and chop together with the parsley and all the other fresh herbs (use these to taste). Season the inside of the fish with salt and pepper, then scatter over the chopped herb mixture. Moisten the fish with 5 tablespoons of olive oil, pour over the wine, then cook in the preheated oven for about 35 minutes.

Meanwhile, trim and wash the zucchini, cut them into thin rounds and cook for 2 minutes in a pan of boiling water. Drain and refresh under cold running water, then lay them out to dry on paper towels.

Crumb the bread in a blender and mix in the grated Parmesan. Just five minutes before the fish is cooked, take the dish out of the oven and cover the bass with the sliced zucchini, arranging them like scales. Sprinkle over the breadcrumbs and cheese mixture, trickle over 2 tablespoons of oil and return the fish to the oven, increasing the temperature to 450°F. Leave in the oven for 5 minutes or more, until the breadcrumbs are well browned.

Take the fish out of the oven, carefully transfer it to an oval serving dish, decorate with a few slices of lemon and some parsley sprigs, and serve immediately.

Fish Medallions

Haché di mare

---

8 oz monkfish tail
5 oz swordfish steak
2 egg yolks
salt and pepper
flour
olive oil
2 scallions
½ cup dry white wine
⅔ cup tomato passata (sieved tomatoes)
a small bunch of fresh parsley
fresh basil

SERVES 4

PREPARATION AND COOKING TIME:
ABOUT 30 MINUTES

Remove the skin from the fish, cut the flesh into small pieces and mince, using the finest blade of the food processor. Place in a bowl, add the egg yolks, and mix well. Season and divide the mixture into 4 equal parts, shaping each into a medallion shape. Roll the medallions in the flour, very carefully shaking off the excess. Heat 3 tablespoons of oil in a shallow pan and brown the medallions on both sides.

Trim the scallions and cut into thin rounds, then add them to the pan with the fish medallions. Cook for a few minutes. Pour over the white wine, partially evaporate it, then add the tomato passata. Season again and cook for a further 5 minutes.

Meanwhile, finely chop the parsley and 4 or 5 basil leaves. Place the fish medallions on individual plates, spoon about a quarter of the sauce over each one, sprinkle with chopped herbs and serve immediately.

RIGHT: *Sea bass with zucchini* (top); *Steamed whiting* (center, recipe on page 125); *Fish medallions* (bottom).

Fillets of John Dory with Lettuce and Peas

Filetti di San Pietro con lattuga e piselli

---

1 ¼ lb John Dory fillets
flour
1 egg, beaten
4 tablespoons butter
olive oil
salt and pepper
1 ¼ cups frozen peas
4 oz lettuce
Worcestershire sauce

SERVES 4

PREPARATION AND COOKING TIME:
ABOUT 40 MINUTES

Wash the fish well, removing the skin. Dry, then dip them first in the flour, shaking off any excess, then in the beaten egg.

In a frying pan, heat the butter with 3 tablespoons of oil until very hot, put in the fillets and cook for about 3 minutes on each side. Remove them from the pan, season and keep warm.

Meanwhile, cook the peas in boiling salted water, wash the lettuce and shred it. Put the vegetables into the cooking juices in the frying pan and heat quickly, stirring with a wooden spoon. Season and add a few drops of Worcestershire sauce. Serve the fish fillets surrounded by the vegetable garnish.

Fillets of Salmon au Gratin

Salmone in filetti, gratinato

---

1 ½ lb salmon fillets
½ cup dry white wine
fresh thyme
fresh marjoram
salt and pepper
olive oil
1 shallot
1 × 14 oz can chopped tomatoes
6 slices white bread
1 small bunch fresh parsley

SERVES 6

PREPARATION AND COOKING TIME:
ABOUT 1 HOUR, PLUS 2 HOURS MARINATING

Wash the fillets, then remove any skin and lay them on a long, deep platter. Pour on the wine and cover thickly with sprigs of thyme and marjoram, season and leave to marinate for about 2 hours.

Preheat the oven to 375°F. Transfer the marinated salmon fillets to a baking dish and strain and reserve the marinating liquid. Mix the liquid with 4 tablespoons of oil and pour over the fish. Cook in the oven for about 25 minutes.

Meanwhile, peel and finely chop the shallot and color it lightly in 1 tablespoon of oil in a saucepan. Add the chopped tomatoes without their juice, season and cook over high heat for about 15 minutes until the mixture has reduced and thickened.

Crumb the bread in a blender. Take the salmon fillets out of the oven and sprinkle them with the breadcrumbs and a trickle of oil, then cook under a hot broiler until the breadcrumbs have formed a golden crust. Transfer the fish to a warmed serving platter, scatter over some finely chopped parsley and pour over the sauce. Serve at once.

LEFT: *Fillets of salmon au gratin* (top); *Sea bream with mustard sauce* (center, recipe on page 130); *Fillets of John Dory with lettuce and peas* (bottom).

Sea Bream with Mustard Sauce

Orate alla senape

---

4 small sea bream, cleaned and gutted
salt and pepper
fresh basil
fresh rosemary
1 medium onion
½ garlic clove
olive oil
⅔ cup dry white wine
a little light fish stock (can be made from a bouillion cube)
4 tablespoons wholegrain mustard

SERVES 4

PREPARATION AND COOKING TIME:
ABOUT 40 MINUTES

Preheat the oven to 375°F.
Wash the fish, inside and out, and dry well. Season and place a few basil and rosemary leaves inside. Arrange the bream well spaced out in a flameproof baking dish. Finely chop the onion and garlic and sprinkle these over the fish. Moisten with a trickle of olive oil.

Cook in the preheated oven for 10 minutes, then baste the bream with the wine and a ladleful of stock. Cook for another 10 or 15 minutes, then take the baking dish out of the oven and remove the fish.

Put the baking dish on the burner, bring the cooking juices to the boil and stir in the mustard. Stir, simmering for 1 or 2 minutes, then pour the sauce over the bream and serve.

Trout with Artichokes

Trotelle con carciofi

---

4 trout, cleaned and gutted
fresh rosemary
fresh sage
fresh parsley
salt and pepper
olive oil
2 artichokes
lemon juice
2 medium onions
1 carrot
¼ cup dry white wine

SERVES 4

PREPARATION AND COOKING TIME:
ABOUT 40 MINUTES

Preheat the oven to 400°F.
Wash the fish, inside and out, then dry with paper towels. Inside each fish, place a sprig of rosemary, a sage leaf and a parsley stalk. Season, then lay the trout in a baking dish, trickle over a little olive oil and cook in the oven for 10 minutes.

Trim the artichokes, removing the tough outer leaves and the spiny parts. Cut them in half and, if necessary, discard the chokes. Place the prepared artichokes in water acidulated with a little lemon juice. Peel the onions, trim, scrub and wash the carrot, then drain and dry the artichokes. Chop all the vegetables.

In a frying pan, heat 3 tablespoons of oil, put in the chopped vegetables and sweat over moderate heat until tender. Moisten with the wine, bring to the boil then, before it evaporates, briefly remove the trout from the oven and pour the mixture over them.

Return the baking dish to the oven and cook for a further 15 minutes. Serve the trout straight from the dish, with all the vegetables and herbs.

RIGHT: *Trout with artichokes* (top); *Aromatic hake steaks* (center, recipe on page 132); *Mussels with saffron* (bottom, recipe on page 132).

Mussels with Saffron

Cozze ai pistilli di zafferano

2½ lb mussels
olive oil
1 garlic clove
1 small red chilli pepper, chopped
1 shallot
1 bay leaf
1 cup whipping cream
small pinch of powdered saffron
1 teaspoon saffron strands, soaked for 10 minutes in a
tablespoon of water
salt and pepper

SERVES 4

PREPARATION AND COOKING TIME:
ABOUT 35 MINUTES

Scrub the mussels, remove the beards and any impurities from the shells, then wash thoroughly under running water. Discard any that are open. In a shallow pan, heat 3 tablespoons of oil with a halved and lightly crushed clove of garlic and the chilli pepper. Add the mussels, cover and set the pan over high heat until they open (discard any that do not open). When they have opened, take the pan off the heat and remove the top shell of each mussel, leaving them still attached to the half shell. Keep warm.

Meanwhile, strain any mussel liquor, return it to the heat, add the finely chopped shallot, bay leaf, cream and the powdered saffron. Cook this sauce, stirring with a wooden spoon, until thick and reduced by about half.

Now add the mussels, immersing them in the sauce. Add the saffron strands, cover and cook over high heat for 5 minutes. Season then divide the mussels between individual plates and serve.

Aromatic Hake Steaks

Tranci di nasello aromatici

1¼ lb hake steaks
3 slices white bread
½ tablespoon capers
fresh rosemary
fresh sage
celery leaves
2 anchovy fillets
green olive paste
olive oil
salt and pepper
4 tablespoons butter

SERVES 4

PREPARATION AND COOKING TIME:
ABOUT 35 MINUTES

Preheat the oven to 400°F.
Rinse the fish and dry carefully on paper towels. Crumb the bread in a blender and transfer to a bowl. Drain and finely chop the capers, the leaves from a sprig of rosemary, a sage leaf, 3 celery leaves and the anchovy fillets and add these to the bowl. Stir, then add about 2 tablespoons olive paste, 3 tablespoons of olive oil and a pinch of salt and pepper. Stir to blend all the ingredients properly, then coat the fish with the paste, pressing it down well to make sure that the hake steaks are completely and uniformly covered.

Heat the butter in a large frying pan and brown the fish steaks on both sides, without cooking them through. Transfer the fish to a baking dish, spacing them out well, and finish cooking in the oven for about 10 minutes. Serve very hot.

Light Seafood Stew with Lemon

Bocconcini di mare al limone

---

3 salmon fillets
4 large cuttlefish or squid, about 12 oz
salt and pepper
8 oz jumbo shrimp
1 shallot
olive oil
¼ cup dry Martini
rind of 1 lemon, chopped

SERVES 4

PREPARATION AND COOKING TIME:
ABOUT 40 MINUTES

Wash and dry the salmon fillets and cut into bite-sized pieces. Clean the cuttlefish or squid, removing the ink sacs. Wash carefully and cut into thin strips. Wash the shrimp, peel, and break off the heads. Peel and finely chop the shallot, and color it in 3 tablespoons of oil. Add the cuttlefish or squid and cook over medium heat for about 5 minutes. Season and add the pieces of salmon and continue to cook for 6 or 7 minutes. Finally, add the shrimp and cook all the seafood for another 5 minutes.

Before removing the mixture from the heat, add the Martini and the lemon rind. Pour the stew into a warmed serving dish. If you wish, garnish with slices of tomato and celery leaves. Serve immediately.

Soused Sole

Sfoge in saor

1¾ lb sole, gutted and cleaned
flour
olive oil
salt
2 large onions, very thinly sliced
white wine vinegar
½ cup pine nuts
½ cup golden raisins
chopped fresh parsley

SERVES 4

PREPARATION AND COOKING TIME:
ABOUT 45 MINUTES, PLUS MARINATING

To skin the sole, make small incisions at the head and tail on both sides of the fish. Lift up a flap of skin and pull it sharply towards you (if it is too slimy, grip it with a cloth). Turn over the sole and repeat on the other side. Dip the skinned sole in flour, shaking off the excess. Fry in deep hot oil until golden on both sides, then drain on a double thickness of paper towels. Season with salt.

Discard the frying oil and clean the frying pan to eliminate any burned bits. Pour in half a glass of fresh oil and soften the sliced onions, without letting them take on any color. Add 2 tumblers of vinegar, simmer for 2–3 minutes, then turn off the heat and add the pine nuts and raisins. Arrange the sole in an earthenware dish and cover completely with the sousing liquid. Cover the dish with plastic wrap and leave to marinate in the refrigerator for a day, or, better still, 48 hours.

Just before serving, sprinkle the dish with a pinch of chopped parsley, if you like.

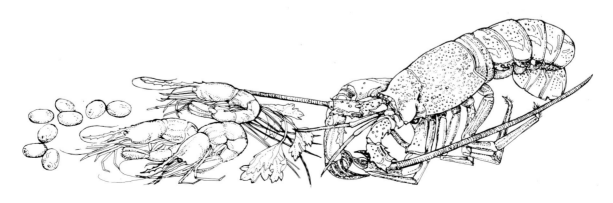

Salmon and Shrimp Stew

Zuppa di scorfano e canocchie

---

1 lb salmon fillets
8 oz cooked shelled small shrimp
12 oz mussels
12 oz clams
olive oil
2 garlic cloves
fresh rosemary
1 medium onion
2 celery stalks
2 carrots
½ cup dry white wine

SERVES 6–8

PREPARATION AND COOKING TIME:
ABOUT 1 HOUR 20 MINUTES

Wash and dry the salmon fillets and shrimp. Clean the mussels and clams, removing any beards or impurities and discarding any that are open. Put the mussels and clams in separate pans, each with 2 tablespoons of oil, a chopped garlic clove and a sprig of rosemary. Cook until they are open (discard any that do not open). Remove the mussels and clams from the two pans and strain the juices through a cheesecloth to remove any residues.

Carefully trim and chop the onion, celery and carrots and sweat in a large saucepan with 3 tablespoons of oil until soft. Add 1 cup of water and the wine and bring to the boil. Cut the salmon fillets into good-sized chunks and add to the broth. Cook over medium heat, turning them only occasionally, for about 5 minutes.

Carefully add the shrimp, mussels and clams and heat through for 5 minutes. Arrange in a suitable dish and serve immediately.

Broiled Langostinos with Sweet Pepper Sauce

Grigliata di gamberoni al ragù di peperoni

---

8 langostinos
salt and pepper
olive oil

FOR THE SAUCE
1 small onion
olive oil
½ each red and yellow pepper
½ cup pine nuts
fresh basil
2 tomatoes, peeled and chopped

SERVES 4

PREPARATION AND COOKING TIME:
ABOUT 30 MINUTES

Shell the langostinos, leaving the heads on, and arrange them on a plate. Season and moisten with a trickle of olive oil. Cover the plate with another inverted plate and leave to marinate in the refrigerator for about 15 minutes.

Meanwhile prepare the sauce. Peel and thinly slice the onion and sweat with 2 tablespoons of oil. Wash and seed the red and yellow peppers, remove the membrane and cut them into tiny dice. Add them to the pan with the onion and sauté over high heat for about 2 minutes. Season then add the pine nuts and a few washed and drained basil leaves, roughly torn with your hands. Cook, stirring, for about 1 minute, then put in the chopped tomatoes. Lower the heat, cover the pan and cook for about 10 minutes to reduce the sauce.

Heat the broiler and, when it is searing hot, drain the langostinos and broil them for about 8 minutes, turning them over halfway through. As soon as they are ready, divide them between individual plates and serve piping hot, accompanied by the pepper sauce.

RIGHT: *Salmon trout "en papillotte"* (top, recipe on page 136); *Broiled langostinos with sweet pepper sauce* (bottom).

Salmon Trout "En Papillotte"

Trota salmonata al cartoccio

10 oz mussels
olive oil
1 garlic clove
5 oz uncooked shrimp
1 shallot
salt and pepper
1 × 7 oz can chopped tomatoes
1 salmon trout, about 2¼ lb, cleaned and gutted
fresh sage
fresh mint
fresh rosemary
1 egg white

SERVES 6
PREPARATION AND COOKING TIME:
ABOUT 45 MINUTES

Preheat the oven to 400°F.
Scrub the mussels and wash thoroughly, removing any beards or impurities. Discard any that are open. Put them in a pan with 2 tablespoons of olive oil and the chopped garlic clove. Cover and heat until the mussels have opened (discard any that do not open). Take the pan off the heat and remove the top mussel shells, leaving the mussels attached to the half shell. Strain any cooking juices into another pan and keep them warm.

Shell the shrimp, peel and finely chop the shallot and sweat it in a shallow pan with 2 tablespoons of oil. Add the shrimp and cook over high heat until browned all over, then season with salt and pepper and moisten with the mussel juices. Bring to the boil, stir, then add the chopped tomatoes and simmer until the sauce is well thickened.

Meanwhile, wash, dry and fillet the fish, then lay the fillets side by side on a sheet of heavy baking parchment. Finely chop a few sage, mint and rosemary leaves and sprinkle them over the fillets. As soon as the shrimp sauce is ready, pour it evenly over the fillets, then add the mussels on their half shells and season to taste. Place another sheet of parchment over the fish, brush the edges with egg white, and seal the packet lightly. Lightly oil a baking sheet and slide on the *papillotte*. Trickle over a little oil, then bake in the preheated oven for about 20 minutes.

Transfer the *papillotte* to a suitable platter and serve, opening it in front of the assembled company.

RIGHT: *Gratin of turbot.*

Gratin of Turbot

Rombo gratinato

3½ lb turbot, gutted and cleaned
fish stock (see method)
4 oz sole fillets
⅓ cup whipping cream
salt and pepper
thyme
butter for greasing

FOR THE SAUCE
¼ cup all-purpose flour
2 tablespoons butter
1 cup fish stock
salt
1 slice white bread made into breadcrumbs, and butter, for
gratin topping
lemon rounds, for garnish

SERVES 6

PREPARATION AND COOKING TIME:
ABOUT 1½ HOURS

Halve the turbot lengthways and fillet it. Cut the fillets into six equal slices. Use all the bones and head to make about 1 quart of fish stock, and reserve it. Purée the sole fillets in a food processor and transfer to a bowl. Add the cream, a pinch of salt and pepper, and stir thoroughly. Preheat the oven to 400°F. Sprinkle the slices of turbot with a pinch of thyme, then cover them with the sole mixture. Arrange in a well-buttered ovenproof dish, adding a ladleful of stock. Cover with foil and bake for about 10 minutes. Take the turbot out of the liquid, cover and set aside (all this can be done a day in advance).

Just before serving, prepare the sauce. Mix the flour and butter to a paste and whisk in the fish stock. Season with salt. Put the pan on the heat and simmer for 6–7 minutes, whisking continuously. Lay the turbot slices on a buttered ovenproof dish and sprinkle with the breadcrumbs. Dot with a little butter and place under the broiler just to give the top a light golden color. Serve hot, with the sauce.

Florentine-style Fillet of Perch

Filetti di pesce persico fiorentina

---

2 lb fresh young spinach
coarse cooking salt
4 tablespoons butter
olive oil
salt and pepper
nutmeg
flour
scant 1 cup milk
1 garlic clove
2 sage leaves
*16 small or 8 large fillets of perch, weighing about 2 lb in
all, divided in half lengthways*
breadcrumbs
parsley

SERVES 4
PREPARATION AND COOKING TIME:
ABOUT 1¼ HOURS

Preheat the oven to 357°F. Wash the spinach
thoroughly under running water. Cook for about
5 minutes in an uncovered saucepan with only the
water that remains on the leaves after washing and a
little coarse cooking salt, until the leaves are tender,
stirring occasionally with a wooden spoon. Drain the
spinach and cool under running water. When it has
cooled, squeeze it dry and chop it coarsely.

Heat half the butter and 2 tablespoons of olive oil
in a large frying pan and, as soon as the fat is hot, put
in the spinach and fry lightly, seasoning with a little
salt, pepper and nutmeg. Sprinkle in a little flour and
heat the milk before pouring that in too. Stir and
simmer for a few seconds, then transfer the contents
of the pan to a heatproof dish. Keep warm in the oven
with the door open.

Flour the fish and shake them to remove any
excess. Clean and dry the pan that was used for the
spinach and melt the rest of the butter and 3
tablespoons of olive oil in it, flavoring with the lightly
crushed garlic and the sage leaves. Fry the fish until
golden brown and season with a little salt and a pinch
of pepper.

Remove from the pan and arrange on the bed of
spinach. Strain the juices in the pan and pour over the
fish. Sprinkle lightly with breadcrumbs and bake for
a couple of minutes. Serve garnished with parsley.

Trout in Herbed Breadcrumbs

Trote al pangrattato aromatico

---

4 cleaned trout, about 8 oz each
2 large sprigs fresh rosemary
1 sprig fresh parsley
1 sprig fresh sage
1 garlic clove
4 slices fresh white bread
salt and pepper
juice of ½ lemon
a little olive oil
lemon slices for garnish

SERVES 4
PREPARATION AND COOKING TIME:
ABOUT 50 MINUTES PLUS THAWING

Wash and dry the trout on paper towels. Finely
chop the leaves of 1 rosemary sprig, the parsley,
3 sage leaves and the garlic clove. Crumble the bread
into breadcrumbs, then mix the breadcrumbs with
the chopped herbs and place on a large plate or tray.

Preheat the oven to 375°F. Slit the trout
lengthways, remove the backbone, and open them
out. Sprinkle the insides with a little salt and pepper.
Rub with a little lemon juice and brush with a little
olive oil.

Coat the fish thoroughly in the herbed
breadcrumbs, place them on a lightly greased baking
tray and cook in the oven for about 20 minutes or
until golden brown. Arrange the trout on a warmed
dish, garnish with parsley and slices of lemon, and
serve immediately.

RIGHT: *Florentine-style fillet of perch.*

Fish Whirls

Girandole di pesci

---

1 small red pepper, diced
½ small onion, chopped
salt and pepper
fresh thyme
olive oil
4 oz button mushrooms
1½ tablespoons butter, plus extra for greasing
2 shallots
parsley
dry white wine
2 hard-boiled egg yolks
chervil
chives
3 egg whites
2 slices white bread, made into crumbs
8 very thin slices of monkfish, about 8 oz
8 small fillets of sole, about 7 oz
8 small slices of fresh salmon, about 7 oz
butter for greasing

FOR THE BRUNOISE
1 zucchini
1 small carrot
1 small leek
butter
salt

SERVES 4

PREPARATION AND COOKING TIME:
ABOUT 45 MINUTES

Brown the diced pepper with the chopped onion, salt and a sprig of thyme in 1 tablespoon oil. Cook for 15 minutes, then purée. Stew the mushrooms in the butter with a chopped shallot, parsley, salt, pepper and a dash of wine. Take off the heat and purée. Rub the hard-boiled egg yolks through a strainer and mix them with some chopped chervil, thyme, chives and salt and pepper. Bind each of these mixtures with an egg white, and add a slice of crumbed bread to the pepper and mushroom mixtures.

Preheat the oven to 350°F. Spread the monkfish slices with the pepper mixture, the sole with flavored egg, and the salmon with the mushroom mixture. Roll up each slice and secure with a toothpick. Arrange the fish whirls in a buttered baking dish and add a chopped shallot and half a glass of wine. Cook in the oven for about 8 minutes.

Meanwhile, cut the zucchini, carrot and leek into very fine dice (brunoise). Soften in about 1½ tablespoons butter and scatter them over the fish whirls as soon as these come out of the oven. Serve immediately.

Hot Fish Carpaccio

Carpaccio caldo di pesce

---

2 slices white bread
7 oz very thin slices of fresh salmon
7 oz very thin slices of swordfish
7 oz very thin slices of monkfish
salt and pepper
chopped fresh parsley and mint
butter

SERVES 4

PREPARATION AND COOKING TIME:
ABOUT 15 MINUTES

In a food processor, reduce the bread to fine white crumbs. Arrange the slices of fish in a large oven-to-table dish, alternating according to the pinkness of the flesh. Season with salt and pepper and sprinkle with the breadcrumbs mixed with ½ tablespoon of chopped parsley and mint.

Dot with small flakes of butter and place under the broiler for 2 minutes, then serve, garnishing the dish as you like.

LEFT: *Hot fish carpaccio* (top); *Fish whirls* (bottom).

Baked Stuffed Salmon Trout

Arrosto di trota salmonata

2 lb salmon trout
7 oz sole fillets
½ cup whipping cream
1 egg white
3 oz small shrimp, cooked and shelled
1 oz shelled and skinned pistachios
olive oil

FOR THE SAUCE
1 lb 2 oz mussels
1 garlic clove
olive oil
¼ cup all-purpose flour
4 tablespoons butter
1 cup fish stock (see method)
1 shallot
dry white wine
2 egg yolks
¼ cup whipping cream

SERVES 8
PREPARATION AND COOKING TIME: 2 HOURS

Fillet the trout and keep the bones to make a stock. Purée the sole fillets in a food processor and place in a bowl. Work in the cream and egg white, and season with salt and pepper. When the mixture is smooth, add the shrimp and chopped pistachios.

Preheat the oven to 400°F. Brush a sheet of parchment paper with butter and lay the trout on it. Spread the sole mixture all over the trout. Cover with the second fillet, brush with melted butter and season with salt and pepper. Enclose the fish in the paper and tie the opening with several turns of string. Lay it in an ovenproof dish, trickle on a little oil and bake in the hot oven for about 40 minutes.

Meanwhile, make stock with the trout bones, appropriate vegetables and 3 cups of water, then strain it. Scrub the mussels and remove any impurities; discard any that open. Open them in a tablespoon of very hot oil, flavored with the garlic (discard any that do not open). Shell them and strain the juices. Make a sauce with 2 tablespoons butter, the flour and 1 cup stock. Brown the shallot in the remaining butter, then add the mussels. Pour on the wine and ½ cup mussel juices. Reduce the sauce by half, stir it into the stock and thicken with the egg yolks and cream. Season to taste. Take the trout out of the oven, leave to rest for 10 minutes, coat with the sauce and serve.

Tuna Tart

Torta di tonno

3½ cups all-purpose flour, plus extra for dusting
8 oz butter, softened and diced, plus
extra for greasing
1 egg
FOR THE FILLING
1 lb potatoes
14 oz tomatoes
8 oz zucchini
1 slice of fresh tuna (14 oz)
olive oil
freshly ground black pepper
oregano
1 small bunch fresh parsley

SERVES 8
PREPARATION AND COOKING TIME:
ABOUT 1½ HOURS, PLUS RESTING THE PASTRY

Sift the flour onto a work surface and make a well. Put in a pinch of salt and the diced, softened butter. Incorporate the butter, then add the egg and knead a little, rolling it into a ball. Wrap in plastic wrap and place in the refrigerator for 30 minutes.

Butter and flour a 10 inch springform cake pan. Roll out the dough on the floured surface to about ⅛ inch thick and use to line the tin, leaving enough overhanging to fold in to make a ring after the pan has been filled.

Peel the potatoes and cut the tomatoes and zucchini into rounds. Skin the tuna and cut into bite-sized pieces. Cover the base of the pan with about half the potatoes, then make an even layer of half the zucchini then the tomatoes. Trickle over a little olive oil, and season with the pepper and oregano.

Arrange the pieces of tuna on the tomatoes in a single layer. Continue to make layers of the vegetables, finishing with tomatoes. Season with salt, pepper and oregano and moisten with about 3 tablespoons of olive oil.

Fold the overhanging pastry inwards, pinch up the edges and bake in the oven preheated to 400°F for about 1 hour. Take the tart out of the oven, sprinkle with finely chopped parsley leaves and serve.

RIGHT: *Baked stuffed salmon trout.*

Delicious Swordfish

Pisci spata a ghiotta

¼ cup raisins
flour
4 swordfish steaks, about 1¼ lb
olive oil
salt and pepper
1 medium onion
2 garlic cloves
1 celery stalk
¼ cup pine nuts
1 tablespoon capers
green olives
14 oz ripe but firm tomatoes, peeled and deseeded
2 bay leaves

SERVES 4

PREPARATION AND COOKING TIME:
ABOUT 50 MINUTES

Soak the raisins in tepid water. Meanwhile, lightly flour the fish and fry in a pan of hot oil. Season with salt and pepper and, when the steaks are well browned, take them out of the pan and keep warm. Finely chop the onion with the garlic cloves and celery. Soften the vegetables in the oil you used for the fish, adding the pine nuts, the squeezed-out raisins, drained capers and a handful of olives. Brown the mixture well, then finally add the tomatoes. Season the sauce to taste, cover and cook over medium heat for about 10 minutes.

Preheat the oven to 400°F. Arrange the swordfish in an ovenproof dish, coat it with the sauce, season again, and add the bay leaves. Add enough tepid water to cover the fish, then cook in the oven for about 15 minutes. Take the fish out of the oven as soon as it is ready and serve with fresh crusty bread.

LEFT: *Sicilian dried cod.*

Sicilian Dried Cod

Piscistuoccu a missinisa

2¼ lb dried salt cod, already softened
olive oil
1 medium onion, thinly sliced
14 oz chopped tomatoes
1 lb 2 oz potatoes, sliced into rounds
4 oz black olives
2 oz capers
4 oz zucchini, sliced
1 small carrot, sliced
1 medium celery stalk, trimmed and cut into sticks
black and cayenne pepper
salt

SERVES 6

PREPARATION AND COOKING TIME:
ABOUT 2½ HOURS

Remove any bones from the salt cod, then cut the fish into even pieces. In a heavy frying pan or terracotta casserole, soften the sliced onion in a little oil. Purée and strain half the tomatoes and add them to the pan with a glass of water. Cover and bring to the boil, then add the pieces of cod, sliced potatoes, olives, capers, zucchini and carrot, the rest of the chopped tomatoes and finally the celery. Season with plenty of black pepper and a pinch of cayenne, cover and cook over medium heat for about 2 hours, adding a ladleful of hot water from time to time.

When the cod is cooked, taste it and add salt if necessary. Serve the dish very hot with its sauce (there should be plenty). Accompany the cod with crusty bread, sprinkled with a little olive oil, then toasted in the oven.

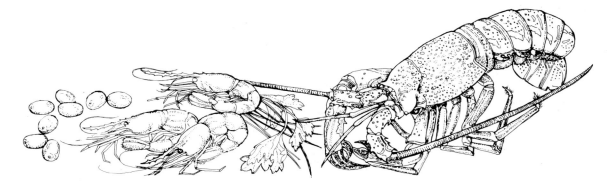

Baked Monkfish with Rosemary

Pescatrice al rosmarino

1½ lb monkfish tail
salt and pepper
fresh rosemary
olive oil
½ cup dry white wine
1 small bunch fresh parsley

SERVES 6

PREPARATION AND COOKING TIME:
ABOUT 40 MINUTES

Preheat the oven to 375°F. Wash and dry the monkfish and place it in a flameproof baking dish. Season and add a few sprigs of rosemary. Moisten with 4 tablespoons of oil and the wine, then bake in the oven for about 25 minutes.

Meanwhile, finely chop the leaves from a branch of rosemary and the parsley. When the fish is cooked, take it out of the oven, remove from the baking dish and keep warm. Remove the sprigs of rosemary from the cooking juices, and put in the chopped herbs. Place the dish on the heat, bring the sauce to the boil and cook for about 2 minutes.

To serve, cut slices from the fish and place on a platter, accompanied by the sauce. If you wish, garnish with a few tender lettuce leaves, a sprig of rosemary and half a lemon, cut into a flower.

Aromatic Sea Bream

Dentice aromatico

---

1 sea bream, about 2½ lb
salt and pepper
chopped fresh herbs (thyme, sage, marjoram)
8 large lettuce leaves
4 oz bacon strips
8 anchovy fillets, chopped
olive oil
1 lb tomatoes
¼ cup dry white wine

SERVES 4

PREPARATION AND COOKING TIME:
ABOUT 45 MINUTES

Preheat the oven to 425°F. Rinse the bream under running water, then dry by patting it with a double thickness of paper towels. Season inside and out with salt, then with a pinch of chopped herbs.

Blanch the lettuce leaves in boiling water. Refresh and lay out half on a tea towel. Arrange half the bacon on top, then finally put on the sea bream. Cover the fish with the remaining bacon rashers and wrap it in the rest of the lettuce leaves, to make a green parcel.

Place the fish in a greased shallow baking dish and scatter over the chopped anchovies, then trickle on a little olive oil. Place the baking dish in the preheated oven and cook for about 10 minutes.

Blanch the tomatoes, peel and dice then add to the fish as it cooks and sprinkle with the white wine. Season with salt and pepper. After about 20 minutes, remove the fish from the oven, drain it, place on a serving platter and keep warm. Rub the sauce through a food mill, then pour it over the fish.

Serve immediately.

RIGHT: *Aromatic sea bream.*

146

Meat

The *piatto di mezzo* or 'middle dish' is the Italian term for the central course of a full meal. Italian cooking is noted for its many ways with veal, but here are also recipes for beef, lamb (treated in Italy as a special-occasion dish), pork, poultry and game, a northern specialty. These dishes range from simple roasts to elaborate recipes with sumptuous sauces suitable for the grandest occasion.

Stuffed Roast Veal with Spinach

Arrosto farcito agli spinachi

---

12 oz leaf spinach, frozen
4 oz beef
4 oz pork
2 oz fairly lean bacon
1 slice white bread, soaked in milk
2–3 sprigs fresh parsley
2 eggs
1 cup grated Parmesan cheese
salt and pepper
nutmeg
1 whole boned breast of veal, about 3 lb
olive oil
2 celery stalks
1 medium carrot
1 small onion
3 garlic cloves
1 sprig fresh rosemary
1 sprig fresh sage
butter
½ cup dry white wine
½ cup chicken stock (can be made from a bouillion cube)
½ teaspoon cornstarch

SERVES 8–10
PREPARATION AND COOKING TIME:
ABOUT 2½ HOURS

Cook the spinach in its own liquid, drain well and spread it out on a board to cool. Squeeze out the moisture thoroughly, chop and put it in a large bowl.

Grind or finely chop the beef, pork, bacon and the drained and squeezed bread and add the mixture to the spinach. Chop the parsley very finely and add this to the mixture. Bind to a smooth mixture with the eggs and the Parmesan cheese, and season with a little salt, pepper and nutmeg.

Preheat the oven to 400°F. Sprinkle a little salt on the breast of veal, then spread the prepared stuffing uniformly over it, stopping about ½ inch from the edges. Roll the meat up, enclosing the stuffing completely, then sew up the opening with kitchen thread. Tie the rolled meat with string, brush it all over with olive oil and put it in a roasting pan just large enough to hold it. Surround it with the chopped celery, carrot and onion, lightly crushed garlic, rosemary and 3 or 4 sage leaves. Dot with butter and

roast for about 1½ hours, turning the meat four or five times, basting often and from time to time moistening with a little of the dry white wine.

When the meat is cooked, remove it from the roasting pan and take off the string. Skim off some of the fat from the cooking juices, dilute with the cold stock in which you have dissolved the cornstarch and the remaining white wine, and simmer gently for a few minutes. Strain through a fine strainer into a warmed sauceboat.

Serve the sauce with the roast, which should preferably be carved at the table.

Valdostana Chops

Costolette alla Valdostana

---

4 thick veal chops, each weighing 8 oz
4 oz Fontina cheese, thinly sliced
flour
2 eggs, beaten
salt
breadcrumbs
butter for frying

SERVES 4
PREPARATION AND COOKING TIME:
ABOUT 30 MINUTES

Cut the chops almost right through horizontally, leaving them joined at the bone side. Insert thin slices of the cheese into the chops and beat them lightly together again with a meat mallet. Coat them first with flour, then with beaten egg mixed with a little salt, and then with breadcrumbs, shaking off any excess.

Fry the chops in plenty of butter until they are golden on both sides. Drain thoroughly and serve at once on a warm serving dish.

RIGHT: *Stuffed roast veal with spinach.*

Veal Steaks Hunter-style

Bistecca alla cacciatora

----

4 veal steaks, weighing 1¼ lb in all
flour
1 medium onion
¼ cup olive oil
salt and pepper
1 lemon
robust red wine
2 tomatoes
2 large cep mushrooms (or fresh porcini)

SERVES 4
PREPARATION AND COOKING TIME:
ABOUT 1 HOUR

Lightly coat the steaks in flour. Peel the onion and slice it very thinly. Put the onion into a casserole dish large enough to hold all the steaks in a single layer and soften it in the oil. Immediately add the steaks and color on both sides. Season with salt and pepper, flavor with a little lemon zest and moisten with half a glass of wine. When this has evaporated, add the deseeded and chopped tomatoes and the trimmed and coarsely chopped ceps (you can substitute dried mushrooms soaked in tepid water, squeezed dry and roughly chopped for the fresh ceps). Cover and cook the steaks over medium heat for about 15 minutes, then serve them with the prepared sauce.

You can use beef steaks instead of veal if you prefer. In this case, after adding the tomatoes and mushrooms, cover the meat with a little stock and cook over very low heat for about 3 hours, shaking the casserole frequently to prevent the meat from sticking to the bottom. The perfect accompaniments for this dish are puréed potatoes, green vegetables braised in butter or the classic Tuscan 'fagioli all'uccelletto' (white beans with tomatoes and olive oil).

Blanquette of Veal with Fava Beans and Sausage

'Bianchetto' di vitello con fave e salsiccia

1¼ lb cubed stewing veal
flour
olive oil
1 medium onion
butter
1 garlic clove
1 sprig fresh sage
½ sprig fresh rosemary
½ cup dry white wine
salt and pepper
1½ cups chicken stock (or use a bouillion cube)
2 cups shelled fresh fava beans
8 oz sausages

SERVES 4
PREPARATION AND COOKING TIME:
ABOUT 2 HOURS

Lightly coat the veal pieces in flour and brown in 3 tablespoons of olive oil. Drain. Thinly slice the onion and fry gently in 2 tablespoons butter and 2 tablespoons of olive oil. Finely chop the garlic clove, a large sage leaf and the leaves of half a sprig of rosemary and add to the pan. Cook for a few seconds, then add the veal.

Pour over the white wine and allow it to evaporate rapidly. Season with salt and pepper and pour over the hot stock. Stir and cook over moderate heat for about 1½ hours, stirring occasionally and adding a little more stock if necessary.

Meanwhile, parboil the beans in salted water for 5 minutes. Drain thoroughly. Cut the sausages into small pieces (about 2 inches) and brown in a tablespoon of olive oil.

About 15 minutes before removing the veal from the heat, stir in the beans and sausage pieces and cover the pan. Check and adjust the seasoning according to taste just before serving.

LEFT: *Veal steaks hunter-style.*

Veal Shank Stew

Ossibuchi in forno

---

2 lb shank or shin of veal, cut into ossobuco pieces
flour
olive oil
1 sage leaf
½ garlic clove
1 medium onion
½ celery heart, trimmed
butter
8 oz peeled tomatoes
2 fresh basil leaves
½ bay leaf
salt and pepper
3 cups good meat stock
a little chopped parsley for garnish

SERVES 4

PREPARATION AND COOKING TIME:
ABOUT 2¼ HOURS

Preheat the oven to 375–400°F. Nick the meat around the bones with the point of a sharp knife, then flour the veal pieces and shake off any excess flour.

Heat 4 tablespoons of olive oil in a large frying pan with the sage and garlic and put in the veal pieces. As soon as they are slightly brown, arrange them in an ovenproof dish which is large enough to hold the meat in a single layer. Leave them to one side covered with foil.

Finely chop the onion and celery and fry in 2 tablespoons butter in the frying pan used for the meat. Purée the tomatoes and add to the other ingredients in the frying pan. Mix, and put in the basil and the bay leaf, a little salt and freshly ground pepper. Simmer for about 10 minutes over moderate heat. Remove the garlic, basil and bay leaf and pour the sauce over the meat. Bring the stock to the boil and pour that in too.

Cover the dish with foil and put in the oven for about 1½ hours. From time to time check that the sauce has not all evaporated and add a little boiling water if necessary. Also make sure the meat is not sticking to the bottom of the dish. Turn the meat over once halfway through cooking. The sauce should be fairly thick by the end. Heat a serving dish and arrange the meat on it. Pour over the sauce, sprinkle with parsley and serve.

Loin of Veal in White Wine

Bianco costato al vino bianco

---

1 loin of veal, about 2½ lb
flour
oil
2 medium onions, finely chopped
4 garlic cloves
3 bay leaves
3 chicken bouillon cubes
2 small tomatoes, skinned and chopped
1 quart dry white wine
1 teaspoon cornstarch
salt and pepper

SERVES 6

PREPARATION AND COOKING TIME:
ABOUT 4½ HOURS

Preheat the oven to 400°F. Tightly bind the loin of veal with kitchen twine and coat in flour. Heat 3 tablespoons of oil in a roasting pan and add the veal, browning it on all sides. Add the onions, the whole garlic cloves, bay leaves, the crumbled bouillon cubes and the tomatoes. Pour on the white wine, cover and cook in the preheated oven for about 2 hours.

Turn the meat every 30 minutes during cooking. After 2 hours, pour enough water into the pan to cover the meat. Re-cover the pan and cook for a further 2 hours, still turning the meat every 30 minutes. Remove the meat from the pan and discard the twine. Place on a serving dish and keep warm.

Strain the cooking juices into a saucepan and add a teaspoon of cornstarch dissolved in 3 tablespoons of cold water, stirring constantly. Simmer gently to form a smooth gravy. Taste and adjust the seasoning according to taste.

Pour some of the gravy over the meat and the rest into a gravy-boat. Serve with fresh vegetables.

RIGHT: *Stuffed fillet of veal with vegetables.*

Stuffed Fillet of Veal with Vegetables

Filetto farcito alle verdure

1½ lb broccoli
salt and pepper
1 whole fillet of veal, 2 lb
1 small carrot
1 zucchini
4 oz cooked ham, sliced
2 oz pancetta, sliced (Italian bacon)
1 medium onion, peeled and chopped
olive oil
dry white wine
milk

SERVES 6

PREPARATION AND COOKING TIME:
ABOUT 2 HOURS

Trim the broccoli, discarding the most fibrous part, divide into florets and cook in boiling salted water. Make a slightly oblique cut in the veal fillet and open it out to form a rectangle about ½ inch thick. Flatten it with a mallet to make it as regular a shape and thickness as possible. Peel the carrot and dice finely. Trim and finely dice the zucchini. Sprinkle the prepared meat with the diced vegetables, then cover it with all but 2 slices of ham. Drain the broccoli and gather it into a single bunch, wrapping the ends of the stalks in the remaining ham. Lay the bunch on one of the short sides of the meat and, starting from that point, roll up the fillet. Cover the roll with the pancetta slices and tie the whole thing up with kitchen twine. Season with salt and pepper.

In a flameproof casserole just large enough to hold the veal, soften the onion in 2 tablespoons oil. Put in the meat and brown well all over on high heat (about 15–20 minutes), then add the wine and milk. Reduce the heat to low and cook the veal for 30–40 minutes.

Take the meat out of the sauce and cut off twine. Strain the cooking juices. Slice meat and arrange on a serving plate. Serve the strained juices separately.

Sweet and Sour Ossobuco

Ossibucchi in agrodolce

½ cup raisins
14 oz small pickling onions, peeled
salt and pepper
flour
6 pieces shank or shin of veal (ossobuco)
olive oil
1 garlic clove
2 bay leaves
dry white wine
hot chicken stock (can be made from a bouillion cube)
parsley, washed, trimmed and finely chopped

SERVES 6
PREPARATION AND COOKING TIME:
ABOUT 1¾ HOURS

Soak the raisins in tepid water. Rinse the onions under running water, then boil for 3 minutes in salted water. Lightly flour the pieces of ossobuco, shaking off the excess. In a large frying pan, heat 4 tablespoons oil with the whole garlic clove, lightly crushed, and the bay leaves, then put in the ossobuco and brown it. Moisten with a glass of wine and, when it has evaporated, add the well-drained soaked raisins and the cooked onions. Pour in 2 ladles of hot stock, season with salt and pepper, then cover and cook over low heat for about 1 hour 20 minutes, moving the meat frequently with a wooden spoon to prevent it from sticking to the bottom of the pan. If it dries out too much during the cooking, add a little more stock.

Take the ossobuco off the heat and transfer to a warmed serving dish. Sprinkle with a tablespoon of chopped parsley and serve immediately with the onions and all the cooking liquid.

Veal with Ham and Sage

Saltimbocca alla romana

---

8 small slices of veal, about 1 lb in all
4 slices of raw ham, about 4 oz
8 sage leaves
3 tablespoons butter
salt
dry white wine

SERVES 4
PREPARATION AND COOKING TIME:
ABOUT 20 MINUTES

Bat out the veal slices. Lay half a slice of ham in the middle of each one, and place a sage leaf on the ham. Thread a wooden cocktail stick through the veal, ham and sage to hold everything together.

Heat the butter in a large frying pan and, when it is foaming, put in the saltimbocca in a single layer. Brown on both sides over high heat, then season with salt and moisten with a quarter glass of wine. When it has evaporated, the meat should be ready (it takes only 5–6 minutes). Carefully drain the meat, transfer to a plate, remove the cocktail sticks, and keep warm.

Place the pan containing the cooking juices on the heat and deglaze with a ladleful of hot water. Simmer for 1 minute, pour the sauce over the meat and serve with peas or other buttered vegetables, as you like.

RIGHT: *Veal with ham and sage.*

Breaded Veal Escalopes with Ham and Parmesan

Cotolette alla bolognese

---

4 slices of leg of veal
salt and pepper
1 egg
breadcrumbs
6 tablespoons butter
4 slices of raw ham
3 oz Parmesan cheese

SERVES 4

PREPARATION AND COOKING TIME: 30 MINUTES

Pound out the slices of veal into thin escalopes and salt lightly. Break the egg into a shallow plate, add a pinch each of salt and pepper and beat with a fork. Spread plenty of breadcrumbs on a sheet of paper towels. Melt about 5 tablespoons butter in a large frying pan. Dip the veal escalopes in the beaten egg, then in the breadcrumbs, pressing the meat with the back of your hand so that the coating adheres firmly. Lay the escalopes in the foaming butter and brown slowly on both sides then, leaving them in the pan, cover with the ham slices and thin flakes of Parmesan cheese. Cover and cook over moderate heat until the cheese has melted completely, covering the veal with a soft white coat.

Meanwhile, in another pan, melt the remaining butter. Drain the escalopes, transfer to a warmed serving dish and pour on the melted butter. Serve at once, before the cheese cools and hardens. If you wish, accompany the dish with a green vegetable sautéed in butter or a fresh salad.

LEFT: *Breaded veal escalopes with ham and Parmesan.*

Veal Stew with Sausage and Dried Mushrooms

Bocconcini di vitello stufati

---

1 medium stalk celery
1 small carrot
1 medium leek
olive oil
1 oz dried mushrooms (porcini), soaked
1 bay leaf
12 oz stewing veal, cut into bite-sized pieces
7 oz Italian boiling sausage, cut into chunks
⅔ cup dry white wine
hot chicken stock (can be made from a bouillion cube)
salt and pepper
zest of ½ lemon
parsley

SERVES 4

PREPARATION AND COOKING TIME:
ABOUT 1 HOUR 15 MINUTES

Trim and chop the celery, carrot and leek and soften in 3 tablespoons oil. Squeeze dry and chop the softened mushrooms, then add them to the pan, together with a bay leaf and the veal. Brown over high heat for 3–4 minutes, then add the pieces of sausage, stirring to blend well. When this has taken on a little color, moisten with the wine and, when it has partly evaporated, add a ladleful of hot stock. Cover, reduce the heat, and cook for about 1 hour, or until the meat is tender.

Season the cooked stew with salt and pepper, then stir in the lemon zest, carefully washed and finely chopped, and a bunch of parsley leaves. Serve hot, with puréed potatoes and steamed zucchini.

Cold Roast Veal in Piquant Sauce

Lombata di vitello in salsa picante

1¾ lb boned veal T-bone, trimmed of all fat
and skin
salt and pepper
olive oil

FOR THE SAUCE
1 medium red pepper, roasted
½ tablespoon capers, drained
3–4 gherkins
fresh basil
½ cup olive oil
2 tablespoons vinegar
salt

SERVES 8
PREPARATION AND COOKING TIME:
ABOUT 1 HOUR 20 MINUTES, PLUS COOLING

Preheat the oven to 400°F. Season the meat generously with salt and pepper, then place in a roasting pan just large enough to hold it. Pour on 3 tablespoons oil and roast in the hot oven for about 1 hour 10 minutes, or until it is cooked through. Take the meat out of the oven and leave until cold.

Just before serving, prepare the sauce. Remove the charred skin from the red pepper, then coarsely chop it and put into a blender with the drained capers, gherkins, a large bunch of basil, the oil, vinegar and a pinch of salt. Blend at maximum speed until you have a perfectly smooth emulsified sauce.

Using a very sharp knife, or preferably a slicer, carve the meat into thin slices. Serve on a bed of mixed leaf salad, dressed with the piquant sauce.

Veal and Eggplant Rolls

Involtini alle melanzane

---

1 lb eggplant
salt and pepper
1 medium onion
olive oil
1½ oz cooked ham
2 slices white bread softened in milk
¼ cup grated Parmesan cheese
fresh oregano
4 large slices of veal, or 8 small ones about 1 lb
10 oz tomatoes
flour
2 tablespoons butter
dry white wine
fresh basil

SERVES 4
PREPARATION AND COOKING TIME:
ABOUT 1 HOUR

Peel and finely dice the eggplant, then place in a colander, sprinkle with salt and leave for about 30 minutes to draw out the juices. Chop the onion and brown it and the diced eggplant in 3 tablespoons hot oil. Transfer the mixture to a food processor, together with the cooked ham and squeezed bread, and purée until smooth. Transfer to a bowl and mix in the Parmesan cheese and some chopped oregano leaves. Season the mixture with salt and pepper. Pound the veal slices until they are large and thin, then spread the eggplant mixture over the slices of veal. Roll them up and secure carefully with wooden toothpicks.

Skin the tomatoes (to do this easily, cut a cross in each one and plunge into boiling water for a few seconds), discard the seeds and chop the flesh. Roll the veal rolls in flour, shaking off the excess. Heat the butter with 3 tablespoons oil until foaming, then put in the rolls and brown evenly. Moisten with half a glass of wine and, when it has evaporated, add the chopped tomatoes and season with salt and pepper. Drain the veal rolls and reduce the sauce, adding a large bunch of chopped basil.

Pour the sauce over the veal rolls and serve hot. A mixed salad makes an excellent accompaniment to this dish.

RIGHT: *Chicken kebabs with herbs* (top left, recipe on page 209); *Veal and eggplant rolls* (top right); *Cold roast veal in piquant sauce* (bottom).

Cold Roast Veal with Savory Sauce

Arrosto freddo con salsa saporita

2¼ lb veal rump
3 shallots
3 anchovy fillets, drained and chopped
1 teaspoons capers, rinsed
2 oz black olives, drained and pitted
1 hot chilli pepper
1 garlic clove
fresh sage
fresh rosemary
olive oil
salt and pepper
dry white wine
1 slice of white bread
2 tablespoons vinegar

SERVES 8

PREPARATION AND COOKING TIME:
ABOUT 1 HOUR 25 MINUTES

Preheat the oven to 400°F. Tie up the meat with several turns of kitchen twine. Place the shallots in a roasting pan with the anchovies, capers, olives and whole chilli. Add the garlic, a sprig of sage and rosemary, and 4 tablespoons olive oil. Set the pan over high heat and heat the vegetables, then season the veal with salt and pepper, put it in the pan and brown all over. Sprinkle with wine, then transfer the pan to the oven. Cook about 1 hour, occasionally basting all over with a ladleful of hot water. When the meat is cooked, lift it out of the juices, remove the twine and leave to cool.

Remove the chilli, sage and rosemary from the cooking juices and put all the remainder into a blender. Add half a glass of cold water, the bread and vinegar. Blend at maximum speed to make a dense, smooth sauce. Transfer to a bowl and serve the sauce as an accompaniment to the thinly sliced cold veal.

Frittata Roll with Veal Mousse

Frittata alla spuma di vitello

---

7 oz boneless veal
1 egg white
⅔ cup whipping cream
salt and pepper
5 large eggs
butter for greasing

SERVES 6

PREPARATION AND COOKING TIME:
ABOUT 50 MINUTES

Preheat the oven to 400°F. Purée the veal in a food processor, then transfer it to a bowl. Mix in the egg white, the cream and a pinch of salt and pepper. Place the mixture in the freezer for about 10 minutes.

Meanwhile, prepare the frittata. Break the eggs onto a plate, season with salt and pepper and beat with a fork. Line a rectangular baking dish with waxed paper, grease with a little butter, then pour in the beaten eggs. Cook in the hot oven until the frittata has set, then turn it out and remove the paper.

Take the bowl of veal mixture out of the freezer and, using a whisk, work it until foamy. Spread this mousse over the frittata, then roll it up, starting from a long side. Wrap the roll in parchment paper, twist the ends of the paper and tie with a few turns of twine. Lay the roll in a roasting pan filled with two fingers of water and cook in the hot oven for 30 minutes.

Take the roll out of the oven and carefully remove the paper. Cut the roll into even slices, arrange on a serving dish and serve hot.

ABOVE LEFT: *Cold roast veal with savory sauce.*

Beef Rolls with Peas

'Braciole' di manzo ai piselli

---

about 1½ lb lean beef in 8 slices
salt and pepper
about 10 oz ham, in 16 slices
4 oz mild Provolone cheese, rind removed
8 fresh basil leaves
1 garlic clove
flour
4 tablespoons butter
olive oil
1 sprig fresh sage
1 medium onion
½ cup dry white wine
12 oz tomatoes
1 beef bouillion cube
super-fine sugar
2 cups shelled peas

SERVES 8

PREPARATION AND COOKING TIME:
ABOUT 2¾ HOURS

Lightly pound the slices of beef, taking care not to split them. Sprinkle with salt and pepper, then lay 2 slices of ham on each beef slice – they should not overlap the edges of the beef. Cut the Provolone cheese into eight small sticks and arrange them on the ham. Beside each one place a small basil leaf and a thin sliver of garlic. Roll up the beef slices and tie them with kitchen twine. Roll them one at a time in flour, shaking them well to remove the excess.

In a saucepan, heat the butter, 2 tablespoons of oil and 2 sage leaves. When the fats are melted and thoroughly hot, put the beef rolls in the pan, and brown them lightly on each side. Then add the onion sliced very thinly; cover and sauté gently for about 10 minutes. Moisten with the white wine and let it reduce by about two thirds.

Add the peeled and puréed tomatoes. Shake the pan to make sure nothing sticks to the bottom, then season with the crumbled bouillion cube, a grinding of pepper and a pinch of sugar. Replace the lid and simmer very gently for about 1½ hours, adding a little boiling water every now and again, if required.

Cook the peas in boiling salted water for 3–4 minutes, drain and add to the beef rolls. Add a little boiling water to the beef rolls and continue cooking for another 30 minutes.

Finally remove the sage leaves from the pan, and cut the twine away from each beef roll. Serve on a warmed serving dish. If any of the tomato and pea sauce remains, it may be used to accompany pasta.

Very Smooth Rissoles

Polpettine vellutate

---

12 oz lean pork
4 oz veal
4 oz sausage
2 oz mortadella sausage
3 slices white bread soaked in chicken stock
a handful of fresh parsley
1 garlic clove
lemon rind
1 large egg or 2 small ones
½ cup grated Parmesan cheese
salt and pepper
ground nutmeg
olive oil
breadcrumbs
6 tablespoons butter
1 small onion
2 small pieces dried mushroom (porcini)
¼ cup flour
2½ cups light chicken stock
celery leaves

MAKES 16 RISSOLES

PREPARATION AND COOKING TIME:
ABOUT 1½ HOURS

Grind the pork, veal, sausage, mortadella and the well-squeezed slices of bread finely.

Chop a handful of parsley with half a garlic clove and a piece of lemon rind, then add the chopped flavorings to the meats, mix thoroughly with the egg and the Parmesan cheese, salt lightly and season with a little pepper and ground nutmeg.

Form into 16 patties or rissoles, moistening your hands with a little olive oil. Press the rissoles in breadcrumbs, then arrange them in a buttered casserole dish and sprinkle with 2 tablespoons melted butter. Leave them in a cool place for about 10 minutes. Preheat the oven to 400°F.

Chop the onion and soften it in the remaining butter in a small pan. Add the pieces of dried mushroom and, after a few seconds, the sifted flour, stirring to prevent lumps from forming. Add the hot stock, pouring it in a trickle and, still stirring, bring the sauce to the boil. Lower the heat and let it simmer for 15 minutes.

Put the rissoles in the hot oven and cook them for about 15 minutes. Cover the rissoles with the strained sauce, sprinkle with the finely chopped celery leaves and serve them immediately.

Leg of Beef with Cloves

Garofolato di bue

---

2 garlic cloves
parsley
marjoram
2 oz salt pork, cut into small dice
2¼ lb leg of beef
3 tablespoons each carrot, celery and onion, chopped
3 oz raw ham
olive oil
salt and pepper
3 cloves, ground in a pestle and mortar
nutmeg
robust red wine
1¾ cups tomato passata (sieved tomatoes)

SERVES 6–8

PREPARATION AND COOKING TIME:
ABOUT 2½ HOURS

Chop 1 garlic clove with the leaves from a bunch of parsley and marjoram. Roll the diced bacon in this mixture and insert it into the meat, then tie the beef up with kitchen twine.

In a deep, heavy saucepan make a bed of the chopped vegetables and the ham, chopped with a garlic clove and a few parsley leaves. Lay the meat on this bed, moisten with a trickle of oil and color lightly over moderate heat. Season with salt and pepper, the ground cloves and a grating of nutmeg. When the meat is uniformly browned, moisten with a glass of wine and evaporate this over high heat. Add the tomato passata and enough cold water to cover the meat. Lower the heat, cover and continue to cook for about another 2 hours or until the meat is tender but not pulpy, and the sauce nicely thickened.

Remove from the heat and serve, cut into thick slices, with the sauce.

RIGHT: *Leg of beef with cloves.*

Roast Beef with Tomato and Garlic Sauce

Filetto alla pizzaiola

---

1 large ripe tomato, weighing about 5 oz
olive oil
1 garlic clove
a few fresh basil leaves
2 oz Mozzarella cheese
butter
12 oz fillet of beef, finely sliced

SERVES 4
PREPARATION AND COOKING TIME:
ABOUT 20 MINUTES

Preheat the oven to 375°F. Cut the tomato in half horizontally, remove the seeds and then dice. Heat 2 tablespoons of olive oil and fry the garlic. Add the tomato, basil leaves and a pinch of salt. Fry over high heat without overcooking. Dice the Mozzarella cheese. Liberally butter a shallow baking dish and place the slices of beef on it, setting them well apart. Pour over a trickle of olive oil and place in the oven for about 2 minutes. The meat should remain almost pink.

Remove from the oven and sprinkle with the cubes of Mozzarella cheese and tomato. Reheat in the oven just long enough for the cheese to melt a little. Arrange the beef on individual warmed plates and serve at once.

Fillet Steak with Piquant Sauce

Controfiletto con salsa piccante

---

4 tablespoons cooking fat
1 small onion
extra cooking fat
¼ cup flour
1 cup light beef stock
1–2 shallots
½ cup white wine vinegar
3–4 gherkins
olive oil
4 fillet steaks, each weighing about 5 oz
Worcestershire sauce

SERVES 4
PREPARATION AND COOKING TIME:
ABOUT 45 MINUTES

Cut the cooking fat into small cubes and finely chop the onion. Melt an extra 2 tablespoons cooking fat in a small saucepan, then add the cubes of cooking fat and the chopped onion. Mix with a wooden spoon and brown gently for a few minutes, then sprinkle with the sifted flour, stir, and moisten with the hot stock, poured in a trickle; stir continuously with a small whisk until the sauce is well blended. Simmer gently for at least 15 minutes, then strain the sauce.

Meanwhile finely chop the shallots and put in a small saucepan, add the vinegar, then simmer very slowly for about 10 minutes. Strain into the sauce, stirring well with the whisk; add the thinly sliced gherkins and, still stirring, simmer for a few more minutes. Remove from the heat and keep warm.

Brush the fillet steaks with olive oil and broil them briefly on both sides under a very hot broiler so that they are rather rare. Salt the steaks, season them with a dash of Worcestershire sauce, then serve with the prepared sauce.

Fillet of Beef with Mushrooms and Parmesan

Filetto con funghi e grana

---

*4 oz roast lean fillet of beef, cut into very
thin slices*
1 medium mushroom (preferably cep)
1 oz Parmesan cheese, flaked
celery leaves
½ garlic clove
anchovy paste
mild mustard
herb vinegar
salt and pepper
olive oil

SERVES 1
PREPARATION TIME: ABOUT 20 MINUTES

Arrange the fillet slices in a ring on a plate which
you have chilled in the refrigerator. Trim the
mushroom and wipe it with a damp cloth. Cut into
slices and arrange the best ones on the slices of meat,
the others in the center of the plate. Pile the flaked
cheese on top and surround with the celery leaves.

Rub the bottom of a bowl lightly with half a garlic
clove, put in ¾ inch anchovy paste, a little mustard
on the end of a teaspoon, 3–4 drops of vinegar and a
pinch each of salt and pepper. Combine the
ingredients with a fork and dilute with a tablespoon
of olive oil. Pour this dressing over the slices of meat
and serve.

Meatloaf with Olives

Polpettoncino alle olive

---

2 slices white bread
milk
14 oz minced beef
½ cup grated Parmesan cheese
1 egg
salt and pepper
nutmeg
4 stuffed olives
breadcrumbs
olive oil
frisée

SERVES 4–6
PREPARATION AND COOKING TIME:
ABOUT 1 HOUR

Soak the 2 slices of bread in a little milk. Preheat the
oven to 375°F.

Squeeze the bread well then add it to the meat and
grind both together. Place the mixture in a bowl, add
the Parmesan cheese, the egg, a pinch of salt, a
grinding of pepper and one of nutmeg. Mix well with
a wooden spoon. The mixture should be rather firm.
Shape it into a loaf about 7 inches long, pressing
the olives into the mixture.

Roll the meatloaf gently in the breadcrumbs to
coat it, then place in a lightly oiled rectangular baking
pan, sprinkle with a little olive oil and bake for about
35 minutes until the surface is lightly browned.

Remove the loaf from the oven and let it rest for
about 10 minutes before cutting it into slices.
Arrange on a serving dish and garnish with tender
leaves of frisée.

Fillet Steak with Bearnaise Sauce

'Tagliata' di manzo con salsa bearnaise

2 tablespoons white wine vinegar
4 tablespoons white wine
1 shallot
a few sprigs fresh tarragon
a few sprigs fresh chervil
a few sprigs fresh thyme
1 bay leaf
1 beef bouillion cube
2 egg yolks
8 oz butter
a few sprigs fresh parsley
2 large beef fillet steaks, each weighing 12 oz
olive oil
1 sprig rosemary
salt and pepper

SERVES 4

PREPARATION AND COOKING TIME:
ABOUT 45 MINUTES

Pour the vinegar and wine into a small pan; add a teaspoon each of finely chopped shallot and tarragon, half a teaspoon of chopped chervil and thyme together, a small piece of bay leaf and a quarter of a crumbled bouillion cube. Simmer until the liquid is reduced to a third, then strain and cool. Place the saucepan in a water bath, add the 2 egg yolks and beat with a small whisk until creamy.

Remove from the water bath and, proceeding as for mayonnaise, add the butter (first melted and still warm) little by little. Do not add more butter until the previous addition has been completely absorbed; halfway through add a tablespoon of lukewarm water. When you have used up all the butter, stir a teaspoon each of chopped fresh tarragon and chopped fresh parsley into the sauce, which should be creamy, then pour the sauce into a sauceboat and keep it warm.

Slightly flatten the two fillet steaks, then brush them on both sides with olive oil and broil for about 6 minutes on each side, first at high heat, then moderate, to allow the meat to cook through without burning on the outside. Brush them with a little oil using a sprig of rosemary during cooking.

Remove the meat from the broiler, season with pepper and salt and serve on a serving board. Slice the meat in front of the guests and accompany it with the hot Bearnaise sauce.

Painter's Steak Tartare

Tartare del pittore

1 lb fillet steak
4 egg yolks
12 round slices lemon
32 capers in oil
1 pickled carrot
6 stuffed olives
4 anchovy fillets in oil
a handful of chopped parsley and a few sprigs
2 baby artichokes in oil
salt and pepper
olive oil
a little lemon juice, strained
tomato ketchup
mustard
Worcestershire sauce

SERVES 4

PREPARATION TIME: ABOUT 40 MINUTES

Grind or finely chop the steak and form four individual heaps on separate chilled dinner plates. Make a well in the center of each heap.

Place an egg yolk, in half an eggshell, in the center of each well. Surround each tartare with six half-slices of lemon and on these arrange 8 capers, well drained from their oil, 3 slices of carrot, 3 olive halves, an anchovy fillet, well dried, a teaspoon of chopped parsley, and half an artichoke, divided into two again.

Garnish with sprigs of parsley and serve with salt, freshly ground pepper, olive oil and lemon juice, tomato ketchup, mustard and Worcestershire sauce for guests to help themselves.

FAR LEFT: *Fillet steak with bearnaise sauce.*

Broiled Meatballs with Onion

'Delizie' cipollate, alla griglia

---

1 small onion
1 garlic clove
butter
1 sprig fresh rosemary
1 sage leaf
a few young, fresh fennel leaves
2 slices fresh white bread
cold beef stock (can be made from a bouillion cube)
12oz ground beef
salt and pepper
olive oil
breadcrumbs

SERVES 4

PREPARATION AND COOKING TIME:
ABOUT 1¼ HOURS

Preheat the oven to 400°F. Finely chop the onion and garlic and fry gently in 2 tablespoons butter, taking care not to let them brown. Remove from the heat and place in a bowl to cool. Meanwhile, chop the rosemary leaves together with the sage and a little fennel. Add the herbs to the cold onion. Soak the bread in the stock, then squeeze well and add to the bowl together with the ground beef, salt and pepper.

Combine all the ingredients together until smooth and make 16 equal-sized meatballs. Brush them all over with olive oil, then coat evenly with breadcrumbs.

Broil the meatballs quickly, turning them over once. Arrange them in a greased ovenproof dish, pour over a trickle of olive oil, then bake for 10–12 minutes or until they are cooked through.
Serve on a bed of vegetables cooked in butter, garnished with fennel leaves.

Stuffed Cold Beef

Controfiletto freddo, farcito

---

2 medium stalks celery, sliced
1 small pimiento
1 tablespoon capers
1 × 3 oz jar artichoke in oil
thick mayonnaise
1 teaspoon mustard
Worcestershire sauce
24 thin slices cold roast beef
olive oil

SERVES 6

PREPARATION TIME: ABOUT 30 MINUTES

Drain the celery, dry it carefully on paper towels and place it in a bowl. Drain and dry the pimiento in the same way, cut it into short, thin strips and mix it with the celery. Add the finely chopped capers and artichoke, cut into small pieces.

Bind the mixture with mayonnaise and fold in the mustard and a dash of Worcestershire sauce. Taste and adjust the seasoning.

Spread the slices of meat on a work surface and place some of the prepared mixture on each slice. Roll the meat up and arrange the rolls on a plate. Brush each roll with a very little olive oil and garnish as desired.

Serve with a fresh mixed green salad and a simple vinaigrette dressing.

RIGHT: *Autumn stew.*

Autumn Stew

'Fusello' d'autunno

2 large carrots
1 celery stalk, trimmed
1 small onion
1 large garlic clove
olive oil
4 tablespoons butter
1½ lb stewing beef
flour
½ cup Marsala wine
1 quart good meat stock
2 tablespoons tomato paste
1 bay leaf
2 red chillies
2 juniper berries
1 clove
1 small piece cinnamon stick
8 oz baby onions
¼ beef bouillion cube
nutmeg

SERVES 4

PREPARATION AND COOKING TIME:
ABOUT 3 HOURS

Peel the carrots, cut them in half lengthways and cut them into 1 inch lengths. Then, using a small knife with a curved blade, pare the edges and chop the trimmings together with the celery, onion and garlic. Heat in a large shallow saucepan in 4 tablespoons of olive oil and 2 tablespoons butter. Fry gently without browning over moderate heat. Remove and leave aside.

Cut the beef into large cubes, flour and brown them in the pan, stirring occasionally with a wooden spoon. Pour in the Marsala and let it evaporate, keeping the heat moderate and the pan uncovered.

Boil the stock. When nearly all the Marsala has been absorbed in the other pan add the tomato paste and stir, then pour in the boiling stock. Turn the heat down to simmer. Put the bay leaf, chillies, juniper berries, clove and cinnamon in a small cheesecloth bag, and add to the pan. Cover and simmer for about 2 hours, stirring from time to time and adding a little boiling water if necessary.

When the meat is half-cooked, heat a frying pan containing the rest of the butter and 1 teaspoon of olive oil. Put in the carrot mixture and the baby onions and fry gently for a few minutes. Pour in ⅔ cup of boiling water and crumble in the bouillion cube. Add a little grated nutmeg. Cover and cook over moderate heat until all the liquid has disappeared and the vegetables are tender. Add this to the stew 10 minutes before the end of cooking, stirring carefully. Serve with polenta.

Beef in Red Wine

Carbonade

1¾ lb stewing beef
flour
4 tablespoons butter
1 large onion
2½ cups robust red wine
salt and pepper

SERVES 6

PREPARATION AND COOKING TIME:
ABOUT 2 HOURS

Trim the meat of any sinews and fat, then cut it into largish cubes. Coat the cubes of beef with flour and shake off the excess.

Melt the butter in a heavy-based pan and brown the meat. When it is well browned on all sides, take it out of the pan. Cut the onion into small pieces and brown it in the same pan. Return the meat, cover and cook over very low heat for about 1¾ hours, adding the wine a little at a time, and stirring frequently so that the meat does not stick to the bottom of the pan. Season with a pinch of pepper and a good handful of salt (originally this recipe was made with beef preserved in salt).

Apart from salt and pepper, you could season the 'carbonade' with a pinch of aromatic herbs and a little sugar; the strong taste of the wine can be diluted with a ladleful of boiling stock; or substitute bitter beer for the wine (as they do in the Belgian version of this dish), or, failing that, add vinegar to the cooking liquid.

Serve the beef straight from the pan, accompanied by some steaming polenta, cooked slowly in a copper cauldron, or lightly puréed potatoes.

Fillet of Beef with Mushrooms

Filetto di manzo ai funghi

---

1 small onion
2½ oz pancetta (Italian bacon)
olive oil
fresh sage
fresh rosemary
2½ lb beef fillet
10 large cultivated mushrooms
juice of ½ lemon
salt and pepper
dry white wine
¼ cup whipping cream

SERVES 8–10

PREPARATION AND COOKING TIME:
ABOUT 1 HOUR

Preheat the oven to 425°F. Peel and chop the onion and place in a roasting pan. Dice the pancetta and add it, together with 4 tablespoons oil and a small bunch of sage and rosemary. Place the casserole over high heat and soften all the contents, then add the beef and color it evenly all over, turning it with a fork but taking care not to pierce it (so that the juices do not run out).

Meanwhile peel and halve the mushrooms. Add them to the well-browned beef and sprinkle them with the lemon juice. Season with salt and pepper and cook in the hot oven for about 20 minutes, or longer depending on how you like your meat cooked; it should still be more or less rare when served. Baste the meat frequently with its cooking juices and half a glass of wine during cooking.

When the beef is cooked to your liking, drain it, place on a serving dish and keep warm. Discard the aromatic herbs, then place the roasting pan on the heat. Add the cream, allow the sauce to thicken slightly, then season the beef with salt.

Serve immediately, with a selection of steamed and crisp green vegetables.

LEFT: *Beef in red wine.*

Braised Beef in Barolo

Brasato al Barolo

2¼ lb boned shin of beef, in one piece
2 carrots, scraped and cut into large chunks
2 medium onions, each stuck with 2 cloves
2 garlic cloves
1 celery stalk, cut into lengths
bouquet garni (parsley, sage, bay leaf, rosemary)
peppercorns
salt
ground cinnamon
nutmeg
1 × 75 cl bottle of Barolo
2 tablespoons butter
brandy

SERVES 6

PREPARATION AND COOKING TIME: ABOUT
5 HOURS, PLUS MARINATING

Put the meat in a bowl with the carrots, onions, whole garlic cloves, celery, bouquet garni, 5–6 peppercorns, a pinch each of salt and cinnamon and a grating of nutmeg. Pour on the wine, cover the bowl and leave to marinate in a cool place for at least 6 hours (overnight is better).

To cook the braised beef, drain the meat from the marinade. Heat the butter in a large, heavy-based pan, put in the beef and brown it carefully over high heat. Sprinkle with a small glass of brandy and flame it. As soon as the alcohol has evaporated, add the vegetables and the strained wine from the marinade. Cover the pan and cook over very low heat for about 4 hours, or until the meat is very tender.

Just before the end of cooking, pass the sauce, including the bouquet garni, through a food mill back over the beef. Cook for a further 10 minutes, then serve the beef in thick slices, very hot with its sauce and puréed potatoes or polenta, whichever you prefer.

Braised Beef with Cabbage and Barbera

Tapulon

1½ oz salt pork
3 tablespoons butter
olive oil
3 garlic cloves, crushed
2 bay leaves
1 lb savoy cabbage
1¼ lb stewing beef
fennel seeds
1 teaspoon ground cloves
peppercorns
1 glass of Barbera wine
hot beef stock (can be made from a bouillion cube)
salt

SERVES 4

PREPARATION AND COOKING TIME:
ABOUT 1 HOUR

Sweat the salt pork with the butter and 2 tablespoons oil in a large saucepan. Add the crushed garlic cloves and bay leaves and brown them. Shred the cabbage, cut the meat into 2 inch cubes and add them to the pan. Mix, season with a pinch of fennel seeds, the ground cloves and a grinding of pepper, and brown the cubes of meat over high heat until it is very dry and completely sealed.

Moisten with a glass of Barbera and, when this has evaporated, add a ladleful of hot stock. Taste, add salt if necessary, then cover the pan and cook over medium heat for about 1½—2 hours, or until the meat is tender. Check from time to time to make sure that the meat does not dry out too much; add a ladleful of hot stock if it does. The 'tapulon' should be neither too dry nor too moist. Serve it immediately.

RIGHT: *Braised beef in Barolo.*

174

Braised Beef Shank

Stracotto di stinco di manzo speziato

---

2 lb boned beef shank
2½ cups robust red wine
cinnamon, sticks and ground
peppercorns
6 cloves
1 large onion, peeled
olive oil
flour
salt and pepper
hot beef stock (can be made from a bouillion cube)

SERVES 6

PREPARATION AND COOKING TIME:
ABOUT 2¼ HOURS, PLUS MARINATING

Cut the meat into cubes, trim off any sinews and fat and place in a bowl. Pour in the wine and add 2 cinnamon sticks, ½ tablespoon peppercorns and 6 cloves. Cover the bowl with plastic wrap and leave to marinate in a cool place for about 12 hours.

When you are ready to cook the meat, roughly chop the onion, place in a heavy-based pan with 3 tablespoons oil, and soften. Drain the meat from the marinade and remove any peppercorns sticking to it. Lightly flour the meat, then brown the pieces in the pan with the onion, turning them to color on all sides. Season with a pinch each of salt, pepper and ground cinnamon. Strain the marinade and pour it into the pan with the meat, then add 3 ladles of hot stock. Cover and cook over very moderate heat for about 2 hours, or until the meat is tender. If the sauce seems too liquid at the end of cooking, increase the heat and reduce it. If it seems too thick, dilute it with a little more stock.

Serve the beef very hot, straight from the pan, accompanied by some steaming polenta or lightly puréed potatoes, whichever you prefer.

Fillet of Beef on Crôutons

Filetti di manzo su crostini

---

4 slices white bread
4 slices of beef fillet, about 1 lb
olive oil
salt and pepper
1 shallot, finely chopped
3 gherkins
mustard
½ cup whipping cream
beef stock (can be made from a bouillion cube)

SERVES 4

PREPARATION AND COOKING TIME:
ABOUT 30 MINUTES

Using a 2 inch round pastry cutter, cut out four circles of bread, then toast them lightly in the oven or under the grill.

Gently pound the beef into four even medallions. In a frying pan, heat 2 tablespoons oil, then brown the meat for about 1½ minutes on each side. Season with salt and pepper and keep warm. In the same pan, and in the meat juices, soften the chopped shallot. Add the gherkins, cut into rounds, and 2 teaspoons mustard. Finally, add the cream and half a ladle of stock. Stir with a wooden spoon and cook until the sauce has thickened.

Lay the beef medallions on the crôutons, arrange on a serving plate, coat with the sauce and serve. Some crunchy green beans and a mixed leaf salad go well with this dish.

LEFT: *Braised beef shank* (top); *Sweet and sour ossobuco* (bottom, recipe on page 156).

Meat Patties with Artichokes

Medaglioni di carne con i carciofi

2 fresh artichokes
a little lemon juice
1 small onion
1 small garlic clove
1 sprig fresh parsley
olive oil
⅔ cup dry white wine
½ cup meat stock
(can be made from a bouillion cube)
thyme
4 tablespoons butter
½ beef bouillion cube
2 slices white bread, soaked in milk
4 oz ground beef
4 oz ground veal
4 oz ham
¼ cup grated Parmesan cheese
1 egg
ground nutmeg
flour
1 sprig fresh sage

SERVES 4

PREPARATION AND COOKING TIME: 1 HOUR

Top and tail the artichokes and remove the tough outer leaves. Cut them in half lengthways, scoop out and discard the chokes. Place the artichokes in a bowl of water with a little lemon juice.

Sauté about one-third of the onion, the garlic and the parsley in 3 tablespoons of oil. Drain the artichokes, cut into small pieces and add to the pan. Cook gently for a few minutes then add half the wine. When it has been absorbed, add the boiling stock. Season with salt, pepper and thyme. Cover, lower the heat and cook for about 15 minutes.

Meanwhile sauté the remaining onion in a tablespoon of butter. Blend in the crumbled bouillion cube. Drain the bread and process it in a food processor with the beef, veal and ham. Place in a bowl and add the sautéed onion, grated cheese, egg and a little pepper and nutmeg. Blend thoroughly and divide into four patties. Coat in flour.

Heat the remaining butter, 2 tablespoons of oil and 2 sage leaves and fry the patties over low heat, until browned on both sides. Add the remaining wine and cook until the liquid has reduced by about two-thirds. Serve topped with the artichokes.

Savory Meatballs in Red Wine

Polpettine saporite al vino rosso

10 oz boneless veal
10 oz boneless beef
2½ oz raw ham
4 slices white bread, soaked in milk
1 tablespoon grated Parmesan cheese
chopped parsley
salt and pepper
flour
1 small onion
1 small stalk celery
½ medium carrot
4 tablespoons olive oil
1 bay leaf
1 clove
fresh sage
scant 1 cup robust red wine
12 oz chopped tomatoes
hot beef stock (can be made from a bouillion cube)

SERVES 6

PREPARATION AND COOKING TIME:
ABOUT 1½ HOURS

Pass the veal, beef and ham through a grinder and place in a bowl. Squeeze out the bread and add it, together with the Parmesan cheese, a pinch of chopped parsley, and salt and pepper to taste. Blend the mixture and form it into balls, flattening them slightly. Roll in a little flour.

Chop together the onion, celery and carrot; soften the chopped vegetables in the oil with the bay leaf, clove and a small bunch of sage. Add the meatballs, brown them over high heat, then moisten with the wine. When this has partially evaporated, add the chopped tomatoes and half a ladleful of hot stock. Reduce the heat, cover and cook the meatballs for about 50 minutes.

Serve hot, accompanied by a potato purée and a green vegetable, such as spinach or broccoli.

RIGHT: *Guinea fowl with bay leaves* (top right, recipe on page 213); *Savory meatballs in red wine* (bottom).

Breast of Pork with Cabbage

Punta di maiale alle verze

---

1 garlic clove
chopped mixed herbs (sage, rosemary, parsley)
salt and pepper
2 lb breast of pork
1 medium onion, chopped
olive oil
1¼ cups dry white wine
2 lb savoy cabbage
hot chicken stock (can be made from a bouillion cube)
½ cup tomato passata (sieved tomatoes)
2 bay leaves

SERVES 8
PREPARATION AND COOKING TIME:
ABOUT 2 HOURS 20 MINUTES

Preheat the oven to 400°F. Finely chop the garlic and mix it with 2 tablespoons chopped herbs. Season with salt and pepper, then rub this mixture liberally over the meat. Roll it up and tie like a rolled roast with kitchen twine. Place the meat in a roasting pan just large enough to hold it and the chopped onion, moisten with a trickle of oil, then roast in the hot oven for about 1 hour 20 minutes, basting the meat from time to time with the wine.

Meanwhile, trim the cabbage and pull off the leaves; boil for 2 minutes in salted water. Drain and add to the meat after the stated cooking time; cover with foil and return to the oven for about another 30 minutes.

Drain the meat, transfer to a serving plate and keep warm. Add a ladleful of hot stock, the tomato passata and bay leaves to the cooking juices, place over moderate heat and cook for about 15 minutes.

Partially slice the meat, coat generously with the sauce and serve with the cabbage.

Pork Chops with Balsamic Vinegar

Braciole di maiale all'aceto balsamico

---

6 pork chops, each weighing about 6 oz
2 tablespoons mild mustard
flour
1 sprig fresh sage
1 garlic clove
butter
olive oil
½ cup dry white wine
Worcestershire sauce
½ chicken bouillion cube
1 tablespoon balsamic vinegar
a few sprigs fresh parsley for garnish

SERVES 6
PREPARATION AND COOKING TIME:
ABOUT 40 MINUTES

Remove excessive fat from the chops, then pound them lightly, taking care not to split the meat. Put the mustard in a bowl and coat the chops with it on both sides. Then coat them with flour, shaking them gently to remove any excess.

Finely chop 2 sage leaves and the garlic. Melt 2 tablespoons butter with 3 tablespoons of oil in a large frying pan and soften the sage and garlic gently, taking care not to brown them. Now put the chops in the pan and allow them to cook and brown. Moisten them with the white wine, and season with a dash of Worcestershire sauce. Then add the crumbled half bouillon cube.

When the meat has absorbed almost all the wine, moisten it with the balsamic vinegar and keep the pan on the heat for a few moments more. Serve very hot, garnished with fresh parsley.

LEFT: *Breast of pork with cabbage* (top left); *Casserole of turkey "haunches"* (top right, recipe on page 213); *Veal stew with sausage and dried mushrooms* (bottom, recipe on page 159).

Pork Chops with Grapes

Costolette di maiale all'uva

---

48 perfectly ripe green grapes
4 pork chops
a little flour
butter
olive oil
½ bay leaf
¼ cup dry white wine
a piece of chicken bouillion cube
¼ cup brandy

SERVES 4

PREPARATION AND COOKING TIME:
ABOUT 1 HOUR

Using a short, sharp knife, peel and seed the grapes if necessary. Remove any sinews and membranes from the chops. Pound the chops lightly and flour them all over, shaking off any excess.

Heat 2 tablespoons butter and 1 tablespoon oil in a large frying pan and flavor with the bay leaf. Put the chops into the hot fat and brown on both sides, turning them over without piercing them. Splash over a little white wine from time to time.

When the wine has almost entirely evaporated, put in the grapes. Turn up the heat, crumble in the piece of bouillion cube and shake the frying pan frequently from side to side to allow all the chops to absorb the flavor. Pour in the brandy and set it alight.

Finally, arrange the chops on a serving dish with the grapes on one side, together with the sauce from the pan. Serve at once.

Pork and Liver Roulades

Involtini di fegato e maiale

---

1 small onion
1 garlic clove
butter
5 oz calves' liver
1 oz capers
1 teaspoon anchovy paste
1 tablespoon breadcrumbs
salt and pepper
16 thin slices of pork fillet, weighing about 1 lb
flour
½ cup dry white wine

SERVES 4

PREPARATION AND COOKING TIME: 45 MINUTES

Chop the onion finely together with the garlic and fry in a knob of butter. Chop the liver and place in a bowl. Add the fried onions, thoroughly drain and chop the capers and add these, mix in a heaped teaspoon of anchovy paste and a heaped tablespoon of breadcrumbs. Add salt and pepper and mix thoroughly.

Pound the slices of pork as thinly as possible and spread a little of the liver mixture on one side of each piece. Roll up the meat, sealing the stuffing well inside and tie up with kitchen thread like a small parcel. Flour the roulades, shaking off any excess.

Melt a knob of butter in a frying pan and fry the roulades, browning them well on all sides. Add very little salt, then pour over the wine. Shake the pan vigorously to prevent the meat from sticking to the bottom, then cover. The wine will evaporate leaving a delicious sauce. Serve hot, with boiled new potatoes and a green vegetable.

RIGHT: *Pork chops with oregano.*

Pork Chops with Oregano

Costolette di maiale all'origano

---

4 boneless pork chops, each weighing 5 oz
flour
olive oil
butter
1 garlic clove
1 sprig fresh basil
1 tablespoon spiced white wine vinegar
¼ cup dry white wine
8 oz tomatoes, puréed
½ chicken bouillion cube
pepper
oregano
2 tablespoons capers

SERVES 4

Remove any tendons and sinews from the chops, then pound them lightly. Coat them one at a time in the flour, shaking off any excess.

Put 2 tablespoons of oil and the butter in a frying pan wide enough to contain the chops in a single layer. Heat the fats with the lightly crushed garlic clove and the basil; remove the flavorings when they have browned. Arrange the chops in the pan and brown them over vigorous heat. Moisten them with the vinegar, then add the white wine. Cook until the liquid is reduced by two-thirds.

Add the tomatoes, season with the crumbled bouillion cube and a grinding of pepper, flavor with a pinch of oregano and sprinkle over the capers. Shake the pan to prevent the sauce sticking and reduce it, turning the chops once only.

Arrange on a hot serving dish, pour over the sauce and garnish according to taste. Serve immediately.

Loin of Pork in a Bread Crust

Arista di maiale in crosta di pane

3 lb loin of pork
10 oz cooked ham, thinly sliced
chopped fresh sage
chopped fresh parsley
salt and pepper
olive oil
2 lb bread dough (can be made from a package)
2 eggs
3 tablespoons grated Parmesan cheese
4 tablespoons butter
1 oz toasted flaked almonds

SERVES 12
PREPARATION AND COOKING TIME:
ABOUT 2 ½ HOURS

Preheat the oven to 400°F. Using a long, very sharp knife, make deep vertical and horizontal cuts in the meat and open it up into a rectangle. Cover the rectangle with one-third of the ham slices, then roll up the meat to make a roast, and tie with several turns of kitchen twine. Place in a roasting pan, season generously with the chopped herbs and salt and pepper, and trickle on some olive oil. Roast in the hot oven for 50 minutes. Remove and set aside to cool.

Meanwhile, put the bread dough in the bowl of an electric mixer. Add 1 egg, the Parmesan cheese and 3 tablespoons oil. Knead slowly with the dough hook to make a smooth, elastic dough. Leave to rise in a warm place until the pork is completely cooked. Roll out the dough to make a rectangle slightly larger than the meat.

Chop the remaining ham, then mix with the butter to make a mousse. When the meat is cooked and cold, cut off the twine, roll out the dough to a thickness of ½ inch and lay the meat on the dough. Spread the meat and dough with the ham mousse, then roll up the dough and brush with beaten egg.

Preheat the oven to 375°F. Place the roll on a baking sheet lined with baking parchment. Shape the pastry trimmings into a braid and lay it on the roll. Brush again with egg and sprinkle with almonds. Bake in the oven for about 40 minutes, or until the dough is cooked and golden.

LEFT: *Loin of pork in a bread crust.*

Pork Sausage Parcels

Involtini di Lonza

1 eggplant
12 slices pork sausage with wide shape
4 oz Provola cheese
oil for frying
12 fresh basil leaves
2 anchovy fillets in oil, broken up
flour
olive oil
butter
1 small onion, sliced
3 tablespoons Marsala wine
½ cup chicken stock (can be made from a bouillion cube)
salt and pepper

SERVES 6
PREPARATION AND COOKING TIME:
ABOUT 1 ¼ HOURS

Peel the eggplant and cut it into 12 equal slices about ⅛ inch thick. Arrange the slices on a tilted plate, sprinkle with salt and leave for about 30 minutes for the juices to drain off.

Lightly pound the slices of sausage with a meat mallet. Cut the Provola cheese into 12 equal pieces. Rinse the slices of eggplant under running water, drain and dry them. Fry them in plenty of oil, then drain thoroughly.

Arrange the slices of sausage on a tray, keeping them well apart from each other, and place a slice of eggplant on each slice of sausage. Place a leaf of fresh basil, a piece of Provola cheese and a small piece of anchovy fillet one on top of the other in the center of each piece of eggplant. Roll the meat tightly around the other ingredients and secure with kitchen twine. Coat the parcels in flour.

Heat 3 tablespoons olive oil and a large knob of butter in a large frying pan. Add the sliced onion, discarding it as soon as it has browned. Fry the parcels until golden brown. Pour in the Marsala wine and the boiling stock. Season with salt and pepper and cook until the liquid has reduced to form a thick sauce. Remove from the heat, discard the kitchen twine from the parcels and serve immediately.

Rissoles with Tomato Sauce

Polpettine al pomodoro

---

2 slices white bread, soaked in milk
1 lb sausage meat
4 oz ham, diced
¾ cup grated Parmesan cheese
2 eggs
salt and pepper
ground nutmeg
olive oil
1 medium onion
1 garlic clove
1 lb firm ripe tomatoes
5–6 fresh basil leaves
sugar

SERVES 6

PREPARATION AND COOKING TIME:
ABOUT 1¼ HOURS

Drain the bread and grind with the sausage meat and ham. Place the ground mixture in a bowl and stir in the grated Parmesan cheese, the eggs, a pinch of salt and pepper and a little ground nutmeg. Mix thoroughly to form a smooth paste. Make 24 rissoles from the mixture, shaping them with your hands, and place them on an oiled baking pan. Sprinkle with a little oil and leave to stand in a cool place for at least 15 minutes.

Meanwhile finely slice the onion and fry it gently with the lightly crushed garlic clove in 4 tablespoons of oil. Stir in the coarsely chopped tomatoes, a few basil leaves, a little salt and pepper and a pinch of sugar. Bring slowly to the boil and then lower the heat, half-cover the pan and cook for about 15 minutes, stirring occasionally.

Preheat the oven to 400°F. Process the sauce in a blender and pour it back into the pan. Test and adjust the seasoning according to taste. Bake the rissoles in the oven for 12–13 minutes, transfer to the sauce in the pan and cook gently for a further 4–5 minutes. Place in a warmed dish, garnish with fresh basil and serve.

Cotechino "in a Galley"

Cotechino in galera

---

1 cotechino (fresh pork sausage, salted and spiced), about 1¼ lb
1 large slice of leg of pork, 10 oz
7 oz sliced raw ham
½ medium onion
olive oil
chicken stock
dry Lambrusco wine
salt

SERVES 6–8

PREPARATION AND COOKING TIME: 2¼ HOURS

Prick the cotechino in several places with a toothpick, put it in a pan of cold water and cook over medium heat until half-cooked. Drain and remove the skin.

Cover the pork with the slices of ham and lay the cooled cotechino in the center. Roll it up in the meat and tie up the roll with kitchen twine.

Chop the onion and soften it in 2 tablespoons oil. Add the meat roll, but do not let it color. Pour in a mixture of equal quantities of stock and wine sufficient to cover the meat. Salt lightly, cover the pan and cook over medium heat for 1 hour.

To serve, cut off the twine and cut the roll into quite thick rounds. Transfer to a serving dish with the very hot sauce and serve with puréed potatoes.

RIGHT: *Cotechino "in a galley".*

Cotechino in Béchamel Sauce with Vegetables

Cotechino in salsa con verdure

---

2 cotechino sausages
1 medium leek
2 medium carrots
2 medium stalks celery
5 oz mushrooms
olive oil
vegetable or chicken stock
salt

FOR THE BÉCHAMEL SAUCE
2 tablespoons butter
4 tablespoons flour
1¼ cups hot milk
salt
3 egg yolks

SERVES 6
PREPARATION AND COOKING TIME:
ABOUT 2 HOURS

Prick the cotechino in several places with a toothpick, place in a pan of cold water and cook over very moderate heat for about 1½ hours. (You can even do this a day in advance.)

To serve the cotechino, trim and wash the leek and cut into rounds. Scrape the carrot and slice it; peel the celery and cut into thin strips. Trim the mushrooms to remove any dirt, wash, drain and slice thinly. Sweat the leek, carrot and celery in the butter and 1 tablespoon oil. When they are lightly browned, add the mushrooms and soften all the vegetables, adding a small ladleful of stock. Season with a little salt.

Meanwhile, make the béchamel. Make a roux with the butter and flour, then stir in the hot milk. Cook over moderate heat for about 5 minutes, then remove from the heat, season with salt and thicken with the egg yolks.

Remove the skin from the cooked cotechino and cut into rounds. Spread the vegetables over the bottom of an ovenproof serving dish. Arrange the cotechino rounds on top, then cover thickly with the béchamel. Place under a hot grill for a couple of minutes, to brown the dish. Serve immediately.

LEFT: *Cotechino in béchamel sauce with vegetables* (top); *Fillet of beef with mushrooms* (bottom, recipe on page 173).

Sausage and Pepper Kebabs

Spiedini di salsiccia e peperone

---

12 oz spicy sausages
6 small bell peppers
mustard
flour
butter
olive oil
1 garlic clove
2 sage leaves
3 tablespoons dry white wine
1 head frisée

SERVES 4
PREPARATION AND COOKING TIME:
ABOUT 30 MINUTES

Cut the sausages into 32 equal-sized pieces, without removing the skin. Wash the bell peppers, discard the seeds and stalks, and cut into 24 equal-sized pieces in all. Spread a little mustard on one side of each piece of sausage.

Thread the pieces of sausage and pepper on to eight thin wooden skewers, alternating four pieces of sausage and three pieces of pepper on each one. Each piece of pepper should be against the mustard side of the sausage and the kebabs should be compact.

Lightly coat the kebabs in the flour, shaking off any excess. Heat the butter and 2 tablespoons oil in a frying pan and add the garlic and sage leaves. Place the kebabs in the frying pan one at a time and cook over moderate heat until browned on all sides. Just before removing the kebabs from the heat, sprinkle them with a little white wine. Allow the wine to evaporate quickly.

Serve the kebabs on a bed of tender frisée leaves.

Broiled Lamb Chops

Costolettine d'agnello grigliate

---

12 lamb loin chops
1 small onion
1 large garlic clove
1 sprig fresh sage
1 small celery stalk
olive oil
salt and pepper
juice of 1 large lemon
Worcestershire sauce
1 teaspoon mustard
oregano

SERVES 4

PREPARATION AND COOKING TIME:
ABOUT 1 HOUR

Remove the fat from the chops, and any tendons or membrane, but leave the bony part at the base of each one. Arrange them in a large, deep dish which can hold them in a single closely packed layer.

Slice the onion very thinly, and chop the garlic, 2 sage leaves and the celery rib very finely. Sprinkle these ingredients over the chops and season with a grinding of pepper. Pour over 4 tablespoons of olive oil mixed with a tablespoon of lemon juice and a pinch of salt. Cover the dish with plastic wrap and leave to stand in a cool place (not the refrigerator) for about 30 minutes.

Meanwhile, put a large pinch of black pepper and a pinch of salt into a deep dish. Add the strained juice of half a lemon, 4 tablespoons of oil, a light dash of Worcestershire sauce, the mustard and a small pinch of oregano and beat until smooth.

Heat the broiler. Wipe the chops and broil them to taste. Arrange them on a warmed dish, dress them with the sauce, then serve.

Lamb and Artichoke Stew

Agnello e carciofi in umido

1¾ lb boned leg of lamb
1 medium onion
2 garlic cloves
1 sprig fresh sage
butter
olive oil
½ cup Marsala wine
8 oz tomatoes, peeled and finely chopped
⅔ cup meat stock (can be made from a bouillion cube)
1 teaspoon cornstarch
1 lemon
Worcestershire sauce
3 medium artichokes
a few sprigs fresh parsley
ground thyme

SERVES 6
PREPARATION AND COOKING TIME:
ABOUT 2 HOURS

Cut the lamb into pieces the size of a small egg. Finely chop two-thirds of the onion, a garlic clove and 2 sage leaves and fry them in 2 tablespoons of butter and 2 tablespoons oil. Add the lamb and cook for at least 5 minutes, stirring frequently. Add the wine and cook until it has been absorbed, shaking the pan occasionally. Stir in the tomatoes and the cold stock in which the cornstarch has been dissolved. Add a small piece of lemon rind, a pinch of salt and a dash of Worcestershire sauce. Cover and cook for 1¼ hours, adding more stock if necessary.

Meanwhile, cut off the stalks and tips of the artichokes, remove the tough outer leaves and place the artichokes in a bowl of water with the juice of half the lemon. Thinly slice the remaining onion, finely chop the garlic clove and a small handful of parsley, and sauté them in the remaining butter and 2 tablespoons oil.

Discard the chokes from the artichokes, and cut each into six pieces. Add them to the pan. After a few minutes stir in ⅔ cups boiling water, a little salt and thyme. Cover and cook the artichokes over moderate heat until slightly *al dente*. When the meat has been cooking for about 1 hour, add the artichokes and complete cooking. Pour into a serving dish and garnish with parsley. Serve immediately.

191

Braised Lamb

Stufadin di agnello

¾ oz dried mushrooms (porcini)
3 lb 5 oz boned lamb
1 large onion
4 tablespoons butter
olive oil
1 celery stalk, cut into even pieces
1 large carrot, scraped, washed and cut into small chunks
salt and pepper
dry white wine

SERVES 6

PREPARATION AND COOKING TIME: 2½ HOURS

Soften the mushrooms in tepid water. Remove any sinews and skin from the lamb, then cut the meat into even pieces. Peel and chop the onion and soften in a large, heavy-based pan with the butter and a tablespoon of oil. Add the pieces of lamb and brown them, then add the mushrooms, celery and carrot. Season with salt and plenty of pepper, cover and cook gently over the lowest possible heat for about 2 hours.

Towards the end of cooking, take the lamb out of the liquid and add half a glass of wine to the sauce. When this has evaporated, serve the lamb, straight from the pan if you wish. Polenta makes a particularly good accompaniment to this dish.

Lamb Stew with Flowers

Spezzatino di agnello, fiorito

1¾ lb boned leg or shoulder of lamb
⅔ cup dry white wine
2 large sage leaves
1 sprig rosemary
2 garlic cloves
butter
olive oil
1 small onion
½ cup Marsala wine
petals of 7–8 edible white daisies (optional)
1 piece lemon rind
⅔ cup meat stock
8 oz tomatoes, skinned
salt and pepper
1 teaspoon cornstarch
extra fresh edible daisy petals

SERVES 4–6

PREPARATION AND COOKING TIME:
1½ HOURS, PLUS OVERNIGHT MARINATING

Dice the lamb into 1½ inch cubes. Put the meat in a bowl and pour over the wine. Add the sage leaves, rosemary and 1 lightly crushed garlic clove. Cover the bowl with plastic wrap and leave to marinate overnight in a cool place.

The following day, remove the lamb from the marinade and pat it dry on paper towels. Heat 2 tablespoons of butter and 2 tablespoons of oil in a large frying pan and finely chop the onion together with the remaining garlic clove. Fry these without browning them, put in the meat cubes and lightly brown them all over. Pour over the Marsala and let it reduce almost completely. Then put in the daisy petals and a piece of lemon rind, which should later be discarded.

After a few minutes, pour over the boiling stock and purée the tomatoes before adding them too. Stir and season with salt and pepper. Dissolve the cornstarch in 3 tablespoons of cold water and stir into the pan. Simmer the stew for about 1 hour, adding a little more boiling stock if necessary.

Serve on a warm dish, garnished with daisy petals.

RIGHT: *Braised lamb.*

Chicken Livers with Egg and Lemon

Cibreo di regaglie

14 oz chicken livers
2 tablespoons butter
chicken stock (can be made from a bouillion cube)
salt and pepper
3 eggs
flour
juice of ½ lemon

SERVES 4

PREPARATION AND COOKING TIME:
ABOUT 45 MINUTES

Clean the livers, eliminating any greenish spots. (If you get your chicken livers from a butcher and can get them, the cockscombs can be used in this recipe too.) Toss the livers into boiling water for 2 minutes, then drain. If you are using the cockscombs, they should be boiled with the chicken livers then skinned and chopped. Coarsely chop the livers, keeping them separate. Melt the butter, add the cockscombs, if you are using them, and when they are lightly browned, moisten with a glass of stock. Cover and cook over moderate heat for about 30 minutes, then add the chopped livers. Season with salt and pepper and cook for a few minutes more.

Meanwhile, beat the eggs with a teaspoon of flour, the lemon juice and a small ladleful of hot stock, adding the stock a little at a time so that the eggs do not curdle.

Take the livers and cockscombs off the heat, mix in the eggs to thicken slightly, and serve.

LEFT: *Chicken livers with egg and lemon.*

Liver with Herbs

Fegato agli aromi

4 large slices calves' liver, together weighing 12 oz
2 fresh sage leaves
½ sprig rosemary
a bunch of fresh parsley
a handful of fresh basil
salt and pepper
2 slices fresh white bread
butter
olive oil

SERVES 4

PREPARATION AND COOKING TIME:
ABOUT 30 MINUTES

Remove the thin membrane and any nerves from the slices of liver. Finely chop together 2 sage leaves, the rosemary sprig, a small bunch of parsley and 4 basil leaves; put the chopped mixture in a bowl and add a generous grinding of pepper. Crumble bread finely and mix with the herbs. Spread the mixture over a plate and roll the slices of liver in it, one by one, coating them as evenly as possible and shaking off any excess.

Heat 2 tablespoons of butter and 3 tablespoons oil in a large frying pan and when hot put in the liver slices; brown and cook them on both sides, adding salt only when the meat is cooked. While they are cooking, do not prick the slices of liver but turn them carefully with a spatula.

Finally arrange them on a serving dish and serve immediately, garnishing them with a few parsley sprigs and more fresh basil leaves.

Sweetbreads with Mushroom Sauce

Animelle di vitello ai funghi

2–3 dried cep mushrooms (or porcini)
1 lb calves' sweetbreads
salt
juice of 1 lemon
4 tablespoons butter
breadcrumbs
4 oz fresh mushrooms
1 small onion
1 garlic clove
a little parsley
olive oil
4 tablespoons Marsala wine
a piece of chicken bouillion cube
thyme
½ cup light cream
½ teaspoon cornstarch

SERVES 4

PREPARATION AND COOKING TIME:
ABOUT 1½ HOURS

Soak the dried mushrooms in cold water for about 1 hour. Wash the sweetbreads and simmer them for about 20 minutes in a saucepan of lightly salted boiling water to which 2 tablespoons of strained lemon juice have been added. Remove from the water with a slotted spoon and place in a bowl of cold water. When they are cool enough to handle, remove the membrane, veins and any nerves. When the sweetbreads are completely cold, remove from the water and drain thoroughly. Dry, and cut into fairly thick slices.

Melt half the butter and brush the slices of sweetbread with this. Then coat them evenly with breadcrumbs, shaking off any excess.

Trim and wash the fresh mushrooms. Finely chop the onion with the garlic, and a few parsley leaves. Heat 3 tablespoons of oil in a frying pan and gently fry this mixture until the onion is lightly colored. Then drain the dried mushrooms thoroughly, setting aside the water in which they soaked, and finely chop before adding these to the frying pan too. Finely slice the fresh mushrooms and add them to the other ingredients after a short time. Fry for a few minutes, then pour in 4 tablespoons of water from the dried mushrooms and the Marsala. Crumble in a piece of bouillion cube and add a pinch of thyme. Simmer until the liquid has reduced by at least two-thirds before dissolving the cornstarch in the cream and adding this to the sauce. Stir in and simmer gently for a few minutes.

Meanwhile, fry the slices of sweetbread in the rest of the butter and a tablespoon of olive oil until golden brown on both sides. Sprinkle with salt when they are cooked. Arrange on a warmed serving dish and pour over the mushroom sauce. Sprinkle with a little chopped parsley and serve.

Kidney with Mushrooms

Rognoncino ai funghi

---

1 slice bread
butter
1 large mushroom cap (preferably cep)
olive oil
½ garlic clove
4 oz calves' kidney, fat removed, thinly sliced
flour
¼ cup meat stock
1 tablespoon whipping cream
Worcestershire sauce
chopped parsley

SERVES 1

PREPARATION AND COOKING TIME:
ABOUT 20 MINUTES

Preheat the oven to 400°F. Remove the crust from the bread; brush with 2 teaspoons of melted butter, then brown it in the oven for 3–4 minutes. Divide it into four triangles, lay them on a plate and keep hot.

Wipe the mushroom cap with a damp cloth and slice it. Heat a small frying pan with a knob of butter, half a tablespoon of oil and half a garlic clove (which you then discard). Put the kidney and mushroom in the pan and brown them lightly over high heat for a couple of minutes.

In another frying pan melt the remaining butter, mix in a little flour, then moisten with the hot stock. Bring to the boil, stirring all the time, then add the kidney and the mushroom, a tablespoon of cream and a dash of Worcestershire sauce. Keep over a very low heat for 2–3 minutes, taste and adjust the seasoning if necessary.

To serve, spoon on to a warmed plate, sprinkle with a pinch of chopped parsley and garnish with the four croûton triangles.

Sweet and Sour Calves' Liver

Fegato di vitello all'agrodolce

---

6 slices calves' liver
4 tablespoons butter
1 sprig fresh sage
salt
1 tablespoon pine nuts
10 capers
1 macaroon cookie
1 dry biscuit (zweiback)
1 teaspoon white wine vinegar
juice of ½ lemon
4–5 tablespoons chicken stock (or use a bouillion cube)
mild mustard
a little flour
olive oil
½ garlic clove
a little chopped parsley

SERVES 6
PREPARATION AND COOKING TIME:
ABOUT 40 MINUTES

Trim the slices of liver, removing membrane and tendons but reserving the scraps.

Heat a small frying pan with 2 tablespoons butter and a small sage leaf. As soon as it is hot, add the scraps of liver, brown them lightly, then put them with the other contents of the pan into a mortar. Add a large pinch of salt, the pine nuts, capers, macaroon, dry biscuit and the vinegar. Pound to a pulp, adding the strained lemon juice.

Put the mixture into a small saucepan, dilute with the boiling stock and flavor with the mustard. Bring to the boil over low heat, stirring all the time, then taste and adjust the seasoning. Keep warm.

Flour the liver slices, shaking to remove any excess. Melt the remaining butter and 3 tablespoons of oil, flavored with 2 sage leaves and half a garlic clove, in a frying pan that will just hold the liver. Brown the liver slices lightly on both sides until they are cooked through (about 3–5 minutes).

Salt them after cooking, then arrange them in a dish. Pour over the sauce, sprinkle over some parsley and serve.

Venison Alpine-style

Cosciotto di capriolo 'alpestre'

---

1 haunch or leg of venison, well hung
1 carrot
1 celery stalk
1 sprig fresh rosemary
3–4 fresh sage leaves
1 bay leaf
2 garlic cloves
½ cup white wine vinegar
2 large onions
about 4 oz butter
¼ cup flour, more for dusting
at least 2 cups good meat stock
1 teaspoon sugar
olive oil
salt and pepper

SERVES 6
PREPARATION AND COOKING TIME:
ABOUT 2 HOURS, PLUS 24 HOURS MARINATING

Wash and thoroughly dry the haunch of venison, then remove the bone from the meatiest part. Sew the meat up and arrange in a dish, preferably earthenware, just large enough to hold it. Slice the carrot and celery finely and place all round the meat, with the chopped rosemary and sage leaves. Put in a bay leaf and lightly crush the garlic cloves before adding them too. Pour in the vinegar and cover the dish. Leave in a cool place to marinate for 24 hours, during which time the haunch should be turned over three or four times.

The following day finely slice the onions and lightly fry in 4 tablespoons of butter in a saucepan. Mix 2 tablespoons of butter with the flour and, when the onions begin to brown, stir this in. Mix and fry for a few seconds, then stir in ⅔ cup of boiling stock. Mix well and add the sugar. Cook the gravy for a few minutes.

Heat the remaining butter with 3 tablespoons of oil in a frying pan. Remove the venison from the marinade, dry and flour it all over and seat it in the hot fat. Carefully drain it and place it in the onion sauce. Add salt and pepper and pour in ⅔ cup of boiling stock. Cover and cook over low heat for about 1½ hours, adding more boiling stock if necessary.

Remove the meat from the saucepan. Blend the juices and pass them through a fine strainer. Serve the meat hot, with the sauce.

Venison Stew

Lombo di capriolo in umido

3–4 shallots
1 sprig fresh rosemary
4 oz fatty raw ham
4 oz butter
12 venison loin chops
¼ cup red wine vinegar
½ cup robust red wine
1 quart good meat stock
2–3 juniper berries
1 clove
1 piece cinnamon stick
1 bay leaf
meat extract
¼ cup flour
2 tablespoons Marsala wine

SERVES 6
PREPARATION AND COOKING TIME:
ABOUT 1¾ HOURS

Finely chop the shallots together with the rosemary leaves and the ham and put in a saucepan. Add about half the butter and fry gently for a few seconds without browning. Add the venison chops and brown gently. Turn them over carefully with a fork, without pricking the surface. Pour over the vinegar and allow it to evaporate almost entirely before pouring in the wine. When that in turn has completely evaporated, pour in about 2½ cups of boiling stock. Add the juniper berries, clove, cinnamon, bay leaf and ½ teaspoon of meat extract. Cover the pan and simmer for about 1 hour, diluting with more stock if necessary.

Meanwhile prepare a sauce by heating the rest of the butter and incorporating the flour with a wooden spoon. Pour in 1¼ cups of boiling stock gradually, as if for a béchamel sauce. Remove the juniper berries, clove, bay leaf and cinnamon from the stew and pour the sauce into the stew. Shake the pan so that the sauce blends well with the meat juices, then put in the Marsala wine and simmer for a further 20 minutes.

Serve hot, with polenta or potatoes.

Baked Rabbit with Vegetables

Coniglio al forno, con verdure

4–6 rabbit pieces, about 1¾ lb
olive oil
1 bay leaf
1 small onion
1 small carrot
1 small celery stalk plus a few leaves for garnish
4 tablespoons butter
2 large garlic cloves
1 sprig fresh sage
1 chicken bouillion cube
salt and pepper
1¼ cups dry white wine
2 teaspoons cornstarch
parsley

SERVES 4
PREPARATION AND COOKING TIME:
ABOUT 1¾ HOURS

Put the rabbit pieces into a greased large frying pan, and add half a bay leaf. Cover the pan, put it over low heat and draw out some of the moisture from the meat. Drain well and leave to dry on a plate covered with a double sheet of paper towel. Preheat the oven to 400°F.

Slice the onion very thinly and cut the carrot and the celery into thin rounds. Mix these vegetables together and put them in the bottom of a small buttered baking pan just large enough to contain the rabbit pieces. Add the large garlic cloves, lightly crushed, and 2 or 3 sage leaves. Pack the pieces of rabbit closely on top of the vegetables and season with the crumbled bouillion cube and a generous grinding of pepper. Moisten with the white wine in which you have dissolved the cornstarch, then dot with the remaining butter cut into small pieces.

Seal the pan with foil, and bake in the oven for 1 hour or a little longer, until the rabbit is tender and the gravy reduced. Serve sprinkled with chopped parsley and garnished with a few celery leaves.

RIGHT: *Venison alpine-style* (top right, recipe on page 197); *Venison stew* (bottom left).

Roast Stuffed Rabbit

Coniglio ripieno al forno

———

1 rabbit, complete with its offal (liver, lungs, heart)
salt and pepper
olive oil
1 garlic clove
1 small onion
a bunch of aromatic herbs (basil, bay leaf, rosemary)
1 lb vermicelli
¼ cup grated Pecorino cheese
4 oz Mozzarella cheese, diced

SERVES 6

PREPARATION AND COOKING TIME:
1 HOUR 40 MINUTES

Preheat the oven to 350°F. Wash and dry the rabbit and season inside and out with salt and pepper. Wash the liver, lungs and heart and cut into small pieces. Chop the garlic and onion and soften in a tablespoon of oil, then put in the offal pieces and brown them. Add the bunch of herbs, season with salt and pepper and cook until tender.

Cook the vermicelli in plenty of boiling salted water until it is *al dente*, drain, then toss in the onion mixture to flavor. Season with the Pecorino and diced Mozzarella cheeses and salt and pepper. Twirl small portions of pasta round a fork and stuff the rabbit with these. Sew up the opening, lay the rabbit in a roasting pan and trickle over a little olive oil. Roast in the preheated oven for about 1 hour 10 minutes.

When the rabbit is cooked, cut it into thick slices with a very sharp knife, and serve with a fresh salad or with baby vegetables roasted in the oven.

Rolled Roast Rabbit with Capers

Rotolo di coniglio con capperi

———

1 rabbit, weighing about 3 lb
salt and pepper
2 plump chicken legs
3 slices white bread, soaked in milk
2 oz green olives, pitted
1 tablespoon capers, drained
1 egg
a bunch of sage
a bunch of rosemary
1 garlic clove
olive oil
dry white wine

SERVES 6–8

PREPARATION AND COOKING TIME:
ABOUT 1½ HOURS

Preheat the oven to 400°F. Wash and dry the rabbit thoroughly and then, using a pointed, very sharp knife, bone it completely, taking care not to pierce the flesh; you should end up with a regular rectangular shape. Season with salt and pepper. Bone the chicken legs, remove the skin, then pass both the chicken and the well-squeezed bread through a grinder and transfer to a bowl. Mix in the chopped olives, drained capers, egg, and season with salt and pepper.

Spread the rabbit flesh with this stuffing, then roll it up like a rolled roast. Tie with several turns of kitchen twine and lay in a roasting pan. Add a bunch of sage and rosemary, the garlic clove and 4 tablespoons oil. Roast in the hot oven for about 1 hour, basting the meat from time to time with its cooking juices and a little wine (about half a glass will be enough).

When the rabbit is cooked, remove the twine and slice the roll. De-grease and strain the sauce and serve it and the rabbit hot, accompanied by roast potatoes, if you wish.

RIGHT: *Roast stuffed rabbit.*

Rabbit with Lemon

Coniglio al limone

1 rabbit, weighing about 3½ lb

1 medium leek

2 shallots

olive oil

1 sprig of thyme

dry white wine

juice of 2 lemons

SERVES 6

PREPARATION AND COOKING TIME:
ABOUT 1 HOUR

Wash the rabbit thoroughly and then cut it into even pieces. Dry with paper towel.

Trim and peel the leek and slice it with the shallots. Soften the vegetables in 3 tablespoons oil, then add the rabbit pieces. Brown well over high heat, then flavor with the thyme, a pinch each of salt and pepper and a glass of wine. Cover, reduce the heat and cook the rabbit for about 30 minutes. Add the lemon juice and cook for a further 20 minutes or so.

When the rabbit is tender, transfer to a serving dish and serve hot, coated with the strained sauce.

Pigeon, Perugia-style

Piccioni alla perugina

4 pigeons

4 oz sliced raw ham

1 large onion

cloves

3 bay leaves

olive oil

hot chicken stock (can be made from a bouillion cube)

vinegar

SERVES 4

PREPARATION AND COOKING TIME:
ABOUT 1 HOUR

Singe the pigeons by passing them quickly over a high flame to burn off any remaining feathers. Wrap the birds in the slices of ham. Stud the onion with 3–4 cloves, halve it and place in a heavy-based pan. Add the bay leaves and a pinch of salt and

LEFT: *Turkey rolls* (top left, recipe on page 214); *Frittata roll with veal mousse* (top right, recipe on page 163); *Rabbit with lemon* (bottom).

pepper, pour over 4 tablespoons oil, then place on the heat and brown the onion before adding the pigeons. Brown them evenly, then add a ladleful of hot stock and reduce it. Add half a glass of vinegar, then reduce the heat to the minimum, cover the pan with a very tight-fitting lid to seal it almost hermetically, and cook the pigeons for about 50 minutes. They should be tender but not mushy.

Serve hot, with the strained cooking juices.

Hare Trento-style

Lepre alla trentina

1 hare, about 3½ lb

2 quarts red wine

rosemary

sage

bay leaves

juniper berries

1 onion

lemon rind

vinegar

cloves

sugar

ground cinnamon

olive oil

2 oz salt pork

flour

breadcrumbs

chicken stock (can be made from a bouillion cube)

SERVES 6

PREPARATION AND COOKING TIME:
ABOUT 2 HOURS, PLUS MARINATING

Clean the hare and reserve the offal. Joint the hare and marinate it for 48 hours in two-thirds of the wine, the herbs, bay leaves, juniper berries, ½ onion, lemon rind and vinegar. In another bowl, marinate the offal in the remaining wine with lemon rind, cloves, sugar and cinnamon.

Drain the hare pieces and roll them in flour and breadcrumbs, shaking off any excess. Strain the marinade. Chop the salt pork and brown it in a tablespoon of oil with the rest of the onion and the hare. When they are well-colored, add the chopped offal and a glass of stock. Season with salt and pepper and cook over medium heat, moistening with a little strained wine, for about 50 minutes–1 hour or until the hare pieces are cooked through and tender.

Serve hot, with the pan juices.

Pheasant with Port and Mascarpone

Fagiano al porto e mascarpone

---

1 pheasant, about 2 lb
2½ cups dry white wine
peppercorns
salt
2 bay leaves
1 large onion
olive oil
2 chicken livers
scant 1 cup port
scant 1 cup chicken stock
3 oz mascarpone cheese

SERVES 4
PREPARATION AND COOKING TIME:
ABOUT 1 HOUR, PLUS OVERNIGHT MARINATING

The night before, clean, wash and dry the pheasant and place in a bowl. Pour over the white wine, add a tablespoon of peppercorns, cover and leave in a cool place to marinate overnight.

To cook the pheasant: drain it well, reserving the strained marinade liquid, salt it lightly inside and put the bay leaves in the cavity. Tie up the bird with several turns of twine to prevent it from falling apart during cooking.

Peel and finely chop the onion and brown it in a heavy-based pan with 4 tablespoons oil. Add the pheasant and color it well on all sides. Trim the chicken livers, discarding any membrane, then add to the pan. Pour in the port and half the reserved marinade liquid, reduce by half, then add the stock. Melt the mascarpone into the cooking liquid, cover, lower the heat and cook gently for about 1 hour. Check the pheasant from time to time, basting it with a little sauce each time. If it dries out too much, add a few more ladles of stock.

When the pheasant is cooked, remove the bay leaves and purée the sauce in a blender. Serve the pheasant, carved into slices, with the very hot sauce.

Country-style Chicken

Pollo alla contadina

---

4 oz mushrooms
4 oz baby onions
1 chicken, weighing about 2¼ lb
flour
butter
olive oil
1 bay leaf
Worcestershire sauce
scant 1 cup dry white wine
2 tablespoons Marsala wine
1 teaspoon tomato paste
1 chicken bouillion cube

SERVES 4
PREPARATION AND COOKING TIME:
ABOUT 45 MINUTES

Peel the mushrooms and wash them well; also wash and peel the onions. Divide the chicken into eight pieces. Flour them, shaking off any excess, then brown them in a large frying pan in 2 tablespoons butter and 2 tablespoons oil. Add the onions and the quartered mushrooms, flavor with a bay leaf and a dash of Worcestershire sauce, then fry them for a few moments.

Pour in the white wine and Marsala, in which you have dissolved the tomato paste and the bouillion cube. Stir the mixture and cover the pan. Cook over a moderate heat for about 30 minutes.

Serve hot, with a selection of vegetables.

Chicken with Ham au Gratin

Pollo alla coppa, gratinato

1½ lb chicken meat, skinned and boned
flour
6 tablespoons butter
salt and pepper
⅔ cup dry white wine
2 oz thinly sliced raw ham
1 teaspoon chopped fresh parsley
¼ cup grated Parmesan cheese
⅔ cup milk
nutmeg

SERVES 6

PREPARATION AND COOKING TIME: ABOUT 1¼ HOURS

Cut the chicken (preferably leg and thigh meat) into pieces about 2½ inches long. Flour lightly, shaking off any excess, and brown on all sides in 4 tablespoons of the butter. Add salt and pepper. Pour in the wine and allow to evaporate over high heat. Shake the pan to prevent the meat from sticking.

Cut the ham into short thin strips. Remove from the heat and cut the chicken pieces into short but thicker strips and arrange, alternating with the ham, in a large buttered ovenproof dish. Sprinkle the chopped parsley and Parmesan cheese over the meat.

Preheat the oven to 400°F. Make a béchamel sauce by melting the remaining butter in a pan, stirring in 4 tablespoons of flour and adding the milk; season with salt and grated nutmeg. Pour the sauce over the meat and bake for about 20 minutes, until the surface is golden brown. Serve immediately.

Chicken Legs with Juniper

Cosce di pollo al ginepro

---

butter
1 large onion
salt and pepper
4 chicken legs, together weighing about 2¼ lb
1 bay leaf
olive oil
4 juniper berries
small glass gin
scant 1 cup dry white wine
1 teaspoon cornstarch

SERVES 4

PREPARATION AND COOKING TIME: 50 MINUTES

Preheat the oven to 400°F. Butter the base of a casserole dish capable of holding the chicken legs in a single layer. Slice the onion very thinly and place half of it in the bottom of the dish. Season with salt and pepper and place the chicken legs on top, putting the bay leaf between them. Scatter the remaining onion over the top, moisten with the oil, and season with salt and pepper and the juniper berries, broken into small pieces.

Cook in the oven for about 40 minutes. After 15 minutes, pour over the gin, then the white wine in which you have dissolved the cornstarch. Finish cooking, basting often, but without turning.

Serve hot, with crusty bread.

Stuffed Chicken Drumsticks

Fusi di pollo farciti

---

6 chicken drumsticks
3 sprigs fresh sage
1 garlic clove
3–4 slices smoked bacon
1 small onion
1 small carrot
1 small celery stalk
olive oil
butter
salt and pepper
¼ cup dry white wine
⅔ cup chicken stock (can be made from a bouillion cube)
½ tablespoon cornstarch

SERVES 6

PREPARATION AND COOKING TIME: 1½ HOURS

Preheat the oven to 400°F. Rinse and dry the chicken drumsticks. Slit the skin, take out the bones and remove the sinews, turning the meat inside out, without cutting it up. Then push the meat back into shape and insert half a small sprig of fresh sage, a thin strip of garlic clove and a sliver of smoked bacon into each boned drumstick. Stitch up the opening on the drumstick. Cover the base of a flameproof dish with the finely chopped onion, carrot and celery. Arrange the drumsticks on top. Finally, add 2 tablespoons oil, dot with butter and season lightly with salt and pepper.

Bake in the preheated oven for about 45 minutes; turn the drumsticks a couple of times and, halfway through the cooking time, add the dry white wine. Remove the drumsticks from the dish, place the dish on top of the stove and add the stock, with the cornstarch dissolved in it; allow the sauce to simmer for a few minutes, stirring it constantly.

Strain the gravy over the drumsticks and serve. Arrange them, if you like, on top of buttered peas, with a little parsley for garnish.

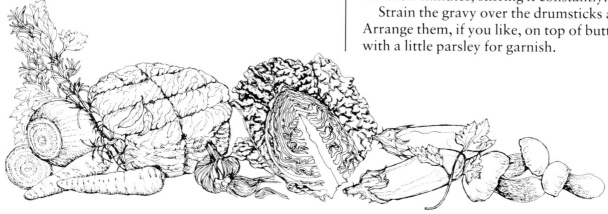

Stuffed Chicken Breasts in Breadcrumbs

Petti di pollo farciti e dorati

———————

6 chicken breasts
12 thin bacon slices
1 sprig fresh sage
1 garlic clove
¾ cup grated Parmesan cheese
2 eggs plus 2 yolks
breadcrumbs
butter
flour
½ cup milk
¼ chicken bouillion cube
½ cup grated Emmental cheese
¼ cup light cream
nutmeg
pepper
olive oil

SERVES 6

PREPARATION AND COOKING TIME:
ABOUT 1 HOUR

Pound the chicken breasts lightly, taking care not to break them. Place 2 slices of bacon on one side of each breast, a small leaf of sage and a sliver of garlic, then close them up into their original shape. Roll them first in the grated Parmesan cheese, then in two of the beaten eggs, lightly salted, and finally in the breadcrumbs, making sure that they are thoroughly coated each time. Trim the edges using a large knife, then lay the chicken breasts on a tray.

Melt 2 tablespoons butter in a small saucepan, add the flour and stir with a wooden spoon to stop lumps forming. Slowly pour in the cold milk and bring the mixture to the boil, stirring continuously, and season with the crumbled bouillion cube. Remove the sauce from the heat, mix in the grated Emmental, the egg yolks and the cream, mixing well after each addition. Season the sauce with a pinch of ground nutmeg and pepper, then keep warm.

Heat two frying pans, and in each one put a knob of butter, 4 tablespoons oil and 2 sage leaves. As soon as the fat is hot, fry the breaded chicken breasts. Remove them from the frying pans and lay them on a plate covered with paper towels to drain.

Transfer to a warm serving dish, garnish to taste, pour the prepared sauce over them and serve at once.

Chicken Breasts with Mushrooms in Marsala

Petti di pollo al marsala, con funghi

———————

12 oz small mushrooms
1 small onion
6 chicken breasts
4 tablespoons butter
olive oil
flour
salt and pepper
⅔ cup Marsala wine
½ teaspoon tomato paste
1 garlic clove
meat extract
salt and pepper
a little chopped parsley

SERVES 6

PREPARATION AND COOKING TIME:
ABOUT 50 MINUTES

Trim the mushrooms, wipe with a damp cloth and slice thinly. Chop the onion very finely and put it in a frying pan large enough to hold the chicken breasts in one layer. Add 2 tablespoons butter and a tablespoon of oil, then fry very gently until the onion is soft.

Remove any sinews from the chicken breasts and flatten them with a meat mallet; flour them, shaking off any excess. Brown them lightly in a pan with the fried onion; season with salt and pepper and moisten them with three-quarters of the Marsala in which you have dissolved the tomato paste.

When the Marsala has formed a creamy sauce and the chicken is cooked, remove the pan from the heat, arrange the chicken breasts on a serving dish, and pour over the boiling sauce, poured through a fine strainer. Cover the dish with foil and keep it hot.

Put the remaining butter in the frying pan you have already used together with a tablespoon of oil, and flavor with the lightly crushed garlic. Add the thinly sliced mushrooms and sauté them gently for a few minutes. Then pour over the remaining Marsala in which you have dissolved a little meat extract on the end of a teaspoon. Add salt and pepper to taste and let the mushrooms absorb all the liquid, becoming tender and flavorful.

Arrange them alongside the chicken breasts, sprinkle over some chopped parsley and serve.

Chicken in Red Wine

Pollo al vino rosso

1 oz dried mushrooms (porcini)
1 chicken, weighing about 3 lb
flour
6 tablespoons butter
olive oil
1 large onion
2 slices bacon
2 tablespoons brandy
¼ cup red wine
salt and pepper
12 oz prepared pie pastry

SERVES 6
PREPARATION AND COOKING TIME: 1¼ HOURS

Soak the mushrooms in a little warm water for approximately one hour.

Meanwhile, carefully wash and wipe dry the chicken, then cut it into serving portions. Coat the portions with flour, shaking off any excess, then fry in 2 tablespoons butter and a tablespoon of oil. When they are browned, remove from the pan, drain on paper towels and keep warm while you make the sauce.

Chop the onion finely and fry it gently in a further 2 tablespoons butter in the previously used frying pan. Drain, wash and squeeze dry the mushrooms and slice them into strips with the bacon slices. Add these to the onion in the pan and fry for a few minutes more. Return the chicken to the pan, stirring to distribute the vegetable mixture, then sprinkle over the brandy. Leave it to evaporate before adding the wine. Stir, reduce the heat to low and season with salt and pepper. Cook gently for 30 minutes, half-covered, and add a little warm water if necessary.

Grease a 9 inch tart pan with a removable bottom with the remaining butter. Roll out the pastry to a circle about 1½ inches larger than the pan, then use this to line it. Prick all over with a fork, cover with waxed paper and baking beans and cook in the oven preheated to 425°F for 20 minutes. Remove the beans and paper and cook for a further 5 minutes until the pastry is browned and crisp. Arrange with pastry shell on a serving dish. Carefully spoon over the chicken sauce. Serve hot.

Chicken with Herbs

Galletti amburghesi, in tegame

---

3 baby chickens or Cornish hens
olive oil
1 sprig fresh rosemary
2 fresh sage leaves
½ garlic clove
salt and pepper
½ cup dry white wine

SERVES 6

PREPARATION AND COOKING TIME:
ABOUT 1 HOUR

Cut the chickens in half (preferably using poultry shears) along the backbone (to one side of it) and flatten them gently with a meat mallet, taking care not to break or shatter the bones.

Place 4–5 tablespoons of oil, the rosemary, sage leaves and garlic clove in a very large frying pan and fry gently for a few minutes. Add the chickens, open side upwards. Sprinkle with salt and pepper, cover the pan and cook over low heat for 10 minutes.

Turn the chickens, sprinkle with salt and pepper again and pour over the white wine. Cover the pan and cook briskly for a further 20 minutes.

Arrange on a warmed dish and serve immediately.

Chicken Kebabs with Herbs

Spiedini piccanti di galletti alle erbe

---

3 chickens, weighing about 3¾ lb
marjoram
sage
rosemary
olive oil
salt and pepper
4 slices white bread
thyme
basil
½ garlic clove

FOR THE SAUCE

7 oz zucchini
½ medium leek
2 tablespoons butter
1 medium red pepper, roasted and skinned
1 hot chilli pepper
hot chicken stock (can be made from a bouillion cube)
salt

SERVES 6

PREPARATION AND COOKING TIME:
ABOUT 40 MINUTES, PLUS MARINATING

Cut each chicken into eight serving pieces. Sprinkle with an aromatic mixture of chopped marjoram, sage and rosemary; moisten with 3 tablespoons oil, season with salt and pepper and leave to marinate for 3 hours.

Meanwhile, make the bread into crumbs in a food processor and mix with a pinch of salt and pepper and a tablespoon of chopped mixed herbs (sage, rosemary, thyme, basil), and the garlic.

Thread four different pieces of chicken onto each skewer; sprinkle with the herbed breadcrumbs, moisten with 3 tablespoons oil, then cook under a very hot broiler for 20 minutes on each side.

Meanwhile, prepare the sauce. Finely dice the zucchini. Slice the leek and soften it in the butter, then add the diced zucchini, the chopped roasted pepper and a piece of chilli pepper. Moisten with 2 ladles of hot stock; season with salt and simmer the sauce for 3 minutes. Finally, purée the spicy sauce in a blender.

Season the kebabs, transfer to a serving dish and serve very hot with the sauce.

LEFT: *Chicken in red wine.*

Chicken in a "Bladder"

Gallina a la canèvera

---

1 medium stalk celery
1 small carrot
1 small onion
cloves
1 oven-ready free-range chicken, about 5 lb
1 orange
1 lemon
1 apple
1 garlic clove
1 tablespoon coarse salt
½ teaspoon sugar
1 cinnamon stick
¼ cup extra virgin olive oil
a length of bamboo, about 12 in
salt

SERVES 8

PREPARATION AND COOKING TIME:
ABOUT 3 HOURS

Cut the celery and carrot into small pieces; stud the onion with a few cloves. Fill the cavity of the chicken with all these, plus a wedge of orange, a wedge of lemon, the apple, cut into small pieces, the garlic, coarse salt, the sugar, a piece of cinnamon and all the olive oil. Tie the chicken legs close to the breast, and insert the piece of bamboo between them. Place the chicken, neck end first in a roasting bag, leaving part of the bamboo protruding from the opening of the bag, and tie up with kitchen twine; the bamboo will act as a vent to allow partial evaporation of the juices that form as the chicken cooks.

Fill a deep saucepan with plenty of salted water, put in the chicken so that the bamboo protrudes at least 4 inches above the water, cover the pan with foil and cook over moderate heat for about 2½ hours.

Cut the chicken into serving pieces and serve with the cooking juices that have formed in the bag.

Chicken with Walnuts and Olives

Sopracosce con noci e olive

---

6 chicken legs
a little flour
butter
3 fresh sage leaves
1 sprig fresh rosemary
½ cup dry white wine
⅔ cup chicken stock (can be made from a bouillion cube)
10 green olives, pitted
10 walnuts
cornstarch
light cream
a little chopped parsley

SERVES 6

PREPARATION AND COOKING TIME:
ABOUT 40 MINUTES

Tie each chicken leg in three places with kitchen twine and coat lightly in flour, shaking off any excess. Heat a large knob of butter in a large frying pan with the sage and the sprig of rosemary. Fry the chicken pieces briskly until crisp and golden on all sides. Pour on the white wine and let the liquid evaporate before adding the stock. Cook over moderate heat for about 20 minutes.

Meanwhile quarter the olives and break the walnuts up into fairly large pieces. As soon as the chicken is cooked and the liquid has reduced, remove the meat from the pan and discard the twine. Place the chicken on a plate and keep hot. Discard the sage and rosemary and add the olives and walnuts to the pan. Dissolve a teaspoon of cornstarch in a little cold water and stir it into the mixture together with 5 tablespoons of cream. Blend thoroughly.

Replace the chicken in the pan and soak in the sauce for a few minutes. Transfer to a hot serving dish, coating the meat with the sauce. Sprinkle with a little chopped parsley, if desired, and serve.

RIGHT: *Chicken in a "bladder"*.

210

Guinea Fowl with Bay Leaves

Faraona all'alloro

---

1 guinea fowl, weighing about 3¼ lb
salt and pepper
1 medium onion
1 garlic clove
2 oz pancetta (Italian bacon)
8 bay leaves
¼ cup olive oil
1½ cups white wine
hot chicken stock (can be made from a bouillion cube)

SERVES 4

PREPARATION AND COOKING TIME:
ABOUT 1 HOUR 20 MINUTES

Singe the guinea fowl over a high flame to remove any remaining feathers or feather ends. Wash and dry the bird, then season both inside and out with salt and pepper.

Chop the onion, garlic, pancetta and bay leaves. Soften this mixture in the oil, then add the guinea fowl and brown it all over, turning it frequently. Sprinkle over about half of the wine. Lower the heat, cover and cook the guinea fowl for about 1 hour (the meat should be falling off the bones), basting it from time to time with the remaining wine and a ladleful of hot stock.

Serve straight from the pan, with the sauce.

Duck in Sauce

Anatra in salsa

2½ oz sliced pancetta (Italian bacon)
2 tablespoons butter
sage
rosemary
2 ducks, about 4¾ lb each
1 lemon
salt and pepper
3 anchovies
1 garlic clove
7 oz Italian sausage
white wine vinegar

SERVES 6

PREPARATION AND COOKING TIME:
ABOUT 3 HOURS

LEFT: *Duck in sauce.*

Preheat the oven to 350°F. Chop the pancetta and brown it in the butter with a few sage leaves and a sprig of rosemary. Take the pan off the heat and add the ducks, the lemon cut into wedges, salt and pepper. Roast in the oven for about 2 hours, basting the ducks frequently with their juices.

Meanwhile, finely chop the anchovies with the garlic and, separately, the Italian sausage. Place all the chopped ingredients in a saucepan and sweat over very moderate heat for about 10 minutes, then moisten with half a glass of vinegar; mix and turn off the heat.

As soon as the ducks are cooked, cut them into serving pieces and arrange in an ovenproof dish. Pour over the sauce, then place in the switched-off but still warm oven for about 20 minutes to give the ducks a fine flavor.

Casserole of Turkey "Haunches"

'Coscette' di tacchino in casseruola

---

2 turkey wings
1 small stalk celery
½ medium carrot
1 small onion, peeled
4 tablespoons butter
1 garlic clove
7 oz chopped tomatoes
hot chicken stock (can be made from a bouillion cube)
salt and pepper
paprika
chopped fresh parsley and sage
⅓ cup whipping cream

SERVES 4

PREPARATION AND COOKING TIME:
ABOUT 1 HOUR 40 MINUTES

Cut off the turkey wing tips, then cut the meat away from the bones, pushing the flesh upwards so that the wings look like 'haunches'.

Chop the celery, carrot and onion, and then soften them in the butter, together with a whole garlic clove. Add the turkey and brown gently, then add the chopped tomatoes, 2 ladles of hot stock, salt, pepper, paprika, and half a tablespoon of chopped herbs. Cover and cook over very moderate heat for about 1 hour, then pour in the cream and cook for about 15 minutes more.

Serve the "haunches" with the cooking liquid and, if you like, some steamed polenta.

Turkey Breast in Pastry

Fesa di tacchino in croste

7 oz smoked bacon (in one piece)
2 lb turkey breast
butter
rosemary
sage
1 celery stalk
1 carrot
1 onion
olive oil
⅔ cup dry white wine
1 small lettuce
8 oz frozen puff pastry, thawed
7 oz cooked ham
mustard
1 egg
1 teaspoon cornmeal
½ cup light cream

SERVES 6–8

PREPARATION AND COOKING TIME: 2 HOURS

Preheat the oven to 375°F. Slice the bacon into strips and cover the turkey with the strips and a little softened butter, then sprinkle over some chopped rosemary and sage. Tie up the turkey securely with kitchen thread. Wash and chop the celery, carrot and onion.

Put the turkey into a roasting pan, add the vegetables, salt and pepper to taste and ⅔ cup oil. Brown for 10 minutes over high heat. Transfer to the oven and cook for 30 minutes; after 15 minutes, pour over the wine and turn the meat over. Turn the oven up to 400°F. When the turkey is cooked, remove from the oven and allow to cool.

Wash and finely slice the lettuce. Roll the pastry into a thin rectangle about 12 × 15 inches. Put it on a greased baking sheet and arrange on it half the ham, half the lettuce and the turkey. Spread mustard over the meat, then cover with the rest of the ham and lettuce. Bring the pastry up around the turkey to enclose it completely, securing it well. Cut away any excess pastry. Brush the top with egg then roll out the excess pastry and use to decorate. Brush the strips with egg then bake for 20 minutes.

Strain the meat cooking juices and reheat, adding the cornmeal and cream to thicken and finish it. Strain again, then serve with the turkey.

Turkey Rolls

Involtini di tacchino

7 oz button mushrooms
1½ tablespoons butter
salt
2 oz raw ham
3 slices white bread
¼ cup grated Parmesan cheese
1 egg yolk
1 tablespoon chopped fresh thyme
1 tablespoon chopped fresh parsley
1 lb 2 oz turkey leg steaks
flour
olive oil
2 shallots
2 garlic cloves
a sprig of rosemary
a sprig of sage
dry white wine

SERVES 4

PREPARATION AND COOKING TIME:
ABOUT 1 HOUR

Trim, wash and drain the mushrooms, cut into quarters and sweat in the butter over very low heat until very dry. Season with salt, then purée in a food processor with the ham. Transfer to a bowl. Make the bread into crumbs in the food processor and add it to the mushroom mixture, together with the Parmesan cheese, egg yolk and the chopped thyme and parsley.

Using a moistened meat mallet, flatten the turkey steaks into a rectangular shape. Divide the mushroom mixture between them, then roll up the turkey, starting from the short side. Secure the rolls with two toothpicks and roll them in flour, shaking off any excess. Heat 3 tablespoons oil with the sliced shallots, lightly crushed garlic cloves and the rosemary and sage. Salt the turkey rolls and brown them all over, then sprinkle with half a glass of wine. Cover and cook for about 15 minutes, then drain the rolls, transfer them to a plate and keep hot. Dilute the sauce with a tablespoon of hot water and reduce it, then strain and pour the sauce over the turkey rolls.

Serve at once, garnished to your taste.

RIGHT: *Turkey breast in pastry.*

214

Vegetables & Salads

Vegetables and salads are often served as a separate course in Italy. They make ideal vegetarian dishes or imaginative side dishes to meat, fish or poultry main courses. Here are recipes for a wide range of vegetables and salads, ranging from the simple to the more ambitious, from the everyday to the exotic – but always absolutely delicious.

Green Beans with Crab

Fagiolini al granchio

1½ lb green beans
1 × 6 oz canned crabmeat
1 lettuce heart
2 anchovy fillets in oil
a handful of fresh parsley
5 or 6 mushrooms in oil
1 tablespoon white wine vinegar
¼ cup mayonnaise
1 teaspoon mustard
Worcestershire sauce

SERVES 6

PREPARATION AND COOKING TIME: 30 MINUTES

Top and tail the beans, then cook in salted boiling water until tender, drain and dry. Flake the crabmeat finely. Remove the tender leaves from the lettuce heart one at a time, and wash and dry each leaf thoroughly.

Now prepare the sauce: finely chop the anchovies with the parsley and mushrooms. Put these in a bowl and incorporate the vinegar then the mayonnaise, flavoring with the mustard and a dash of Worcestershire sauce. Mix carefully after each addition – you should obtain a smooth, fairly runny sauce.

In a salad bowl mix the beans and crabmeat, arrange the lettuce leaves around the outside and serve accompanied by the sauce.

Green Beans and Onions

Fagiolini cipollati

---

14 oz green beans
2 large onions
½ sprig fresh rosemary
1 garlic clove
butter
olive oil
2–3 tablespoons Marsala wine
½ vegetable bouillion cube
nutmeg
1 teaspoon cornstarch
⅔ cup light vegetable stock

SERVES 4

PREPARATION AND COOKING TIME: 45 MINUTES

Slice the onions very thinly and finely chop the rosemary leaves and the garlic. Gently fry the onion in 2 tablespoons of butter and 3 tablespoons oil, taking care not to let them brown. Add the beans.

Pour in the Marsala. Allow to evaporate then crumble in the bouillion cube and season with a little grated nutmeg. Carefully dissolve the cornstarch in the cold stock and pour into the pan. Shake the pan and cover, turn the heat down to the minimum and leave the beans to simmer until the sauce has thickened.

Taste and correct seasoning, then serve.

Country-style Green Beans

Fagiolini alla moda paesana

---

12 oz green beans
1 small onion
1 small carrot
1 celery stalk
1 large garlic clove
2 slices bacon, diced very small
butter
olive oil
8 oz tomatoes, skinned
1 small bay leaf
2 or 3 sprigs fresh parsley
2 fresh basil leaves
a pinch of sugar
grated Parmesan cheese

SERVES 4

PREPARATION AND COOKING TIME: 45 MINUTES

Preheat the oven to 400°F. Finely chop the onion, carrot, celery and garlic. Gently fry together with the bacon in 2 tablespoons of butter and 2 tablespoons of oil. Purée the tomatoes and add to the pan. Tie the bay leaf, parsley and basil together and add these too. Season and add the sugar. Simmer for about 10 minutes with the pan half-covered, then add the beans and leave them to absorb the flavors for about 10 minutes, tossing frequently. Remove the herbs and pour the contents of the pan into an ovenproof dish. Sprinkle with cheese and bake for about 10 minutes. Serve at once.

Green beans with crab (top left);
Green beans and onions (bottom left);
Country-style green beans (top right).

Savoy Cabbage with Onions

Verza cipollata

12 oz savoy cabbage
2 small onions
2 oz cooking fat
rosemary
1 garlic clove
olive oil
½ vegetable bouillion cube
salt and pepper
ground nutmeg
a little dry white wine

SERVES 4

PREPARATION AND COOKING TIME:
ABOUT 45 MINUTES

Bring a large saucepan of water to the boil and add salt. Wash and drain the cabbage carefully and boil for about 5 minutes.

Meanwhile, slice the onions thinly. Blend the fat with a few leaves of rosemary and the garlic clove and fry gently in 2 tablespoons of olive oil. Add the onions and cook gently until transparent.

Drain the cabbage, slice thickly and add to the onions, Flavor with the crumbled bouillion cube, pepper and a pinch of nutmeg, and sprinkle with a little white wine. Cover the pan and allow the wine to evaporate, stirring occasionally. Test and adjust the seasoning according to taste.

Serve immediately.

White Beans with Onion Sauce

Bianchi di spagna con salsa di cipolla

1 × 14 oz can Great Northern beans
1 small onion
butter
1 teaspoon cornstarch
¼ cup milk
10 capers
spring of fresh parsley

SERVES 4

PREPARATION AND COOKING TIME:
ABOUT 30 MINUTES

Rinse the beans thoroughly under warm running water and drain. Chop the onion almost to a paste. Melt 2 tablespoons butter in a small saucepan and fry the onion without browning over low heat for about 15 minutes. Add a tablespoon of warm water, if necessary, to keep the onion soft and to stop it drying out. Sprinkle the cornstarch over the onion and blend in well. Dilute gradually with the cold milk to obtain a smooth, consistent sauce. Season with a pinch of salt and simmer over low heat, stirring constantly, for 5–6 minutes. Remove from the heat and blend at maximum speed until the sauce is completely smooth, then put it in a bowl.

Drain the capers thoroughly, chop them coarsely and add to the chopped parsley. Pour the beans into a serving dish and pour over the onion sauce. Sprinkle with the chopped parsley and capers and serve. This vegetable dish makes a delicate accompaniment to boiled meats.

Haricot Beans with Cheese Sauce

Cornetti gialli con salsa al formaggio

1¼ lb fresh haricot beans
4 tablespoons butter
olive oil
flour
scant 1 cup vegetable stock (or use a bouillion cube)
¼ cup whipping cream
1 egg yolk
¼ cup grated Emmental and Parmesan cheese
salt
ground nutmeg

SERVES 4–6

PREPARATION AND COOKING TIME:
ABOUT 1 HOUR

Heat a pan of water. Pod the beans and wash them thoroughly. As soon as the water is boiling drop them in and cook for about 20 minutes; they should be very tender. Drain and sauté them in a pan with a large knob of butter and 2 tablespoons of oil, keeping the heat low and the pan covered. Stir occasionally and cook for about 10 minutes.

Meanwhile, melt the remaining butter in another pan, fold in 2 tablespoons of flour and stir to prevent lumps from forming; dilute with the hot stock and bring slowly to the boil. Remove the sauce from the heat, stir in the cream beaten with the egg yolk, the grated Emmental and Parmesan cheeses, a little salt and ground nutmeg. Stir well after the addition of each ingredient. Arrange the beans in a shallow dish, pour over the sauce, toss the beans gently and serve.

These beans make an ideal side dish for delicate main courses such as fillet of sole, veal escalopes, chicken and turkey breasts, roast saddle or medallions of rabbit. Green beans can be prepared with the same cheese sauce.

Cauliflower with Tomato and Garlic Sauce

Cavolfiore alla pizzaiola

1 medium cauliflower
1 small onion
2 garlic cloves
olive oil
14 oz skinned tomatoes
a little sugar
salt and pepper
oregano
4 fresh basil leaves
4 oz Mozzarella cheese
4 tablespoons butter
grated Parmesan cheese

SERVES 6
PREPARATION AND COOKING TIME:
ABOUT 1 HOUR

Preheat the oven to 400°F. Wash the cauliflower thoroughly and simmer in an uncovered pan for about 12 minutes.

Meanwhile, finely chop the onion and garlic and sauté in 4 tablespoons of olive oil. After a few minutes add the puréed tomatoes, a pinch of sugar and a little salt and pepper. Stir, and cook for about 15 minutes, stirring from time to time. Then add a pinch of oregano and the finely chopped basil leaves.

When the cauliflower is cooked and tender, remove it from the pan with a slotted spoon and place it on a dish covered with a double layer of paper towels to absorb the moisture. Then place it in a buttered ovenproof dish with high sides that just

contains it. Dice the Mozzarella and scatter the pieces between the cauliflower florets. Melt the butter and pour over the cauliflower and sprinkle with grated Parmesan cheese. Place the dish in the oven for about 10 minutes.

Pour some of the tomato sauce over the cauliflower and serve immediately, and pour the remaining sauce into a sauceboat for serving.

Artichokes Stuffed with Ham

Carciofi ripieni al prosciutto

4 artichokes
juice of 1 lemon
salt
a little flour
2 oz lean ham
butter
1/2 cup milk
1/4 chicken or vegetable bouillion cube
1/4 cup grated Emmental cheese
3 tablespoons grated Parmesan cheese

SERVES 4
PREPARATION AND COOKING TIME:
ABOUT 1 1/4 HOURS

Trim the artichokes and remove the tough outer leaves, but reserve the tender central flesh of the stalks. Cut the artichokes in half lengthways, scoop out and discard the chokes. Place the halves in a bowl of water with half the lemon juice.

Bring a large saucepan of water to the boil. Add salt, the rest of the lemon juice and the flour dissolved in a little cold water. Add the artichokes and stalks and cook for about 20 minutes or until the outer leaves are tender. Drain and cool on paper towels.

Preheat the oven to 375°F. Finely chop the artichoke stalks and the ham. Prepare a béchamel sauce with a knob of butter, a tablespoon of flour and the milk. Blend in the crumbled bouillion cube and the grated Emmental cheese. Stir in the chopped ham and artichoke stalks.

Fill the artichoke halves with the prepared sauce and arrange them in a buttered ovenproof pan. Pour on 2 tablespoons of melted butter, sprinkle with the grated Parmesan cheese and bake in the oven for about 20 minutes or until golden brown. Serve hot.

Casserole of New Potatoes, Artichokes and Peas

Patatine, carciofi e piselli in tegame

---

4 artichokes
juice of ½ lemon
1 small onion
1 small garlic clove
1 sprig fresh parsley
olive oil
dry white wine
⅔ cup vegetable stock (or use a bouillion cube)
salt and pepper
thyme
14 oz new potatoes
4 tablespoons butter
2 sage leaves
12 oz petits pois
2–3 slices bacon
dried mint

SERVES 6

PREPARATION AND COOKING TIME:
ABOUT 2 HOURS

Trim the artichokes, remove the tough outer leaves and put them in a bowl of water, together with the lemon juice.

Chop half the onion finely with the garlic and a handful of parsley and place this in a pan that will hold the artichokes. Add 3 tablespoons each of oil and white wine, and 2 tablespoons stock. Place the artichokes in the pan, stalks upwards, and season with salt, pepper and a pinch of thyme. Put the lid on and place over low heat over a wire mesh or fireproof mat. Cook gently until the artichokes are tender and have absorbed most of the liquid.

Meanwhile, peel the potatoes if necessary and boil them in salted water for 3–4 minutes, then drain well and place in a large heavy-based pan with the melted butter, 2 tablespoons oil and the sage. Cook over very low heat until they are tender and just slightly browned.

Boil the peas for 3–4 minutes. Chop the remaining onion finely with the bacon and sauté the mixture in the remaining butter, taking care that it does not brown. Add the peas and the remaining boiling stock, and season with a pinch of dried mint. Simmer until the peas have absorbed most of the liquid.

Remove the sage, and add the peas to the potatoes. Cut the artichokes into six and add them too, together with their cooking juices. Simmer gently for a further 5 minutes and serve hot.

Fava Beans Lyonnaise

Fave alla lionese

4½ lb fresh broad beans
1 large onion
1 garlic clove
3 slices bacon
olive oil
butter
a little vegetable stock (or use a bouillion cube)
ground thyme
freshly ground pepper

SERVES 4

PREPARATION AND COOKING TIME:
ABOUT 1½ HOURS

Shell and skin the beans, dropping them into cold water as they are done. Boil them for 5 minutes in salted water, then drain well.

Slice the onion very thinly, crush the garlic and cut the bacon into short narrow strips. Heat 2 tablespoons of oil and 2 tablespoons of butter and brown the garlic, then remove and discard it. Put the onion and bacon in the hot fat and fry gently without browning, then add the beans and stir them in for a few minutes with a wooden spoon. Ladle in a little hot stock and flavor with a pinch of thyme and some freshly ground pepper. Stew the beans until they are tender and have absorbed nearly all the liquid, then adjust the seasoning and serve in a hot dish.

RIGHT: *Fava beans lyonnaise.*

Vegetable Ring

Anello di verdure

---

10 oz red bell peppers
12 oz zucchini
olive oil
salt and pepper
grated Parmesan cheese
cornmeal
4 eggs
butter and flour, for the mold
1 large leek
1 lb eggplant
nutmeg
home-made tomato sauce, to accompany

SERVES 8

PREPARATION AND COOKING TIME:
ABOUT 1 HOUR 20 MINUTES

Preheat the oven to 400°F. Scorch the peppers over a high flame, peel them, remove the seeds and cut into thin strips. Trim and wash the zucchini. Dice them finely and brown in 3 tablespoons oil over high heat. Add the strips of red pepper, season with salt and pepper, cook for another 2–3 minutes, then purée the mixture in a food processor and transfer to a bowl. Mix in 2 tablespoons grated Parmesan cheese, 2 tablespoons cornmeal and 2 eggs.

Butter and flour a 9 inch ring mold, then pour in the vegetable mixture. Stand the mold in a roasting pan filled with two fingers of hot water and cook in the hot oven for about 20 minutes.

Meanwhile, trim the leek, slice it finely and soften in 3 tablespoons oil. Cut off the eggplant stalks, finely dice the flesh and add it to the leek. Brown over high heat and season with salt and pepper. Purée these vegetables in a food processor and transfer to a bowl. Mix in 2 tablespoons each of Parmesan cheese and cornmeal, the remaining eggs and a grating of nutmeg. Take the ring mold out of the oven for a moment and add the new mixture to the partially cooked mixture. Return to the oven and cook for a further 30 minutes.

Remove the mold from the oven and invert it onto a plate. Fill the center of the ring with hot tomato sauce, and serve immediately.

Gratin of Potatoes, Mushrooms and Zucchini

Gratin di patate, funghi, zucchini

---

10 oz potatoes
vinegar
8 oz zucchini
7 oz cep mushrooms (or fresh porcini)
butter
fresh sage
salt and pepper
⅔ cup whipping cream
2 egg yolks
1 tablespoon chopped fresh parsley
1 tablespoon grated Parmesan cheese

SERVES 6

PREPARATION AND COOKING TIME:
ABOUT 50 MINUTES

Peel the potatoes, cut into rounds and boil for 2 minutes in plenty of water, acidulated with a tablespoon of vinegar. Drain and set aside.

Trim the zucchini and cut into rounds. Carefully clean the ceps, delicately scraping the stalks and wiping the caps with a damp cloth. If you wish, rinse quickly under cold running water. Slice the mushrooms and brown them in a nut of butter, flavored with a few sage leaves. Season with salt and pepper, then add the zucchini rounds. Brown for about 3 minutes, then transfer to a plate. In the same pan, heat another nut of butter, put in the potatoes, season with salt and brown them. Add the other two vegetables. Pour off any excess fat, sauté the vegetables over high heat for 2 minutes, then transfer to a heatproof dish.

In a bowl, mix the cream and egg yolks with the parsley and a pinch each of salt and pepper. Pour this mixture over the vegetables; dot with flakes of butter and sprinkle on the Parmesan cheese. Place under a hot grill (or in a very hot oven) just until a golden crust forms. Serve hot, with steaks or pork chops.

LEFT: *Gratin of potatoes, mushrooms and zucchini* (top); *Vegetable ring* (bottom).

Deep-fried Vegetables with Piquant Sauce

Fritto misto con salsa picante

---

2 lb 14 oz fennel
salt and pepper
1 lb zucchini
2 eggs, separated
1¾ cups all-purpose flour
nutmeg
scant 1 cup milk
olive oil
FOR THE SAUCE
pickled red pepper
6 gherkins
¼ cup dry white wine
vinegar
Worcestershire sauce
1 cup mayonnaise

SERVES 8
PREPARATION AND COOKING TIME:
ABOUT 1 HOUR

Trim the fennel and discard the most fibrous outer layer. Wash, halve and cook in boiling salted water until *al dente*, then drain. Trim the zucchini, rinse and dry them thoroughly on paper towels and cut into batons the size of half a finger.

To prepare the batter for deep-frying: in a bowl, work the egg yolks (reserving the whites) with the flour, a pinch each of salt and pepper and a grating of nutmeg, then gradually pour in the cold milk in a thin stream. Beat the reserved egg whites until firm, then carefully fold them into the mixture, turning the egg whites from bottom to top and vice-versa.

Cut the cooked, cold fennel into thin sticks. Dip them into the batter, a few at a time, then fry in plenty of very hot oil. As soon as they are ready, take them out with a slotted spoon and drain on a double thickness of paper towels, keeping them hot. When all the fennel is cooked, dip the zucchini in the batter and fry in the same way. When all the vegetables are cooked, arrange them on a plate and keep hot while you prepare the sauce.

Combine the pepper, gherkins, wine, vinegar and a dash of Worcestershire sauce in a blender and blend at maximum speed. Put the mayonnaise in a bowl, add the sauce and mix well. Serve the vegetables and let your guests help themselves to the sauce.

Eggplant Rolls

Involtini di melanzane

---

1 lb eggplant
salt
4 oz leek
7 oz zucchini
2 medium stalks celery
4 oz Emmental cheese
olive oil
fresh white breadcrumbs
chopped parsley

SERVES 6

PREPARATION AND COOKING TIME:
ABOUT 50 MINUTES

Cut off the eggplant stems, then wash and dry the eggplants and cut lengthways into thin slices (you should have about 18). Place in a colander, sprinkle with salt and leave to draw out the juices.

Meanwhile, trim and wash the leek, zucchini and celery. Cut them into thin julienne strips. Cut the cheese into similar strips. Heat 3 tablespoons oil in a frying pan and sauté the vegetables over high heat for not more than 3–4 minutes; they should still be crunchy. Season with salt and leave them to cool.

Preheat the oven to 350°F. Place the eggplant slices under a very hot broiler, turning them over to soften them without cooking. Divide the julienne of vegetables and cheese between the slices and roll them up. Arrange the eggplant rolls in an ovenproof dish and sprinkle with a pinch of salt, breadcrumbs and chopped parsley. Moisten with a trickle of oil, then cook in the oven for 10 minutes; just long enough for the cheese to melt and a crust to form on the rolls. Serve hot.

Golden Eggplant Slices

Melanzane 'indorate'

---

2 medium eggplants
2 eggs
salt and white pepper
½ cup grated Pecorino cheese
1¼ cups fresh breadcrumbs
flour
frying oil

SERVES 4–5

PREPARATION AND COOKING TIME:
ABOUT 40 MINUTES, PLUS 1 HOUR RESTING

Wash and dry the eggplants and cut them in slices about ½ inch thick. Lay on a large tray covered with paper towels and sprinkle them with salt to bring out their juices. Leave to rest in a cool place for about 1 hour, then wash and dry the slices.

Beat the eggs in a bowl with a pinch of salt and pepper. Mix the Pecorino cheese with the breadcrumbs. Roll each slice of eggplant in the flour, then dip it in the beaten eggs and finally in the mixture of breadcrumbs and Pecorino cheese, making sure that each coating covers the slices of eggplant completely.

Heat plenty of vegetable oil in a frying pan; place the slices of eggplant in the pan a few at a time and brown. Remove them with a slotted spoon and, after draining, place them on a plate covered with a double sheet of paper towels to absorb the excess oil; continue to fry the other slices. Finally arrange the eggplant slices on a serving dish.

Yellow Peppers with Aromatic Sauce

Peperoni gialli con trito d'aromi

---

4 yellow bell peppers
1 garlic clove
anchovy paste
15 capers in vinegar
few sprigs fresh parsley
1 sprig fresh watercress
Worcestershire sauce
olive oil

SERVES 4

PREPARATION AND COOKING TIME:
ABOUT 40 MINUTES, PLUS AT LEAST 2 HOURS
RESTING

Wash and dry the peppers, then broil them to scorch the skins, turning them over. Wrap them individually in a double sheet of paper towels and leave them to rest for about 10 minutes. Remove the paper and peel them completely, keeping them under running water. Dry and divide each pepper into three large strips, removing the seeds and the stem. Arrange the strips in a bowl, overlapping them slightly, and prepare the dressing.

Crush the garlic clove in a small bowl, add 1¼ inches of anchovy paste and the finely chopped capers, parsley sprigs and watercress leaves, a pinch of salt, a few drops of Worcestershire sauce and 5 tablespoons of oil. Pour the sauce over the pepper strips, cover the dish with plastic wrap and leave it for at least 2 hours in a cool place.

Serve the peppers sprinkled with chopped parsley in small serving bowls.

Stuffed Zucchini

Tronchetti di zucchine

---

3 zucchini
1 slice very fresh white bread
a little milk
4 oz ground lean beef
1 tablespoon pine nuts
handful of fresh parsley
2 garlic cloves
¼ cup grated Parmesan cheese
1 egg yolk
salt and pepper
ground nutmeg
olive oil
½ cup meat stock
2 tablespoons tomato juice

SERVES 3

PREPARATION AND COOKING TIME:
ABOUT 1¼ HOURS

Trim, wash and dry the zucchini, then cut each one into three. Remove most of the pulp of each one (keep it for a soup or a cream of vegetables), making sure not to cut the outside green part.

RIGHT: *Stuffed zucchini* (top left); *Yellow peppers with aromatic sauce* (top right); *Golden eggplant slices* (bottom).

Prepare the stuffing: soak the slice of white bread in a small amount of milk, then squeeze it and crumble it in a bowl. Add the ground beef, the pine nuts, finely chopped parsley mixed with half a garlic clove, the Parmesan cheese and the egg yolk. Mix everything together thoroughly, add salt and pepper and season with ground nutmeg. Use this mixture to stuff the zucchini without overfilling them.

Preheat the oven to 400°F. Heat 4 tablespoons of oil in a frying pan and sauté a garlic clove. When the oil is hot, remove the garlic and throw it away, then place the chunks of zucchini in the pan and fry them lightly on each side.

Arrange them in an ovenproof dish, moisten them with the stock mixed with the tomato juice and a tablespoon of olive oil. Cover and cook in the preheated oven for about 40 minutes, uncovering the dish for the last 10 minutes.

Carefully transfer the zucchini to a warmed serving dish and serve.

Peas with Mortadella

Pisellini con petitella

---

3 shallots, finely chopped
butter
olive oil
1 lb frozen peas
4 oz mortadella sausage
½ vegetable bouillion cube
ground nutmeg

SERVES 6

PREPARATION AND COOKING TIME:
ABOUT 30 MINUTES

Sauté the shallots in a large knob of butter and 2 tablespoons of oil. Cook the peas in salted boiling water for about 4 minutes. Skin the sausage, cut it in half lengthways and slice it thinly into crescents. Drain the peas and add them to the shallots. Stir, season, and add the crumbled bouillion cube and a little nutmeg.

Pour on ½ cup of water, stir and cover the pan. Allow the peas to absorb all the liquid. Stir in the crescents of mortadella, replace the lid on the pan and cook for a further 2 minutes. Serve in a warmed dish.

Stewed Potatoes, Peppers, Eggplants and Tomatoes

Ciammotta

---

8 oz potatoes
8 oz eggplant
8 oz bell peppers
olive oil
7 oz firm ripe tomatoes
1 garlic clove, chopped

SERVES 4

PREPARATION AND COOKING TIME:
1 HOUR 20 MINUTES

Peel and roughly dice the potatoes. Trim and wash the eggplant, slice it fairly thinly, then sprinkle with salt and leave for about 30 minutes to draw out the juices.

Meanwhile, remove the core, seeds and white membrane from the peppers and cut the flesh into

LEFT: *Vegetable mold.*

thin strips. Heat plenty of oil in a deep-frying pan and fry first the potatoes, then the peppers and finally the eggplant, rinsed and dried with paper towels. Put all the fried vegetables in a heavy-based pan. Peel and deseed the tomatoes, chop roughly and add to the casserole. Season with the chopped garlic and a pinch of salt, then cover and stew over medium heat for about an hour. The stew should be fairly dry.

Vegetable Mold

Sformato di verdure

2¼ lb broccoli
1 lb potatoes
vinegar
1¼ lb carrots
1 large onion, peeled and chopped
1½ tablespoons butter, plus extra for greasing
8 slices white bread, soaked in milk
olive oil
2 eggs
1 cup grated Parmesan cheese
7 oz sliced smoked bacon

SERVES 8

PREPARATION AND COOKING TIME:
ABOUT 2¾ HOURS, PLUS RESTING

Preheat the oven to 400°F. Trim the broccoli into florets and discard the fibrous parts of the stalk, then boil until tender. Peel and slice the potatoes, then boil in water acidulated with vinegar. Scrape the carrots and cut them into rounds. Brown the onion in the butter and add the carrots. Season with salt and pepper, cover with cold water, put the lid on the pan and cook until dry. Squeeze out the bread, mix half into the carrots, then purée in a food processor. Brown the potatoes in a little hot oil. Purée the broccoli and the remaining bread in the food processor. Bind the carrot purée with 1 egg and about half the Parmesan cheese, and the broccoli purée with the other egg and the remaining cheese.

Butter a deep mold and line the bottom with a circle of waxed paper. Arrange half the potatoes in the base and line the sides with the bacon, leaving the ends overhanging. Fill the mold with the carrot purée, then the remaining potatoes in a single layer, and finally the broccoli purée. Level the surface and fold over the overhanging bacon. Place in a water bath and cook in the hot oven for 2 hours.

Take the mold out of the water bath and leave to rest for 40 minutes before unmolding and serving.

Baby Onions with Tarragon

Cipollette al dragoncello

---

salt and pepper
2 lb baby onions
butter
2 tablespoons cooking fat
1 tablespoon super-fine sugar
2 tablespoons red wine vinegar
tarragon

SERVES 4

PREPARATION AND COOKING TIME:
ABOUT 1¼ HOURS

Heat plenty of water in a saucepan and salt it as soon as it comes to the boil. Peel and trim the onions and cook them in the water for 15 minutes. Drain them and leave them to dry on paper towels.

Preheat the oven to 350°F. Melt a large knob of butter and the cooking fat in an ovenproof dish. As soon as the fats are hot, add the sugar and wine vinegar. Once the vinegar has evaporated to form a thick syrupy sauce, add the onions and cook briskly for a few minutes. Season with a little salt and pepper to taste and a generous pinch of tarragon.

Place in the oven and cook for about 40 minutes, turning the onions after 20 minutes. Remove from the oven and serve hot.

Braised Celery and Fennel

Sedano e ginocchio

---

12 oz celery heart
1 small leek, white part only
4 oz fennel bulb
butter
olive oil
salt and pepper
ground nutmeg
2 tablespoons grated Emmental cheese

SERVES 4

PREPARATION AND COOKING TIME:
ABOUT 1 HOUR

Bring a large pan of salted water to the boil. Cut the celery into pencil-thick pieces 2 inches long, removing any strings. Wash thoroughly and boil for about 15 minutes.

Meanwhile, wash the leek and fennel, and cut the leek into very fine slices and the fennel into wedges. Place them in a pan with a large knob of butter and 2 tablespoons oil and brown them gently, uncovered. Remove the celery from the pan with a slotted spoon and add it to the other vegetables. Stir and continue cooking, still uncovered, adding a little of the celery water from time to time.

Preheat the oven to 350°F. When the vegetables are tender and there is no liquid left, season to taste with salt, pepper and ground nutmeg. Place in an ovenproof dish, sprinkle with the cheese and cook in the oven for about 10 minutes.

Garnish, if you like, with a few fine fennel leaves and serve immediately.

RIGHT: *Celery root and carrots braised in red wine.*

Celery Root and Carrots Braised in Red Wine

Sedano e carote stufati al vino rosso

---

12 oz celery root
12 oz carrots
1½ oz pancetta (Italian bacon)
1 medium onion
olive oil
½ teaspoon peppercorns
1 cup robust red wine
salt
1 teaspoon sugar
1 teaspoon tomato paste

SERVES 6

PREPARATION AND COOKING TIME:
ABOUT 35 MINUTES

Peel the celery root and cut it into strips. Trim and scrape the carrots and cut into rounds. Finely dice the pancetta; peel and chop the onion. Soften the onion and pancetta in 3 tablespoons oil, with the peppercorns. Add the prepared celery root and carrots and cook over high heat for about 1 minute, mixing with a wooden spoon. Pour in the wine, season with salt, add the sugar and tomato paste, mix and bring to the boil. Lower the heat and cook for about 20–25 minutes, until almost all the wine has been absorbed.

Transfer the vegetables to a serving dish immediately and serve very hot.

Grilled and Fried Red Radicchio

Radicchio rosso grigliato e fritto

1 egg
1 tablespoon all-purpose flour
salt and pepper
1 glass of beer
8 firm, compact heads of red radicchio
olive oil

SERVES 4

PREPARATION AND COOKING TIME:
ABOUT 40 MINUTES

To prepare the batter for frying: in a bowl, beat the egg with the flour, a pinch of salt and the beer. Leave to rest while you prepare the radicchio.

For the grilled radicchio, choose the longest, most compact heads. Trim off any withered leaves and scrape the roots, then wash and cut lengthways into quarters. In a dish, mix 4 tablespoons oil with a pinch of salt and a grinding of pepper, put in the prepared radicchio and marinate them in the mixture, turning several times to coat them well all over. Arrange on a broiler rack or in a very hot grilling pan and cook on medium heat, brushing occasionally with oil.

Trim the remaining radicchio, cutting off most of the roots, and cut into quarters. Dip them into the batter, making sure they are completely coated, then fry in plenty of olive oil.

Serve the grilled and fried radicchio together in the same dish, piping hot.

Ring of Spinach

Corona di spinaci

salt
1¼ lb frozen spinach
1 small onion
6 tablespoons butter
4 eggs
½ cup milk
salt and pepper
nutmeg
½ cup grated Parmesan cheese
breadcrumbs

SERVES 6

PREPARATION AND COOKING TIME:
ABOUT 1 HOUR

Bring a small amount of water to the boil in a saucepan, salt it, then plunge in the frozen spinach and cook until defrosted. Drain, rinse under cold running water and squeeze well.

Chop the onion and soften it in 4 tablespoons of the butter in a large frying pan. Finely chop the spinach and cook with the onion for a few minutes, then remove from the heat to a bowl to cool completely. Preheat the oven to 350°F.

In another bowl beat the eggs with the milk, season with salt and pepper and a good pinch of nutmeg. Add the egg mixture and the grated Parmesan cheese to the spinach. Adjust the salt to taste, then pour the mixture into a ring mold, well buttered and sprinkled with breadcrumbs. The mold should be about 1 quart in capacity and 9 inches in diameter.

Put the mold in the preheated oven for about 30 minutes. Rest it for 5 minutes before turning out on to a warmed serving dish.

Serve garnished, if you like, with some fresh tomato sauce.

RIGHT: *Grilled and fried red radicchio.*

Braised Lentils with Saffron

Lenticche stufate ai pistilli di zafferano

1¾ cups lentils
1 large onion
olive oil
¾ oz raw ham, cut into slivers
¼ cup dry white wine
1 pinch of saffron strands
1 pinch of powdered saffron
hot chicken stock (can be made from a bouillion cube)
salt

SERVES 6–8
PREPARATION AND COOKING TIME:
ABOUT 30 MINUTES, PLUS SOAKING THE LENTILS

Soak the lentils for about 6 hours. Peel and halve the onion and place in a saucepan with 3 tablespoons oil and the ham. Drain the lentils and add them to the pan, brown briefly, then moisten with the wine. Add the saffron strands and powdered saffron. When the wine has evaporated, pour in just enough hot stock to cover the lentils. Bring to the boil, then lower the heat, cover the pan and cook for about 20 minutes.

Taste, add salt if necessary, then discard the onion and serve hot.

Salsify in Piquant Sauce

Scorzonera con salsa

---

juice of 1 lemon, strained
flour
2¼ lb salsify (root vegetable)
salt
2 oz cooked ham, sliced
1½ oz Parmesan cheese, in one piece
Worcestershire sauce
mustard
white wine vinegar
olive oil

SERVES 6
PREPARATION AND COOKING TIME:
ABOUT 1 HOUR, PLUS COOLING

LEFT: *Good luck salad* (top); *Braised lentils with saffron* (bottom).

Place a saucepan filled with 3 quarts of water over high heat, add the lemon juice, then sift in 1 tablespoon flour from a height, whisking at the same time so that no lumps form. Add salt. Peel the salsify and cut into 1½ inch lengths, wash and toss into the boiling prepared water. Cook for about 40 minutes, then drain carefully, transfer to a dish, cover with paper towels, and leave to dry and cool.

When the salsify is cold, cut away the woody central part, and cut the rest into small batons. Place these in a salad bowl. Cut the ham into slivers and slice the Parmesan cheese on a mandoline; carefully mix the ham and cheese into the salsify.

In a deep dish, combine a pinch of salt, a generous dash of Worcestershire sauce and 1½ teaspoons mustard. Add 2 tablespoons vinegar and mix with a fork to dissolve the salt, then energetically whisk in 4 tablespoons olive oil. Dress the salsify with this sauce and serve at once.

Good Luck Salad

Insalata del buon augurio

---

2 pink grapefruit
4 heads of Belgian endive
a head of red radicchio
FOR THE DRESSING
½ cup extra virgin olive oil
3 gherkins
½ tablespoon capers
5 chives
salt and pepper

SERVES 6
PREPARATION TIME: ABOUT 20 MINUTES

Working over a bowl to catch all the juices, peel the grapefruit, removing all the pith, and cut into segments, taking great care not to break them. Pull off the endive and radicchio leaves, discard the root ends, then wash the leaves in several changes of water and drain well. If the red leaves are too large, tear them into 2 or 3 pieces. Pile up the leaves on a serving plate and top with the grapefruit segments.

Serve the salad with the following dressing, leaving your guests to help themselves. In a blender, combine the olive oil, reserved grapefruit juice, finely chopped gherkins, the capers, rinsed under running water and thoroughly squeezed, the chopped chives, salt and pepper. Blend for 30 seconds to make a smooth, emulsified dressing for the salad.

Salad of Mussels, Bread and Beans

Insalata di cozze, pane e fagioli

2¼ lb fresh mussels
olive oil
2 large garlic cloves
a little lemon juice
1 × 14 oz can Great Northern beans
2 slices white bread
2 anchovy fillets in oil
1 teaspoon mustard
Worcestershire suace
2 tablespoons white wine vinegar
fresh chervil or parsley for garnish

SERVES 4–5

PREPARATION AND COOKING TIME:
ABOUT 45 MINUTES

Scrape the mussels under cold running water, discarding any that are open, then put them into a saucepan with a tablespoon of olive oil, a lightly crushed garlic clove and a few drops of lemon juice. Cover and place the pan over a high heat. After a few minutes' cooking and when the mussels have opened, remove them from their shells and leave them to cool in a bowl. Discard any that do not open.

Drain and rinse the beans, then dry on paper towels. Add them to the mussels. Heat 3 tablespoons oil and the other garlic clove in a frying pan. Fry the bread until it is lightly toasted, then cut it into ¾ inch squares. Mix these with the mussels and beans.

Crush the anchovies with a fork in a bowl, then, still mixing with the fork, add the mustard and a dash of Worcestershire sauce, a little salt, the vinegar and 5 tablespoons olive oil. Pour the dressing over the salad, mix again and garnish with chervil or parsley. Serve immediately.

Salad with Olives

Insalata olivetta

---

1 small head of Belgian endive
1 heart of escarole
1 head of radicchio
2 tablespoons white wine vinegar
salt and pepper
olive oil
1 oz capers
a little parsley
anchovy paste
2 oz small black olives in brine
a small piece of leek

SERVES 4–5

PREPARATION TIME: ABOUT 20 MINUTES

Trim and wash the endive, escarole and radicchio. Drain and dry, keeping the different types separate. Break up the leaves and arrange in a salad bowl.

Prepare the salad dressing: mix the wine vinegar with a pinch of salt and pepper in a bowl, stirring until the salt is dissolved. Add, a tablespoon at a time, 6 tablespoons of olive oil, stirring vigorously to blend the ingredients. Chop the capers and a few leaves of parsley and add to the vinaigrette together with 1½–2 inches of anchovy paste. Blend thoroughly.

To serve, place the olives in the center of the salad bowl and arrange a few finely cut strips of leek on top of them. Pour over the dressing and toss well to mix everything together.

Country Salad

Insalata rustica

---

12 oz fresh fennel bulb
5 oz small fresh mushrooms
juice of ½ lemon
4 oz ham
3 oz Emmental cheese
1 tablespoon black olive paste
1 tablespoon mustard
anchovy paste
Worcestershire sauce
1 tablespoon red wine vinegar
olive oil

SERVES 4

PREPARATION: ABOUT 40 MINUTES

Wash and dry the fennel, keeping the best leaves for the garnish. Peel the mushrooms and remove the earthy bases of the stalks. As you clean them, drop them into a bowl of cold water into which the juice of half a lemon has been squeezed. Cut the ham into short strips and the Emmental into thin slices.

Put the olive paste in a bowl and add the mustard, anchovy paste and a generous dash of Worcestershire sauce. Dilute with a tablespoon of vinegar and ⅓ cup of olive oil, and stir carefully.

Cut the fennel into thin slices, likewise the mushrooms, which have been well drained. Mix all the ingredients together in a salad bowl, pour over the sauce and toss carefully. Use the reserved fennel leaves for garnish.

Cheese and Fennel Salad

Insalata di finocchi, composta

---

2 fennel bulbs
a few drops lemon juice
½ garlic clove
3 oz Emmental cheese
salt and pepper
1 teaspoon mustard
1 tablespoon white wine vinegar
olive oil
1 chive, chopped

SERVES 4–5

PREPARATION TIME: ABOUT 40 MINUTES

Clean the fennel bulbs, removing the green leaves, small shoots and the first layer, then cut them in half and place them in cold water to which you have added a few drops of lemon juice.

Meanwhile, rub the inside of a salad bowl with the garlic clove. Cut the cheese into very thin slices and place in the salad bowl. Put a pinch of salt, a grinding of white pepper, the mustard and wine vinegar into a small bowl; stir with a fork until the salt has dissolved, then dilute with 4 tablespoons of olive oil and mix all the ingredients together well.

Drain the pieces of fennel bulb, dry them, cut them into thin slices and add them to the cheese. Then add the chopped chive too, and toss the salad gently. Now pour over the prepared dressing and toss the salad again before serving.

Summer Salad

Insalata d'estate

---

2 oz mâche
a bunch of watercress
1 iceberg lettuce
a bunch of radishes
6 soft but not over-ripe tomatoes
1 large carrot

FOR THE DRESSING
1 scallion
salt and pepper
1 tablespoon mustard
balsamic vinegar
½ cup extra virgin olive oil

SERVES 6

PREPARATION TIME: ABOUT 30 MINUTES

Trim the mâche, wash, drain well and place in a large bowl. Trim, wash and coarsely chop the watercress and shred the lettuce. Trim and scrape the carrot and slice thinly on a mandoline. Thinly slice a few of the radishes and add them to the bowl with the watercress and lettuce, the quartered tomatoes and sliced carrot.

Mix all the vegetables together and transfer to a salad bowl. Make three or four radishes into 'flowers' and garnish the salad with these.

To make the dressing, chop the scallion and place in a bowl with a pinch of salt, a grinding of pepper and the mustard. Dilute with about 3 tablespoonsful of vinegar, then whisk in the oil until well emulsified. Dress the salad just before serving and toss well to mix together all the ingredients.

Chef's Salad

Insalata della casa

---

3 eggs
2 slices white bread
7 oz mixed salad leaves
green olives
5 oz palm hearts, sliced into rounds
3 oz arugula
FOR THE DRESSING
about 2 cups loosely packed parsley leaves
1 tablespoon capers, drained
3 anchovy fillets
2 gherkins
1 slice of white bread
vinegar
½ cup extra virgin olive oil

SERVES 6

PREPARATION TIME: ABOUT 30 MINUTES

Hard-boil the eggs: cook for precisely 10 minutes from when the water comes to the boil, then refresh under running water and shell. Cut the bread into small dice and toast in a hot oven. Trim, wash and drain the salad leaves and arrange in a large bowl. Mix in the toasted bread, about 10 olives, segments of hard-boiled egg and the palm hearts. Coarsely chop the arugula and add it to the salad.

Next make the dressing. In a blender, combine the parsley, capers, anchovies, gherkins and the slice of white bread, softened in vinegar and squeezed dry. Finally, add the olive oil and blend on maximum speed for about 1 minute, to make a dense, perfectly blended dressing.

Transfer to a bowl and bring it to the table with the salad. Dress and toss the salad at the table in front of the assembled company.

Snacks

The Italians have perfected the art of snacks and light supper dishes, using cheese and eggs. Probably the most famous of all Italian snacks is the pizza. Here are some recipes for classic pizzas, but with pizza you can always experiment with your own toppings, using whatever you happen to have on hand.

Corn, Ham and Olive Pizza

Schiacciata di maïs, prosciutto e olive

---

1 small onion, peeled
1½ garlic cloves
olive oil
8 oz peeled tomatoes
salt
sugar
6 green olives in brine
4 oz slice of ham
2 oz rindless Emmental cheese
butter
4 oz corn
a pinch of ginger
12 oz pizza dough (see recipe opposite)
a pinch of oregano

SERVES 4

PREPARATION AND COOKING TIME:
ABOUT 15 MINUTES

Preheat the oven to 400°F. Finely slice the onion and garlic clove. Fry in a saucepan with 3 tablespoons oil without browning, then purée the tomatoes and add them to the pan with a little salt and a pinch of sugar. Mix thoroughly and simmer gently for about 15 minutes.

Pit and quarter the olives. Cut the ham into short strips. Finely slice the Emmental cheese. Fry the corn and the remaining garlic in a large knob of butter for just a few seconds and then season with a pinch of ginger.

Roll out the dough to a 10 inch round and place on an oiled baking sheet. Pour over the tomato sauce and put the corn on top. Arrange the ham, olives and cheese over the pizza and sprinkle with oregano. Pour on a thin trickle of olive oil.

Bake for about 15 minutes until golden brown. Transfer to a serving plate or a wooden chopping board and serve immediately, with a mixed salad.

Rustic Pizzas with Cheese and Walnuts

Pizette rustiche ai formaggi e noci

---

3 oz Pecorino cheese
2½ oz Mozzarella or Gruyère
4 oz shelled walnuts
¼ cup dry white wine
black pepper

FOR THE PIZZA DOUGH
1 oz fresh yeast
salt
3½ cups all-purpose flour

SERVES 6

PREPARATION AND COOKING TIME:
ABOUT 40 MINUTES, PLUS RISING

First, make the bread dough: crumble the yeast and dissolve it in a little tepid water with half a teaspoon salt. Sift the flour onto a work surface and make a well. Pour the yeast mixture into the center and add about another 1 cup tepid water. Mix well and knead the dough until smooth. Cover with a clean tea towel and leave to rise in a warm place for about 40 minutes.

While the dough is rising, cut the Pecorino and Mozzarella cheeses into tiny dice, then place the walnuts on a board and chop them coarsely with a heavy knife. Put the well-risen dough into the bowl of an electric mixer fitted with a dough hook or onto the work surface with the cheeses and walnuts, and knead vigorously to mix all the ingredients perfectly. Soften the dough with the wine and flavor with a good grinding of black pepper. Cover and leave to rise again in a warm place for about 30 minutes.

Preheat the oven to 400°F. Divide the dough into 12 pieces of about 2 oz each. Press the dough into well-oiled small pizza pans or ramekins. Leave the pizzas to rise again in a warm place for 1 hour before baking them in the hot oven for about 40 minutes. Carefully unmold the pizzas and serve.

RIGHT: *Rustic pizzas with cheese and walnuts.*

Egg Pizza

Pizza all'uovo

flour
1 lb pizza dough (see recipe on page 244)
olive oil
14 oz firm ripe tomatoes
oregano
½ medium zucchini
4 oz Mozzarella cheese
a slice of lean ham
a few fennel leaves
2 tablespoons grated mild Pecorino cheese
1 egg

SERVES 4
PREPARATION AND COOKING TIME:
ABOUT 45 MINUTES

Preheat the oven to 400°F. Roll out the dough to a round about 12 inches. Lightly grease a baking sheet and place the dough on it. With your fingertips press down the dough just inside the edge all the way round to give it a raised edge.

Blanch the tomatoes in boiling salted water for a few seconds and skin them. Cut them in half, remove the seeds, then chop them coarsely. Season them with salt, pepper and a pinch of oregano. Trim and finely slice the zucchini. Bring the water in which the tomatoes were blanched back to the boil and put in the zucchini slices for a bare 2 minutes. Remove them with a slotted spoon and drain carefully. Dice the Mozzarella into cubes of about ½ inch. Cut the ham into matchstick-sized lengths.

Spread the tomatoes over the surface of the pizza dough and arrange the rounds of zucchini around the outside edge, slightly overlapping. Make a circle of Mozzarella, followed by the ham. Place a few young fennel leaves on the ham. Pour over a trickle of olive oil and sprinkle the pizza tops with the grated Pecorino. Bake for about 15 minutes.

Meanwhile, heat a frying pan with 2 tablespoons of oil. Break the egg into a bowl, keeping the yolk intact. When the oil is hot, put in the egg and cook slowly until the white is firm. Cut the egg out with a pastry cutter 4 inches in diameter. Sprinkle very lightly with salt and remove from the pan with a spatula. Remove the pizza from the oven and place the egg in the center. Garnish with more fennel leaves and serve immediately.

Naples-style Pizza

Pizza alla napoletana

flour
8 oz pizza dough (see recipe on page 244)
olive oil
2–3 medium tomatoes, skinned
a pinch of oregano
2–3 large fresh basil leaves
1 garlic clove

SERVES 1–2

PREPARATION AND COOKING TIME:
ABOUT 30 MINUTES

Preheat the oven to 400°F. Roll out the dough to an 8 inch round. Lightly grease a baking sheet and place the dough on it. With your fingertips, press down the dough just inside the edge to give it a raised edge.

Chop the tomatoes, season with a little salt and a pinch of oregano and spread over the pizza. Wipe the basil leaves with a damp cloth and finely chop them before sprinkling them over the tomato. Finely chop or slice half a garlic clove and sprinkle this on too. Do not spread these ingredients right to the edges of the dough. Drizzle on plenty of good olive oil and bake for about 12 minutes.

Serve the pizza straight from the oven on a flat, warmed plate.

Little Pork "Pizzas"

'Capricciosa' di carne

1 lb ground pork
salt and pepper
extra virgin olive oil
7 oz tomatoes
4 oz Mozzarella cheese
2 oz button mushrooms
fresh oregano
12 black olives
fresh basil

SERVES 4

PREPARATION AND COOKING TIME:
ABOUT 50 MINUTES

Preheat the oven to 400°F. Season the ground pork with salt and divide into four equal portions. Flatten each one and, using a pastry cutter, cut out four 3 inch diameter "pizzas". Arrange these in an oiled baking dish, then arrange on them equal quantities of sliced tomatoes and Mozzarella cheese, sliced mushrooms, oregano leaves and 3 olives per portion. Season with salt and pepper, trickle on a little oil, and bake in the hot oven for 18 minutes.

Garnish the "pizzas" with basil leaves and return them to the oven for 2–3 minutes. Serve at once.

Piquant Mini-pizzas

Pizzette piccanti

6 frozen mini-pizzas
olive oil
capers in wine vinegar
6 anchovy fillets in oil
12 stuffed green olives

SERVES 6

PREPARATION AND COOKING TIME:
ABOUT 20 MINUTES

Preheat the oven to 400°F. Place the mini-pizzas on a baking sheet and moisten each one with a little oil, then place them in the oven, still frozen, for approximately 7–8 minutes.

In the meantime, drain the capers, the anchovies and the olives, and slice the olives into small rounds.

About 2 minutes before the pizzas are ready, when the cheese has melted but not browned, remove them from the oven and place on each one 4–5 capers, 1 anchovy fillet and 2 sliced stuffed olives. Moisten with a little oil, and put them back in the oven for the last 2 minutes, taking care that they do not brown too much.

Remove the mini-pizzas from the oven and serve them hot.

Mushroom Pizza

Pizza ai funghi

12 oz mushrooms
juice of 1 lemon
olive oil
1 garlic clove
salt and pepper
flour
14 oz pizza dough (see recipe on page 244)
a little chopped parsley

SERVES 4

PREPARATION AND COOKING TIME: 45 MINUTES

Preheat the oven to 400°F. Peel or wipe the mushrooms and trim the stalks. As they are ready, put them in a bowl of cold water to which the lemon juice has been added.

Heat 3 tablespoons of oil in a frying pan. Crush the garlic and put it in the hot oil. Fry until the garlic browns, then remove from the frying pan. Slice the mushrooms directly into the hot oil and sauté for

3–4 minutes, seasoning with salt and pepper.

Roll out the dough to a 12 inch round. Lightly oil a baking sheet and place the dough on it. With your fingertips press down the dough just inside the edge to give it a raised edge. Spread the mushrooms over the pizza and pour over a trickle of olive oil. Sprinkle with chopped parsley and place in the oven for about 15 minutes.

Serve hot from the oven, cut into quarters.

Farmhouse Pizza with Ham and Cheese

Pizza rustica con prosciutto e formaggio

12 oz frozen puff pastry, thawed
flour
butter
breadcrumbs
4 oz ham, sliced
1 large firm tomato
2 oz Mozzarella cheese
a few sprigs fresh parsley
2 large fresh basil leaves
2 eggs
5 tablespoons whipping cream
½ cup grated Emmental cheese
salt and pepper
nutmeg
a pinch of fresh marjoram

SERVES 8

PREPARATION AND COOKING TIME:
ABOUT 1¼ HOURS

Preheat the oven to 375°F. Defrost the pastry if frozen. Roll it out on a lightly floured board until it is large enough to line a shallow, buttered 11 × 7 inch baking dish. Prick the pastry with a fork, sprinkle the base with breadcrumbs and then make an even layer of ham.

Now prepare the filling: blanch the tomato in lightly salted boiling water for a few seconds, then skin, cut in half and remove the seeds. Cut the tomato into irregular pieces. Dice the Mozzarella cheese and finely chop the parsley with the basil. In a bowl, whisk the eggs with the cream, the grated Emmental cheese, salt, pepper and a little grated nutmeg. Add a pinch of marjoram and then put the chopped tomato into the bowl together with the diced Mozzarella and the chopped parsley and basil. Mix well and pour into the pie dish. Bake in the lower part of the oven for about 35 minutes and serve hot from the oven.

Pizza of Many Flavors

Pizza capricciosa

---

flour
14 oz pizza dough (see recipe on page 244)
8 oz skinned tomatoes
salt
a pinch of oregano
1 oz diced Mozzarella cheese
3 fresh basil leaves, chopped
20 fresh mussels
6 artichoke hearts in oil, cut into quarters
6 black olives, pitted and cut into quarters
5 oz clams
4 oz baby mushrooms in oil
2 oz capers
2 thin slices ham, cut into strips
a few slivers Emmental cheese
a little chopped parsley
olive oil

SERVES 4

PREPARATION AND COOKING TIME:
ABOUT 40 MINUTES

Preheat the oven to 400°F. Roll out the dough to a 12 inch round. Lightly grease a baking sheet and place the dough on it. With your fingertips, press down the dough just inside the edge to give it a raised edge. Remove the seeds from the tomatoes and slice finely. Spread over the pizza. Lightly sprinkle with salt and flavor with a pinch of oregano.

Top the pizza in eight divisions with eight separate toppings: the Mozzarella cheese sprinkled with the chopped basil, mussels, artichoke hearts, olives, clams, the well-drained mushrooms, the well-drained capers and finally the strips of ham and slivers of Emmental. Sprinkle with the parsley and pour over a trickle of olive oil.

Bake for about 15 minutes, and serve at once.

Vegetable Calzone

Calzone di verdura

---

2 oz raisins
½ oz yeast
2½ cups all-purpose flour
salt
1 lb Belgian endive or spinach beet
1 dried chilli
olive oil

SERVES 6

PREPARATION AND COOKING TIME:
40 MINUTES PLUS RISING TIME

Soak the raisins in tepid water. Dissolve the yeast in ½ cup tepid water. Sift the flour onto a work surface and make a well. Put the dissolved yeast and a pinch of salt in the middle, then mix to a soft, elastic dough and knead energetically for several minutes. Leave the dough to rise at room temperature for about 30 minutes.

Meanwhile, preheat the oven to 350°F. Trim the endive or spinach beet, cut into thin strips and place in a bowl. Squeeze the raisins dry and mix them with the endive, together with a pinch of salt, a crumbled chilli and a trickle of oil. Place the risen dough on the floured work surface and knead for a few more minutes, then roll it out to a thickness of ⅛ in.

Lay half the dough (without cutting it) on an oiled baking sheet. Spread over the vegetables, then fold over the unfilled dough and seal the edges. Trickle a little oil along the borders and bake in the hot oven for about 30 minutes.

RIGHT: *Vegetable calzone.*

Valdostana Fondue

'Fondua' valdostana

12 oz Fontina cheese
²/₃ cup tepid milk
2 tablespoons butter
3 egg yolks
3 slices white bread

SERVES 3

PREPARATION AND COOKING TIME:
ABOUT 20 MINUTES, PLUS 2 HOURS SOAKING

Cut the rind off the cheese, slice it into a bowl and cover it with the milk. Leave it to soak for a couple of hours, stirring occasionally.

Melt the butter in a fondue pan, add the cheese and place over a simmering water bath. Stir continuously until the cheese melts, then raise the heat and stir more briskly, adding the egg yolks one by one, making sure each is perfectly incorporated before adding the next. Continue stirring until the cheese is completely melted and dissolved.

Pour the fondue into warmed individual dishes and serve with toasted bread.

Cod and Mushroom Pie

"Pie" marinara

3 eggs
1½ lb fresh cod fillet
salt and pepper
3¾ cups milk, at room temperature
8 oz small mushrooms
6 tablespoons butter
1 garlic clove
½ cup all-purpose flour
nutmeg
1 slice crustless, slightly dry bread, finely crumbled
2–3 sprigs fresh parsley
8 oz frozen puff pastry, thawed

SERVES 8

PREPARATION AND COOKING TIME:
ABOUT 1 HOUR 20 MINUTES

Preheat the oven to 400°F. Hard boil two of the eggs, cool them under running water and shell them. Arrange the cod fillets in a pan that just holds them so that there are no gaps. Season with salt and freshly ground white pepper, then pour over the milk, covering the fish. Cover the pan and put over low heat. Gradually bring to the boil and as soon as it begins to boil, leave it on the heat for a minute, then remove from the heat but leave covered for about 5 minutes.

Remove the lid. Reserve the milk and cut the fish into large chunks. Make sure there are no scales left anywhere. Put 2½ cups of milk in which the cod was cooked through a fine strainer and reserve it. Trim the mushrooms, rinse under running water and cut into thickish slices. Melt 4 tablespoons of butter in a saucepan and fry the lightly crushed garlic. When it is brown, remove and discard it. Put in the mushrooms and sauté for a few minutes until they begin to brown. Sift on the flour and mix in at once. Then gradually pour in the milk reserved from the fish and, stirring constantly, bring to the boil. Correct the seasoning and add the nutmeg.

Butter a 7 inch soufflé dish, not too deep, and sprinkle with the crumbled bread. Cut the hard-boiled eggs into thin slices. Make a layer of fish in the dish, followed by a little sauce, a few slices of hard-boiled egg and a little parsley. Pour over a little more sauce and repeat until the ingredients have all been used up, finishing with a thin layer of sauce. Melt a teaspoon of butter and pour this over the top.

Roll out the pastry on a lightly floured board until it is about ⅛ inch thick and cover the soufflé dish with this, letting about ¾ inch hang over the edge all round. Beat the remaining egg in a bowl and use it to glaze the surface of the pastry. Bake the pie in the oven for about 30 minutes, then serve.

Fontina Cheese Parcels

Involtini di Fontina, in crosta

12 oz frozen puff pastry, thawed
4 tablespoons butter
½ cup all-purpose flour
1¼ cups milk
salt and pepper
ground nutmeg
¼ cup grated Parmesan cheese
4 oz Fontina cheese
1 egg and 1 egg yolk
8 thin slices raw ham
a pinch of aniseed (optional)

SERVES 4

PREPARATION AND COOKING TIME:
1¼ HOURS

Prepare a béchamel sauce by melting 2 tablespoons of butter in a pan, stirring in 4 tablespoons of flour and adding the milk. Season with salt, pepper and a little ground nutmeg, then blend in the grated Parmesan and the diced Fontina cheese. Allow the cheeses to melt, stirring constantly to form a smooth sauce. Whisk in the egg yolk. Remove from the heat and allow to cool.

Remove the fat from 8 thin slices of raw ham. Spread a heaped tablespoon of the cheese sauce on each slice of ham and roll up. Preheat the oven to 375°F.

Roll out the pastry to a thickness of about ⅛ inch. Cut into eight rectangles the same length as the ham rolls. Place a roll of ham on each piece of pastry and brush the edges of the pastry with beaten egg. Fold up the pastry parcels, making sure that they are tightly sealed.

Arrange on a greased baking sheet and brush with beaten egg. Sprinkle with a pinch of aniseed and bake in the oven for about 20 minutes or until golden brown. Serve hot with a green salad or fresh vegetables of your choice.

Spicy Pasties

Calcioni piccanti

---

8 oz pizza dough (see recipe on page 244)
flour
2 oz Mozzarella cheese
3 oz mortadella sausage
tomato paste
16 baby mushrooms in oil
a little oregano
a little paprika
1 egg yolk
a little olive oil

SERVES 4
PREPARATION AND COOKING TIME:
ABOUT 45 MINUTES

Preheat the oven to 375°F. Roll out the dough to a thickness of ⅛ inch. Cut out 16 circles with a 3 inch pastry cutter. Dice the Mozzarella cheese and mortadella sausage finely and place a few cubes in the center of eight of the dough rounds. Add a scant teaspoon of tomato paste, 2 well-drained baby mushrooms, a pinch of oregano and a tiny pinch each of paprika and salt. Take care to leave a little space around the edges.

Brush the edges of each round with egg yolk and cover with the other eight rounds. Press down firmly to seal in the filling. Grease a baking sheet with oil and place the pasties on it, well apart. Brush the surface with egg yolk and cook for 15–20 minutes, until they are golden brown. Remove from the oven and place on a serving dish.

Serve at once while they are hot from the oven.

Calzone with Ricotta

Calzone con la Ricotta

---

12 oz Ricotta cheese
3 oz spicy salami
4 oz Mozzarella cheese
2 thick slices ham
2 eggs
¼ cup grated Parmesan cheese
¼ cup grated Pecorino cheese
salt and pepper
1 lb pizza dough (see recipe on page 244)
olive oil

SERVES 4–5
PREPARATION AND COOKING TIME:
ABOUT 1 HOUR

Preheat the oven to 400°F. Sieve the Ricotta into a bowl. Cut the salami into small cubes and the Mozzarella cheese into larger cubes. Coarsely chop the ham, then add all these ingredients to the ricotta. Bind with the eggs, the Parmesan and Pecorino cheeses, salt and pepper and mix thoroughly. Taste and, if necessary, adjust the seasoning.

Roll out the dough to a 12 inch round. Place the Ricotta mixture over half the circle to within about ¾ inch of the edge. Fold the other half of the dough over the filling, sealing the two edges by pinching them together. Place the calzone on a greased baking sheet and brush it with olive oil; bake in the oven for about 25 minutes. Serve hot.

Frittata with Truffles

Frittata ai tartuffi

---

4 oz fresh black truffles
6 eggs
¼ cup whipping cream
salt and pepper
olive oil
juice of ½ lemon, strained

SERVES 4

PREPARATION AND COOKING TIME:
ABOUT 30 MINUTES

Wash the truffles well, scrubbing them with a hard brush; dry thoroughly on paper towels, then slice on a mandoline.

Break the eggs, one at a time, first onto a plate to check for freshness, then put them into a bowl. Add the cream, salt to taste, a grinding of pepper and the sliced truffles. Heat a trickle of oil in a cast-iron frying pan, then pour in the egg mixture and cook until set on the bottom. Turn over the frittata to set on the other side, then tip it onto a serving plate so that it does not harden; a perfect frittata should be cooked on the outside and soft on the inside, and the truffles should not be cooked.

Cut the frittata into slices and sprinkle with lemon juice. Serve immediately, before it gets cold. Despite their high price, not all truffles are of good quality; check carefully that they have a fine aroma (indicating freshness) before buying.

Sweet Peppers with Scrambled Egg

Peperoni e uova

---

1 medium yellow and 1 medium red bell pepper
8 oz firm ripe romatoes
salt and pepper
3–4 large fresh basil leaves
olive oil
1 garlic clove
2 eggs
1 teaspoon grated Pecorino cheese

SERVES 4

PREPARATION AND COOKING TIME:
ABOUT 45 MINUTES

Wash and dry the peppers and cut them in half lengthways, discarding the stalks and seeds. Cut them again lengthways into strips approximately ¾ inch wide.

Parboil the tomatoes in lightly salted water. Skin them and cut them in half, discarding the seeds. Chop into small pieces. Wipe the basil leaves with a damp cloth.

Heat 4 tablespoons of oil and the lightly crushed garlic clove in a frying pan. Discard the garlic as soon as it has browned. Fry the peppers gently until tender (about 15 minutes), stirring occasionally during cooking. Stir in the tomatoes and basil leaves and season with a little salt and pepper. Cook on a low heat for a further 15 minutes, occasionally adding a little boiling water if the mixture becomes too dry.

Beat the eggs with a pinch of salt and pepper and stir them into the vegetables. Keep stirring until the eggs have scrambled. Remove from the heat and serve sprinkled with the grated Pecorino cheese.

RIGHT: *Frittata with truffles.*

Shrimp and Salmon Omelette

Omelette di gamberetti e salmone

1 tablespoon tomato paste
²/₃ cup fish stock
2 oz canned salmon
2 tablespoons butter
cornstarch
5 tablespoons dry white wine
Worcestershire sauce
12 fresh shrimp
flour
½ small onion
1 garlic clove
parsley
4 tablespoons olive oil
4 eggs
1 large thin slice smoked salmon, cut in strips
1 celery heart, chopped

SERVES 2

PREPARATION AND COOKING TIME:
ABOUT 50 MINUTES

Mix tomato paste with the fish stock and blend it with the salmon, being careful to remove any skin and bones. Sieve.

Melt a knob of the butter in a saucepan and add the blended mixture, together with a teaspoon of cornstarch dissolved in a tablespoon of the white wine. Stir and season with a splash of Worcestershire sauce and simmer gently for a few minutes. Taste and adjust the seasoning if necessary. Keep the sauce hot.

Shell the shrimp, cut into small pieces and then coat in the flour. Finely chop the onion, a quarter of the garlic clove and a few sprigs of parsley and fry in 3 tablespoons of the oil until transparent. Add the pieces of shrimp and fry gently. Sprinkle with the remaining white wine. Allow almost all the wine to evaporate and then remove the pan from the heat.

Beat 2 eggs in a bowl with a pinch of salt and pepper. Melt a knob of butter and a tablespoon of oil in a frying pan and pour in the eggs. Stir gently so that the eggs set smoothly. Lower the heat and shake the pan gently to prevent sticking. Pour on half the shrimp mixture and fold the omelette in half. Turn onto a heated dish and keep warm while you prepare the second omelette in the remaining butter. Arrange strips of smoked salmon on each omelette, sprinkle with chopped celery and surround with the hot sauce. Serve immediately.

Escarole Tart

Stogliata di scarola

12 oz frozen puff pastry, thawed
8 oz onions
1 garlic clove
4 tablespoons butter
olive oil
4 oz smoked bacon
1½ lb escarole, boiled and drained
1 vegetable bouillion cube
ground nutmeg
about 1 tablespoon breadcrumbs
1¼ cups grated Emmental cheese
3 eggs
3 tablespoons grated Parmesan cheese
flour
²/₃ cup milk

SERVES 8

PREPARATION AND COOKING TIME:
ABOUT 1½ HOURS

Thinly slice the onions, finely chop the garlic clove and fry gently in a knob of butter and 3 tablespoons oil until transparent.

Cut the bacon into short, thin strips and coarsely chop the endive. Add first the bacon then the escarole to the onion and garlic. Cook for about 10 minutes, stirring frequently. Season with the crumbled bouillion cube and a little ground nutmeg and pepper.

Butter a 10 inch round, fluted pie dish and line it with the pastry. Pierce the base with a fork and sprinkle over a heaped tablespoon of breadcrumbs. Preheat the oven to 400°F.

Remove the escarole mixture from the heat and blend in first the grated Emmental cheese and then two of the eggs, stirring vigorously. Pour the mixture into the pastry base and smooth the surface with the back of a spoon. Top with a tablespoon of grated Parmesan cheese.

Prepare a light béchamel sauce by melting 1½ tablespoons butter, stirring in 2 tablespoons of flour and adding the milk. Season with salt and a little nutmeg. Blend in an egg yolk. Pour the sauce into the pie shell and sprinkle on the remaining Parmesan.

Bake for about 40 minutes or until cooked and golden brown. Remove from the oven and leave to stand for 10 minutes before serving.

FAR LEFT: *Shrimp and salmon omelette.*

Cheese Dome

Cupola di formaggio

4 oz cream cheese
4 oz Stracchino cheese
4 oz Robiolina cheese
2 oz soft Gorgonzola cheese
½ cup grated Parmesan cheese
½ cup whipping cream
salt and pepper
4 slices white bread

SERVES 6

PREPARATION TIME: ABOUT 40 MINUTES

Remove the cheeses from the refrigerator at least 2 hours before preparation. Finely dice the cheeses and place them all, including the grated Parmesan, in a bowl. Beat and mix to form a smooth, creamy mixture.

Whip the cream and carefully fold into the cheese mixture. Add a pinch of salt and plenty of pepper. Mix well and then place the mixture in the center of a large, round plate. Mold into a dome shape and decorate it with vertical lines, using a fork.

Cut the slices of bread diagonally into eight triangles and either toast them or fry them gently in butter until golden brown. Arrange some of the toast around the cheese dome and serve the rest separately. Garnish as desired and serve.

Cheese and Walnut Pie

Torta di formaggio e noci

12 oz frozen puff pastry, thawed
a little flour
a little butter
4 oz Emmental cheese
3 oz walnuts
2 eggs plus 1 egg white
1 tablespoon Calvados brandy
salt and pepper
ground nutmeg

SERVES 4

PREPARATION AND COOKING TIME: ABOUT 50 MINUTES, PLUS ANY DEFROSTING TIME

Roll out half the pastry on a floured surface to a thickness of ⅛ inch. Butter a 9 inch pie dish and line it with the pastry.

Cut the Emmental cheese into small pieces and work in a food processor with the walnuts. Place in a bowl and stir in the 2 eggs, the Calvados, a pinch of salt and pepper and a little ground nutmeg. Pour this mixture into the pie shell.

Preheat the oven to 375°F. Roll out the remaining pastry and cover the pie with it. Brush the edges with the lightly beaten egg white and seal the lid to the sides of the pastry. Bake in the lower part of the oven for about 30 minutes or until golden brown. Serve hot.

RIGHT: *Broccoli with scrambled eggs.*

Broccoli with Scrambled Eggs

Broccoletti con le uova strapazzate

---

2 lb green broccoli
olive oil
1 garlic clove
1 small piece red chilli pepper
2 large eggs
2 tablespoons grated Pecorino cheese
salt and pepper

SERVES 4

PREPARATION AND COOKING TIME:
ABOUT 1 HOUR

Trim the broccoli and cut it into pieces, including the tender stalks of the larger pieces. Break the larger heads into florets. Put into lightly salted cold water for 30 minutes, then rinse well. Boil a large saucepanful of water and add salt. Put in the broccoli and cook for 5 minutes. When the broccoli is tender, remove with a slotted spoon, drain carefully and place on a large sloping dish.

In the meantime, heat 4 tablespoons of oil in a frying pan with the lightly crushed garlic and the chilli. Discard the garlic and chilli and replace with the broccoli. Shake the pan to ensure it does not stick to the bottom. Beat the eggs and the Pecorino cheese in a bowl and season with a little salt and pepper. Heat 3 tablespoons of oil in a small frying pan and, when it is hot, pour in the eggs. Continue stirring with a fork until they take on a creamy consistency. Arrange the broccoli on a hot serving dish and top with the scrambled eggs. Serve immediately.

259

Emmental and Artichoke Pie

Teglia di carciofi e quartirolo

---

4 artichokes
juice of ¹⁄₂ lemon
1 small onion
1 large garlic clove
a handful of fresh parsley
olive oil
4 tablespoons butter
¹⁄₂ cup white wine
²⁄₃ cup vegetable stock (or use a bouillion cube)
a pinch of thyme
¹⁄₄ cup flour
²⁄₃ cup milk
salt
¹⁄₂ cup grated Parmesan cheese
2 eggs
8 oz Emmental cheese
1 lb frozen puff pastry, thawed
1 tablespoon breadcrumbs

SERVES 8

PREPARATION AND COOKING TIME:
ABOUT 1¹⁄₂ HOURS

Clean the artichokes, remove the leaves, and as they are ready put them in a bowl of cold water with the juice of half a lemon. Finely chop the onion with the garlic and parsley and fry in the oil and half the butter.

Drain the artichokes well, cut them in half and remove the leaves and the chokes. Slice them thinly and add them to the frying pan, stirring with a wooden spoon. Slice the stalks horizontally and add those too. After a few minutes pour in the wine and allow it to evaporate almost entirely. Bring the stock to the boil and pour it in. Stir well and turn the heat down to the minimum. Season with a pinch of thyme and cover the pan. Cook the artichokes until nearly all the liquid has been absorbed, then sprinkle with the sifted flour. Mix and pour in the boiling milk, stirring constantly. Simmer for a few minutes and add salt to taste. Preheat the oven to 350°F.

Purée the artichoke mixture. Mix the Parmesan cheese and eggs into the purée, stirring vigorously. Cut the cheese into thin slices.

Roll out the pastry to a thickness of ¹⁄₈ inch, then line a buttered 14 × 8 inch baking dish with low sides. Prick the pastry with a fork and sprinkle with a fine layer of breadcrumbs. Arrange

LEFT: *Vegetable pie with cheese.*

the slices of cheese in the dish and then pour over the artichoke purée. Trim the pastry around the edges of the dish and roll out to make a cover for the pie, making sure it sticks to the pastry beneath. Prick the surface with a fork and bake in the lower part of the oven for about 35 minutes until it is cooked and golden brown. Serve piping hot.

Vegetable Pie with Cheese

Pasticcio di verdure allo Sbrinz

1¹⁄₄ lb savoy cabbage leaves
1 lb zucchini
olive oil
1 garlic clove
salt
1 lb turnips
2¹⁄₄ lb fennel
10 oz Sbrinz or other grating cheese such as Emmental
butter for greasing

FOR THE BECHAMEL
6 tablespoons butter
³⁄₄ cup flour
1 quart hot milk
salt
nutmeg

SERVES 8

PREPARATION AND COOKING TIME:
ABOUT 1 HOUR 40 MINUTES

Preheat the oven to 400°F. Choose large, unblemished cabbage leaves; blanch them for 2 minutes, then drain and spread out to dry on clean tea towel. Cut the zucchini into thin rounds and brown them over high heat in 3 tablespoons hot oil flavored with the garlic. Season with salt and turn off the heat. Peel the turnips and cut into rounds. Trim the fennel, then cut into strips. Cook the two vegetables separately until *al dente* and drain.

To make the béchamel, make a smooth paste with the butter and flour and whisk in the hot milk. Season with salt and a grating of nutmeg and simmer for 5 minutes.

To assemble the pie, grate the cheese and flatten the ribs of the cabbage leaves with a meat mallet. Butter an ovenproof dish and line it with the cabbage leaves, leaving an overhang. Make alternating layers of the vegetables, cheese and béchamel, reserving a little cheese and béchamel. Fold over the overhanging cabbage leaves to cover the filling, then spread over the reserved béchamel and cheese. Bake in the hot oven for about 40 minutes.

Baked Omelette

Frittata della fornarina

———————

1 small onion
olive oil
1 very large ripe tomato
1 bunch fresh basil
½ vegetable bouillion cube
4 eggs
salt and pepper
¼ cup grated Parmesan cheese
butter

SERVES 4

PREPARATION AND COOKING TIME:
ABOUT 50 MINUTES

Preheat the oven to 350°F. Finely slice the onions and fry gently in 4 tablespoons of oil. Dice the tomato and add it to the onion with 2 basil leaves and the crumbled bouillion cube. Increase the heat and let the tomato dry out thoroughly. Remove from the heat and leave to cool. Discard the basil.

Beat the eggs in a bowl and season with a little salt and pepper. Add the grated Parmesan cheese and the cold tomato mixture.

Butter a 10 inch round ovenproof dish. Cut out a circle of foil or waxed paper the same size as the dish, butter it and place it in the bottom of the dish, making sure that it sticks well. Pour in the egg mixture and cook in the oven for about 20 minutes.

As soon as the top of the omelette is golden brown, remove the dish from the oven and turn it out on to a plate, discarding the foil or paper. Slice, garnish with fresh basil leaves and serve.

Ligurian Pie

'Torta' ligure

———————

2 fresh artichokes
juice of ½ lemon
1 medium onion
1 garlic clove
a little parsley
about 6 tablespoons butter
olive oil
½ cup vegetable stock (or use a bouillion cube)
5 oz parboiled drained lettuce
½ mushroom-flavored bouillion cube
flour
⅔ cup milk
2 eggs
½ cup grated Parmesan cheese
salt
12 oz frozen puff pastry, thawed
1 tablespoon breadcrumbs

SERVES 6–8

PREPARATION AND COOKING TIME:
1 ½ HOURS

Trim the artichokes and remove the leaves, placing them in cold water with the juice of half a lemon. Chop the onion and soften it, together with a garlic clove and a small bunch of parsley, in a knob of the butter and 2 tablespoons of oil.

Drain the artichokes well, remove leaves and chokes, slice them thinly and add to the mixture in the pan. Brown for a few minutes, then pour over the stock and cook in a covered pan until the artichokes are tender and have absorbed all the liquid. Preheat the oven to 400°F.

Chop the lettuce and sauté it in 2 tablespoons of butter; sprinkle with the mushroom-flavored cube and the flour. Stir, and gradually pour in the boiling milk. Leave to simmer for a few minutes, then stir and pour into a bowl. Stir the artichokes, then add them to the lettuce mixture, mixing well. Add the beaten eggs, the Parmesan cheese and a little salt.

Line a buttered oval baking dish measuring about 12 × 8 inches with the pastry, prick the base and sprinkle with about 1 tablespoon of breadcrumbs. Pour in the prepared mixture and cook in the oven for about 30 minutes. Serve hot.

RIGHT: *Crostini with clams.*

Crostini with Clams

Crostini marinari

10 oz firm ripe tomatoes
salt and pepper
fresh basil
extra virgin olive oil
1 lb clams
2 garlic cloves
6 slices country bread

SERVES 6
PREPARATION AND COOKING TIME:
ABOUT 40 MINUTES

Plunge the tomatoes into boiling water, skin them and dice very finely. Place in a bowl and season with salt and pepper, a handful of coarsely chopped basil leaves and a trickle of oil. Cover the bowl with plastic wrap and leave the mixture to marinate in the fridge for about 30 minutes.

Preheat the oven to 425°F. Meanwhile, wash the clams in several changes of water, then place in a frying pan with a tablespoon of hot oil flavored with the garlic. When the clams have opened, remove them from the frying pan, shell them and set aside. Discard any that do not open.

Rub the bread with garlic and toast in the oven until lightly colored. Place the tomatoes and clams on top. Arrange the crostini on a plate, trickle on a little oil, decorate as you wish, and serve immediately.

Desserts

The Italians are known for their scrumptious desserts. They can be as substantial and elaborate as a pistachio and hazelnut charlotte, or as light and simple as seasonal fresh fruit. And finally, real Italian icecream, made from fresh fruit juice, eggs and cream, is a delight, so different from its manufactured equivalent. It's the perfect way to round off a delicious meal.

Strawberry Mold

Sformato di fragole

---

13 oz strawberries
1/4 cup super-fine sugar
juice of 1/2 lemon
2/3 cup heavy cream
soft lady fingers

FOR THE PASTRY CREAM
1 cup milk
lemon zest
2 egg yolks
6 tablespoons super-fine sugar
1/4 cup all-purpose flour
2 teaspoons vanilla extract

FOR THE MERINGUE
4 egg whites
6 tablespoons super-fine sugar

SERVES 6
PREPARATION AND COOKING TIME:
ABOUT 1 HOUR, PLUS CHILLING

Hull and wash 10 oz strawberries, reserving the rest for decoration. Place in a bowl and sprinkle with the sugar and lemon juice. Cover and leave to marinate in a cool place.

To make the pastry cream: heat the milk with a strip of well-washed lemon zest. In a bowl, mix the egg yolks with the sugar, flour and vanilla. Pour in the hot, but not boiling, milk in a steady stream, pour the mixture back into the milk pan and set over low heat. Simmer, stirring continuously, for 3—4 minutes. Take off the heat and leave to cool, stirring from time to time to prevent a skin forming.

To assemble the dessert: whip the cream very stiffly and fold it into the pastry cream. Remove the strawberries from the marinating liquid and brush the lady fingers with the liquid. In a bowl, make alternating layers of lady fingers, marinated strawberries and pastry cream, ending with a layer of lady fingers. Cover with plastic wrap and chill in the refrigerator for at least 6 hours.

Shortly before serving, make the meringue. Preheat the oven to 475°F. Beat the egg whites with a pinch of salt until very firm, then delicately fold in the sugar. Place the mixture in a piping bag fitted with a star tip. Invert the dessert on to an oven-to-table dish and pipe the meringue all over it. Place in the oven until just lightly browned, decorate with the remaining strawberries and serve immediately.

Strawberry Ice Cream with Meringues

Gelato all meringa

FOR THE ICE CREAM
8 oz strawberries
3/4 cup super-fine sugar
2 1/4 cups milk

FOR THE MERINGUES
4 egg whites
1 cup super-fine sugar
1 teaspoon vanilla extract
butter for greasing

SERVES 6
PREPARATION AND COOKING TIME:
ABOUT 40 MINUTES, PLUS FREEZING THE ICE
CREAM AND COOKING THE MERINGUES

Make the ice cream (this can be done several days in advance): hull, carefully wash and thoroughly drain the strawberries and place them in a blender with the sugar and milk. Blend on full power for 2 minutes, then transfer to an ice-cream maker and churn, following the instructions. When the ice cream is dense and creamy, transfer to the freezer until ready to serve.

You can also prepare the meringues in advance. Preheat the oven to 300°F. Put the egg whites, sugar and vanilla in a bowl. Stand the bowl in a pan containing two fingers of tepid water, place over very low heat and beat the egg whites with a whisk or an electric beater until very stiff. Place in a piping bag fitted with a plain tip. Grease a baking sheet, then pipe onto it walnut-sized meringues, spaced well apart. Cook in the heated oven for about 3 hours, until the meringues are firm and crisp; they should be white but perfectly dry. If they begin to brown, prop the oven door open a little.

To serve, place 3—4 scoops of ice cream in each dish, together with 3—4 meringues.

RIGHT: *Strawberry and apple pie* (top right, recipe on page 269); *Strawberry mold* (left); *Strawberry ice cream with meringues* (bottom right).

Charlotte Meringue with Tangerine Sorbet

Charlotte meringata al sorbetto di mandarino

---

1 × 7 inch sponge cake
⅓ cup Grand Marnier liqueur
10 oz strawberries
¼ fresh pineapple, freshly diced
4 egg whites
salt
½ cup super-fine sugar

FOR THE SORBET
⅔ cup tangerine juice, plus the peel from the squeezed fruit
½ cup plus 1 tablespoon super-fine sugar
1 egg white

SERVES 8
PREPARATION AND COOKING TIME:
ABOUT 2 HOURS

Steep the tangerine peel overnight in the juice, ½ cup sugar and ⅔ cup water. Next day, strain the infusion and churn in an ice-cream maker, following the instructions. As soon as it begins to solidify, add one-third of an egg white beaten with the remaining sugar, and finish churning. Transfer sorbet to freezer.

Slice the cake lengthways into ½ inch slices. Cut five or six of the longest into rectangles as long as the diameter of your charlotte mold; halve them into equal triangles and arrange them like rays in the mold, the points converging in the center. Line the sides with some of the remaining slices, cutting off the excess. Brush the lining sponge with Grand Marnier diluted with a little water. Fill the mold with the strawberries, pineapple and sorbet, alternating the layers with the remaining cake. Chill in the freezer at least 4 hours.

Preheat the oven to 475°F. Just before serving, beat the egg whites with a pinch of salt until very firm, adding the sugar little by little. Invert the charlotte onto an ovenproof plate and cover it with this meringue, then bake in the hot oven for not more than 3–4 minutes.

Zabaglione Coupes with Sweet White Wine

Coppe di zabaione al vino bianco

FOR THE CHOCOLATE SPONGE

2 eggs

6 tablespoons super-fine sugar

¾ cup all-purpose flour

cocoa powder

butter and flour for the pan

confectioners' sugar

⅓ cup Kirsch

7 oz semi-sweet chocolate

½ cup heavy cream

fresh raspberries, for decoration

FOR THE ZABAGLIONE

1 whole egg, plus 8 yolks

½ cup sugar

scant 1 cup dessert white wine

1¾ cup heavy cream

SERVES 8

PREPARATION AND COOKING TIME:
ABOUT 2½ HOURS

Preheat the oven to 350°F. To make the chocolate sponge, beat the eggs and sugar together until they are light and fluffy. Carefully sprinkle on the sifted flour and about 3 tablespoons cocoa to color and flavor it, and continue beating until the mixture forms a smooth batter. Butter and flour an 8 inch jelly roll pan and pour in the batter, smoothing over the top. Bake in the oven for 25–35 minutes until cooked or until it comes away slightly from the edges of the pan and the cake springs back slightly when pushed with a finger. Set aside to cool, then transfer to a piece of non-stick paper dusted with confectioners' sugar. Brush the sponge with a mixture of Kirsch and cold water. Melt the chocolate over gentle heat with the cream, then spread this over the sponge. Using the non-stick paper, roll up like a Swiss roll, starting from one of the longer sides.

Just before assembling the coupes, make the zabaglione: combine the whole egg, yolks, sugar and wine in a bowl, and stand it in a hot water bath over very moderate heat. Beat until the zabaglione is foamy; leave to cool, then fold in the whipped cream. Divide the zabaglione between eight dishes. Slice the sponge into rounds and garnish the zabaglione with these. Top with fresh raspberries.

Strawberry and Apple Pie

Pie di fragole e mele

---

12 oz apples

3 tablespoons butter

¼ cup super-fine sugar

3 tablespoons maraschino liqueur

12 oz strawberries

2 soft amaretti biscuits

6 soft lady fingers

7 oz frozen puff pastry, thawed

beaten egg for glazing

SERVES 6

PREPARATION AND COOKING TIME:
ABOUT 1 HOUR

Peel and core the apples and cut into small segments. In a large saucepan, heat the butter, put in the apples, sprinkle with sugar and brown over high heat. Cook for about 2 minutes, then moisten with the maraschino. Evaporate the liquid completely, and leave to cool.

Meanwhile, preheat the oven to 400°F. Hull the strawberries, wash thoroughly and dry well. Cut into small segments and place in a round pie dish, together with the cold apples and the crumbled amaretti biscuits and sponge fingers.

Roll out the pastry and use it to cover the pie dish, making sure it adheres well to the edges. Cut off the excess and use the trimmings to make decorations. Arrange these on the pastry, glaze with the beaten egg and bake in the hot oven for about 30 minutes.

Place the pie dish on a serving plate and serve the pie straight from the dish.

FAR LEFT: *Charlotte meringue with tangerine sorbet.*

Netted Plums

Prugne nella rete

FOR THE SPONGE CAKE
a little flour
4 tablespoons butter
3 eggs plus 1 egg yolk
1¼ cups sugar
grated rind of 1 lemon
a little vanilla sugar
½ cup cornstarch
1 cup all-purpose flour

FOR THE TOPPING
10 large yellow plums
2 tablespoons sugar
½ cup dry white wine
7 oz plum jam
scant 1 cup Amaretto liqueur

FOR THE CARAMEL
½ cup sugar

SERVES 4

PREPARATION AND COOKING TIME:
ABOUT 2 HOURS

Preheat the oven to 350°F. To make the sponge, grease and flour a 9 inch dome-shaped cake tin. Melt 2 tablespoons of butter and leave it to cool while beating together the whole eggs and yolk with the sugar, until the mixture is light and fluffy. Stir in the grated lemon rind, the vanilla sugar, cornstarch and most of the sifted flour. Lastly, add the cool melted butter. Pour the mixture into the prepared cake pan and bake it in the oven for 35 minutes, or until a skewer inserted into the center comes out clean. Cool on a wire rack.

While the sponge is baking, wash and dry the plums, cut them in half, remove the pits and place them in a pan in a single layer. Sprinkle with the sugar, add the white wine and cook them over moderate heat with the lid on for 5 minutes. Take them out of the pan and drain them on paper towels. Add the plum jam and half the liqueur to the juice left in the pan. Stir over low heat until it becomes a thick syrup.

When the sponge is cool, cut it into three layers, moisten them with the remaining liqueur, spread them with the jam mixture (reserving 2 tablespoons) and reassemble the cake on a serving plate. Spread the remaining jam on top and cover it with the cooked plum halves. Leave it in a cool place (not the refrigerator) while you prepare the caramel.

To make the caramel: place the sugar with 3 tablespoons of water over low heat, stirring gently at first until the sugar is completely dissolved. Cook until the sugar has completely caramelized. Dip a wooden spoon into the caramel and run it crisscross fashion over all the plums, like an irregular net. Serve immediately.

Bananas with Pistachios

Banane 'rosate' al pistacchio

---

4 ripe bananas
2 tablespoons sugar
4 tablespoons rum
¼ cup pistachio nuts
5 tablespoons red fruit or rose hip jam
4–5 edible rose petals

SERVES 4

PREPARATION TIME: ABOUT 20 MINUTES

Peel the bananas and halve them lengthways. Arrange them on a large dish and sprinkle with the sugar and rum. Leave to stand in a cool place.

Meanwhile, parboil the pistachios in salted water for a couple of minutes. Peel them while they are still hot and chop them finely. Put the jam into a bowl and stir until smooth. Place it in the center of a serving dish and arrange the bananas around it. Pour the rum marinade over the bananas and top with the pistachios.

Garnish with 4–5 fresh rose petals (if available) and serve immediately.

RIGHT: *Netted plums.*

Oranges in Grand Marnier

Arance al Grand Marnier

6 large ripe oranges, washed
6 sugar cubes
4 tablespoons Grand Marnier

SERVES 4

PREPARATION AND COOKING TIME: ABOUT 30
MINUTES, PLUS 30 MINUTES CHILLING

Pierce the washed oranges all over with a needle. Rub every side of a sugar cube over each orange. Place the sugar in a saucepan. Peel the oranges, remove all the pith and divide them into segments in a bowl. Squeeze any juice remaining in the peel over the sugar cubes.

Heat the sugar cubes gently until dissolved. When a light syrup has formed, remove the pan from the heat and pour in the Grand Marnier. Stir and allow to cool. Pour the liquid over the orange segments and refrigerate for 30 minutes before serving.

If you like, you can place the oranges in individual goblets and garnish to taste.

Venetian Cake with Cream and Chestnuts

Veneziana con panna e castagne

2¼ lb large round brioche, panettone or plain cake
12 oz peeled, boiled chestnuts
4 oz semi-sweet chocolate
2 oz walnuts
1¼ cups whipping cream
scant 1 cup confectioners' sugar
⅔ cup rum
1 marron glacé

SERVES 10

PREPARATION TIME: ABOUT 1 HOUR

Cut the cake into three equal layers. Purée the peeled, boiled chestnuts (or use a can of already puréed unsweetened chestnuts). Finely chop the chocolate and the walnuts. Whip the cream until stiff, sift in ¾ of the confectioners' sugar, stirring with a top-to-bottom folding movement to avoid deflating the cream.

Place a layer of the cake on a serving plate, moisten it with half the rum, then spread it with half the whipped cream and half the chestnut purée, topped with half the chocolate and walnuts. Cover with the second layer of cake and fill in the same way. Cover with the top layer, place a small bowl in the center and sprinkle the remaining confectioners' sugar over the exposed surface of the cake. Remove the bowl and carefully place the candied chestnut in the center of the cake.

Serve as soon as possible without refrigerating. If you prefer, the cake may be cut into more layers than indicated here – in which case the filling ingredients should be divided equally among all the layers.

Chestnut Pagoda

Pagoda di castagne

8 oz chestnut purée
7 oz fresh Mascarpone cheese or cream cheese
1 cup confectioners' sugar
¼ cup cocoa powder
2 tablespoons brandy
3 tablespoons Amaretto liqueur
⅔ cup whipping cream
1 sponge cake, about 9 in
½ cup Cointreau liqueur
1 tablespoon chocolate sprinkles
1 tablespoon white chocolate chips
6 chocolate buttons

SERVES 8

PREPARATION TIME: ABOUT 1½ HOURS

Place the chestnut purée in a bowl and mix in the Mascarpone cheese, stirring with a wooden spoon until smooth. Sift over it ¾ cup of confectioners' sugar and the cocoa powder, mix well, then add the brandy and Amaretto liqueur, making sure that each tablespoon is thoroughly absorbed before adding the next.

Whip the cream until firm, then fold in the rest of the sifted confectioners' sugar, stirring with a wooden spoon from top to bottom rather than round and round. Spoon the cream into a piping bag with a small round tip, and keep in the refrigerator.

Place the sponge cake on a serving dish and moisten it with the Cointreau, then sieve onto it the mixture of chestnuts and Mascarpone cheese, arranging it in a small heap. Pipe the sweetened whipped cream around the edge, and sprinkle over the chocolate threads. Complete the decoration of the cake by placing the white chocolate chips on top of it and arrange the chocolate buttons evenly spread around it.

Keep the cake in the warmest part of the refrigerator until serving time. If you wish, instead of using sponge cake as a base, you can use any other kind of risen cake such as panettone, Viennese pastry and so on.

Fruit Fantasy

Fantasia di frutta

---

3 firm, ripe tangerines or clementines
2 kiwi fruits
1 small banana
3 red and 3 green maraschino cherries
1 tablespoon sugar
juice of ¹/₂ lemon
2 tablespoons liqueur of your choice

SERVES 2

PREPARATION TIME: ABOUT 30 MINUTES

Wash and dry the tangerines, then cut them in half crossways; use a grapefruit knife to loosen the flesh from the skin, without actually removing it. Peel the kiwi fruits and slice them thinly into 18 slices. Cut the same number of slices from the banana and finally cut both the red and green cherries in half.

Arrange the six half-tangerines in the center of 2 small oval-shaped dishes and decorate with the cherries. Put the slices of kiwi fruit round the outside, topped with the banana slices, and leave to rest for a few minutes (do not place in the refrigerator).

Meanwhile put the sugar in a bowl, add the strained lemon juice and stir until the sugar is dissolved. Mix this cold syrup with the liqueur, stir again, pour over the fruit and serve immediately.

Chocolate and Amaretto Cup

Crema all'Amaretto

---

8 oz semi-sweet chocolate
4 oz macaroons
4 egg yolks
¹/₂ cup sugar
³/₄ cup all-purpose flour
1 quart milk
1 tablespoon of vanilla sugar
4 tablespoons butter, cut into small pieces
2–3 tablespoons Amaretto liqueur
2 oz flaked almonds

SERVES 6–8

PREPARATION AND COOKING TIME:
ABOUT 50 MINUTES

Grate the chocolate and finely crush the macaroons. Whisk the egg yolks with the sugar until they form soft, whitish peaks. Fold in the sifted flour and 2 tablespoons of cold milk and stir until the mixture is smooth and free of lumps. Add the remaining milk and the vanilla sugar. Gently heat the mixture in a saucepan and bring it just to the boil, stirring constantly with a whisk. Cook for a few minutes, remove from the heat and stir in the butter, grated chocolate and crushed macaroons.

Pour the Amaretto liqueur into a serving bowl, making sure that the sides of the bowl are coated in the liqueur.

Pour in the prepared mixture and leave to cool. Top with the flaked almonds, cover with plastic wrap and keep in the refrigerator until ready to serve.

Pistachio and Hazelnut Charlotte

Charlotte di pistacchio e nocciole

FOR THE SPONGE BASE
2 eggs
6 tablespoons super-fine sugar
2 teaspoons vanilla extract
¾ cup all-purpose flour
zest of ½ lemon

FOR THE FILLING
4 oz hazelnuts, toasted and skinned
6 tablespoons super-fine sugar, plus 1 teaspoon
2 oz semi-sweet chocolate
1 cup heavy cream
3 tablespoons gelatin
1 cup milk
3 egg yolks
2 teaspoons cornstarch
4 oz pistachios, blanched and skinned

SERVES 12

PREPARATION AND COOKING TIME:
ABOUT 1¾ HOURS, PLUS CHILLING

Preheat the oven to 425°F. Beat the eggs, vanilla and sugar together until light and fluffy. Sift the flour with well-washed grated lemon zest and fold delicately into the egg mixture. Butter and flour a 9 inch Swiss roll tin and line with waxed paper. Butter and flour the paper, pour in the sponge mixture and level the surface. Bake for about 10 minutes. Turn the sponge onto a tea-towel and set aside.

Grind the hazelnuts finely with 1 tablespoon sugar in a food processor to make a paste. Break the chocolate into pieces and place in a bowl with ¼ cup unwhipped cream and the hazelnut paste. Set the bowl in a pan with two fingers of water and melt the chocolate over very low heat. Soften the gelatin in a little cold water. Heat the milk. Work the egg yolks with the sugar and cornstarch. Add the hot milk, stir in the gelatin, then set over very low heat and heat, stirring continuously; do not let it boil. Divide the cream into two equal parts; add the chocolate mixture to one and the pistachios to the other. Blend the latter until smooth. Whip the remaining cream and fold two-thirds into the pistachio cream. Chill in the fridge for about 20 minutes.

To assemble the charlotte: line a 10 inch spring form pan with some of the sponge base. Fold the remaining whipped cream into the chocolate cream. Take the pistachio cream out of the refrigerator (it should have begun to set) and pour it into the pan. Spread the chocolate cream on top. Cover with slices of sponge. Chill in the refrigerator for about 6 hours. Unmold and serve.

Prune and Apple Tart

Crostata di prugne e mele

FOR THE PASTRY
7 oz butter
2½ cups all-purpose flour
1 egg
6 tablespoons super-fine sugar
2 teaspoons vanilla extract

FOR THE FILLING
8 oz pitted prunes
½ cup rum
1¾ lb apples
2 tablespoons butter
juice of ½ lemon
super-fine and confectioners' sugar
flaked almonds
1 egg, beaten

SERVES 10

PREPARATION AND COOKING TIME:
ABOUT 2 HOURS

Soak the prunes in the rum for about 1 hour. Work the butter and flour together, then place on a work surface and make a well. Break the egg into the center and add the sugar, vanilla and a pinch of salt. Mix quickly, using your fingertips so as not to over-soften the butter (which would make the pastry lose its body). Roll the dough into a ball, wrap in plastic wrap and refrigerate for 30 minutes.

Preheat the oven to 375°F. Make the filling: peel and core the apples and dice finely. Place in a saucepan with the butter, lemon juice, 3 tablespoons super-fine sugar and a little cold water. Cover the pan and cook the apples over high heat for 7 minutes, then add the prunes and the rum they were soaked in. Cook until the fruit is quite dry and the apples are pulpy, then leave to cool.

RIGHT: *Prune and apple tart* (top); *Pistachio and hazelnut charlotte* (bottom).

On a lightly floured work surface, roll the dough into a circle ¼ inch thick. Use it to line completely a greased 10 inch tart pan, cutting off the excess dough. Pour the cooked fruit into the tart pan.

Re-roll the pastry trimmings, then, using a fluted cutter, cut into ½ inch wide strips. Arrange these in a lattice pattern on the fruit and fill the spaces with flaked almonds (about 20). Brush the pastry with beaten egg and sift over a light veiling of icing sugar. Bake in the hot oven for about 40 minutes. Serve the tart at room temperature.

Little Pastry Cases with Chocolate Mousse

Coupelle con mousse al cioccolato

FOR THE PASTRY CASES
4 oz butter
4 egg whites
1 cup confectioners' sugar
1 cup all-purpose flour
2 teaspoons vanilla extract

FOR THE MOUSSE
10 oz semi-sweet chocolate
¼ cup rum
1 cup heavy cream

FOR THE VANILLA SAUCE
1 cup milk
2 egg yolks
6 tablespoons super-fine sugar
½ tablespoon flour
2 teaspoons vanilla extract

SERVES 8

PREPARATION AND COOKING TIME: ABOUT 1
HOUR 40 MINUTES, PLUS CHILLING

First make the pastry cases (you can do this the day before if you keep them in a cool, dry place). Preheat the oven to 400°F. Melt the butter without browning it, then cool. In a bowl, mix the unbeaten egg whites with the sugar, flour, vanilla and cooled melted butter to make a soft paste. Butter and flour a baking sheet; on it place a tablespoon of the mixture, flattening it out with the back of a spoon to make a very thin disc 6–6½ inches in diameter. Place the sheet in the hot oven for about 4 minutes. Remove; the disc should be soft, pale in the center and lightly browned at the edges. Lift it off the tray with a palette knife and mold it around the base of an upturned cup. Leave to cool, then unmold. Repeat the operation until all the paste is used up (you should end up with 8–10 pastry cases).

Break up the chocolate and place in a bowl with the rum. Stand the bowl in a pan with two fingers of tepid water, place over very low heat and melt the chocolate, stirring frequently and gently. Leave to cool. Whip the cream very stiffly. Fold it gently into the cooled chocolate. Refrigerate for about 2 hours.

Finally, prepare the sauce: heat the milk and, meanwhile, mix the egg yolks with the sugar, vanilla and flour. Stir in the hot milk. Pour the mixture back into the pan and heat over very low heat, stirring continuously; on no account let it boil. Turn off the heat and leave the sauce to cool.

Just before serving, divide the mousse and vanilla sauce equally between the pastry cases.

Orange Tart with Whipped Cream

Crostata all'arancia con panna montata

FOR THE CRUST
4 oz butter
2½ cups all-purpose flour
1 egg
1 cup confectioners' sugar
1 teaspoon ground cinnamon

FOR THE FILLING
4 egg yolks
¾ cup super-fine sugar
½ cup all-purpose flour
grated zest of 1 orange
2¼ cups milk
2 tablespoons orange liqueur

TO DECORATE
4 oranges
scant 1 cup heavy cream
4 oz apricot jam

SERVES 6–8

PREPARATION AND COOKING TIME:
ABOUT 1½ HOURS

To prepare the crust: beat the butter into the flour, then place on a work surface and make a well. Break the egg into the center and add the sugar and cinnamon. Knead fairly rapidly to avoid over-softening the butter, then wrap the dough in plastic wrap and leave to rest in the refrigerator for about 30 minutes.

Meanwhile, make the filling: in a bowl, work the egg yolks with the sugar, flour and grated orange zest. Heat the milk and pour it onto the egg mixture in a thin stream, then pour the custard back into the pan and place on the heat. Stirring continuously to avoid lumps, simmer for 5 minutes, then remove from the heat, stir in the liqueur and leave to cool.

Preheat the oven to 375°F. On a lightly floured surface, roll out the dough into a circle ⅛ inch thick and use it to line a buttered and floured 10 inch removable bottomed tart pan. Fill with the orange-flavored custard. Cut off the excess dough and pinch up the edges of the crust. Bake the tart in the hot oven for about 40 minutes.

While the tart is cooking, prepare the decoration: peel 3 oranges, removing all the pith, and cut into rounds. Whip the cream until very stiff. Make a glaze by boiling the jam for 3 minutes with one-third of a glass of water. Peel the remaining orange and cut the zest into very thin strips. Blanch for 2 minutes, then drain very carefully.

Remove the tart from the oven, unmold it onto a serving plate and leave to cool. Arrange the orange rounds on the custard, and brush them with the tepid apricot glaze. Put the cream in a piping bag with a star tip, and pipe it around the edge of the tart, then arrange the strands of orange zest on top.

Mixed Glazed Fruit

Frutta mista glassata

white grapes
strawberries
tangerine segments
dried apricots
canned pineapple rings in syrup

FOR THE FONDANT
10 oz sugar lumps
1 oz glucose

FOR THE CARAMEL AND CRYSTALLIZING
1 ¼ lb super-fine sugar

FOR THE CHOCOLATE GLAZE
5 oz semi-sweet chocolate

SERVES 12

PREPARATION AND COOKING TIME:
ABOUT 1 HOUR, PLUS COOLING

Hull, wash and thoroughly dry all the fresh fruit (use any you wish to use – those given above are suggestions only). Drain the pineapple rings and cut into segments. Prepare the fondant: over moderate heat, dissolve the sugar lumps with the glucose and ½ cup water, and heat to 240°F on a sugar thermometer. Pour on to a marble slab and, working energetically with a spatula, knead until the fondant cools to a soft, translucent white mass. Dissolve it again in a water bath, then dip in about a third of strawberries, clusters of grapes, apricots and any other fruits, coating them well. Place the fruits on a wire rack and leave to dry in a cool place.

Make the caramel: dissolve 1 ¼ cups super-fine sugar with ¼ cup water, and boil to make a syrup at 320°F; dip in a further third of the grapes, tangerine segments and apricots, coating them completely. Arrange the caramelized fruit on a wire rack and leave to drain and dry in a cool place. (While you are caramelizing the fruit, tilt the pan, keeping the base away from the marble surface; the caramel will cool more slowly, allowing you to glaze more fruit. If, however, the sugar does harden before you have finished, reheat it for a few moments.)

To make the chocolate coating: break up the chocolate and melt it in a water bath until it reaches

LEFT: *Orange mousse with chocolate* (top); *Mixed glazed fruit* (bottom).

113°F. Immerse the bowl in cold water and, working the mixture with a wooden spoon, cool to 86–90°F dip the remaining fruit into the chocolate; drain with a small slotted spoon and place the fruit on a wire rack to drain and dry.

Finally, crystallize the pineapple: drain it and boil for 25 minutes in a syrup made with 1 ½ cups sugar and ⅔ cup water. Take out the pineapple, arrange on a wire rack, sprinkle with the remaining sugar and leave to dry in a cool place. (All the glazed fruit should be prepared a day in advance.)

To serve, arrange the fruit in little glass dishes.

Orange Mousse with Chocolate

Mousse d'arancia al cioccolato

1 ¼ lb fine semi-sweet chocolate
1 ½ cups milk
4 egg yolks
½ cup sugar
¼ cup flour
⅓ cup Grand Marnier or other orange liqueur
zest of 3 oranges
1 ¼ cups heavy cream

SERVES 12

PREPARATION AND COOKING TIME:
ABOUT 40 MINUTES, PLUS COOLING

Break up the chocolate and melt it in a water bath until it reaches 113°F on a sugar thermometer. Immerse the bowl in cold water and, working the chocolate with a wooden spoon, cool to 86–90°F. Pour some of the chocolate into glass dishes to coat them. Spread out the remaining chocolate very thinly on a marble surface and leave it to cool.

Prepare the custard: heat the milk. In a bowl, work the egg yolks with the sugar and flour. Pour in the milk in a thin stream, then place over very low heat and, stirring continuously to avoid lumps, simmer for about 3–4 minutes. Take off the heat and stir in the Grand Marnier and the carefully washed and grated orange zest. Leave to cool. Whip the cream until very stiff and fold it into the cooled custard.

Using a knife with a wide, sharp blade, scrape the chocolate off the marble to make flakes. Divide the cold custard between the chocolate-lined dishes, decorate with the chocolate flakes and serve immediately, or keep in the refrigerator.

Filled Panettone

Panettone farcito

---

1 × 2¼ lb panettone
generous cup heavy cream
4 oz toasted flaked almonds
½ cup Cointreau or other orange liqueur
¾ cup super-fine sugar
confectioners' sugar

FOR THE GREEN CREAM
1 tablespoon gelatin
2 oz shelled and peeled pistachios
¼ cup super-fine sugar, plus 1 tablespoon
1 cup milk
3 egg yolks
cornstarch

FOR THE YELLOW CREAM
1 tablespoon gelatin
¼ cup super-fine sugar
2 teaspoons vanilla extract
1 cup milk
3 egg yolks
cornstarch

SERVES 12
PREPARATION AND COOKING TIME:
ABOUT 1¼ HOURS PLUS CHILLING

Cut the panettone into six 1 inch thick rounds (you will only use five of these rounds, including the base and top).

Soften both amounts of gelatin. Make the green cream: chop the pistachios with a spoonful of sugar, put into the milk and heat. In a bowl, work the egg yolks with the ¼ cup sugar and a spoonful of cornstarch. Whisk in the hot pistachio milk, then reheat the cream without boiling and stir in half the softened gelatin. Purée the cream in a blender and leave to cool. Make the yellow cream in the same way, using the remaining gelatin and the vanilla, then leave to cool completely.

Whip the heavy cream until stiff and spread some of it on the edges of the panettone rounds, then sprinkle on the almonds. When the green and yellow creams start to set, fold half the whipped cream into each one and chill in the refrigerator for 1 hour.

Mix the Cointreau with ½ cup water and use this to moisten the panettone rounds. Spread the green cream over two of them and the yellow cream over another two. Reassemble the panettone carefully, alternating the different colored rounds and ending with a plain round of panettone.

Make a caramel by boiling the sugar with a little water until it has dissolved and completely caramelized. Take one strand at a time with two forks and stretch it over two wooden handles, until you have a pile of sugar strands. Arrange this on the top of the panettone, sprinkle with confectioners' sugar and then serve.

Panettone with Sauce

Salsa ai panettone

---

10 oz mixed berry fruits, such as strawberries, raspberries,
blueberries
1½ cups super-fine sugar
¼ cup Grand Marnier or other orange liqueur
1 × 2¼ lb panettone

SERVES 12
PREPARATION TIME: ABOUT 10 MINUTES, PLUS
MARINATING

Pick over the fruits and discard any that are bruised, then wash them thoroughly and drain well. Marinate overnight in the sugar and liqueur.

Just before serving, crush the fruits with a small whisk, leaving them in the marinade, and mix to obtain a thick sauce. Transfer to a bowl and bring to the table for your guests to help themselves. Slice the panettone into plain pieces (ie: as it comes in the box), or cut into ¾ inch slices and briefly toast in a very hot oven. Serve accompanied by the fruit sauce.

RIGHT: *Filled panettone.*

Melon Bavarian Cream

Bavarese di melone

¾ oz gelatin
1 perfectly ripe medium melon
6 tablespoons sugar
2 oz cleaned redcurrants
2 teaspoons vanilla extract
scant 1 cup whipping cream
2 oz strawberry jam

SERVES 8–10

PREPARATION AND COOKING TIME: ABOUT 1¼ HOURS, PLUS AT LEAST 2 HOURS CHILLING

Dissolve the gelatin in cold water. Wash and dry the melon, then halve it and remove the seeds. Remove the pulp with a spoon, without piercing the rind which will be used as a container. Place the pulp in a saucepan and add the sugar and the redcurrants. Place the saucepan on the heat and, stirring occasionally with a wooden spoon, simmer gently until the mixture has the consistency of jam, making sure it does not stick to the bottom of the pan.

Remove from the heat, stir the mixture for a couple of minutes and pour it into a bowl; while it is still warm stir in the vanilla sugar and the gelatin. Mix well to dissolve the gelatin, then let it cool. Whip the cream and fold it into the melon cream when it is cold but not yet firm, mixing with a motion from top to bottom rather than round and round (to prevent the cream from going flat). Pour the strawberry jam into a small bowl and stir vigorously with a spoon to make it smooth.

Spread a layer of the melon Bavarian cream in each half shell of the melon and pour over each layer some of the strawberry jam. Refrigerate for at least 2 hours so that the Bavarian cream will set, then cut each half into 4–5 slices, using a very sharp knife; arrange them on a serving plate and serve.

Redcurrants in Lemon Cream Baskets

'Cestini' con crema e ribes

___

5 large lemons

2 small macaroons

3 egg yolks

1/2 cup sugar

1/4 cup flour

1 1/4 cups milk

1 tablespoon orange liqueur

8 bunches redcurrants

8 fresh mint leaves

7 rolled wafers

SERVES 4

PREPARATION AND COOKING TIME:
ABOUT 1 HOUR

Grate the rind of one lemon. Halve the other 4 lemons and squeeze them, reserving the juice. Scrape out the flesh and trim the bases so that they stand level.

Crumble the macaroons and divide them among the half-lemons. Add to the pan with the lemon rind, egg yolks, sugar, flour and 2 tablespoons of the milk, and beat to obtain a perfectly smooth mixture. Add the rest of the milk and, stirring continuously, bring to the boil. Remove from the heat and add the liqueur, then stand the pan in cold water and stir until the custard is completely cooled.

Wash the redcurrants and dry them on a cloth. Pick off the largest currants and arrange them over the macaroon crumbs in the lemon halves; fill up with the lemon cream, using a piping bag with a plain round tip. Garnish with redcurrants and a mint leaf and arrange on a dish, interspersed with the wafers. Serve immediately, before the cream can absorb any bitterness from the lemon pith.

If you do not wish to use lemon halves as containers, you could substitute individual pastry shells baked blind with dried beans to keep their shape. The baskets will need to be served quickly, before the pastry loses its crispness.

Profiteroles in Spun Caramel

Piramide di bignè

FOR THE PASTRY
4 oz butter, cut into pieces
1¼ cups all-purpose flour
4 eggs
a little butter

FOR THE CUSTARD
2 eggs plus 2 egg yolks
¾ cup super-fine sugar
¼ cup all-purpose flour
2½ cups milk
1 tablespoon vanilla sugar

FOR THE CARAMEL
¾ cup super-fine sugar

MAKES ABOUT 40 PROFITEROLES
PREPARATION AND COOKING TIME:
ABOUT 2 HOURS

Heat ⅔ cup of water, the butter and a pinch of salt in a saucepan. As soon as it boils, remove from the heat, and pour in the flour. Mix and cook over low heat, stirring, until it no longer sticks to the edges of the pan. Turn onto a working surface, spread out and leave to cool.

Preheat the oven to 375°F. Return the mixture to the pan and mix in the eggs, one at a time. When the mixture is thick and smooth, spoon it into a piping bag fitted with a plain tip. Pipe rosettes onto a buttered baking sheet, making sure they are well separated – they will puff up and spread during cooking. Bake for 15 minutes. Before removing from the oven cut open 1 profiterole to check that it is cooked – it should be hollow and slightly crisp and golden in the center. Cool the profiteroles on a rack.

Meanwhile, beat the eggs, yolks and sugar until the mixture forms soft white ribbons. Sift in the flour and add the cold milk and vanilla sugar. Heat gently and allow to thicken, stirring constantly. As soon as the mixture comes to the boil, plunge the pan into cold water to cool. Pipe the mixture into the profiteroles and arrange them on a serving plate.

Dissolve the sugar in 4 tablespoons of water over moderate heat. Let it boil until it has turned light brown, remove from the heat and stir to cool and thicken. When it begins to form threads, pour it over the profiteroles, holding the pan fairly high and moving it in circles so that the caramel falls in spun threads around the profiteroles. If it thickens too much, reheat it gently. Serve as soon as possible.

Chocolate Gateau

Torta 'gianfranco'

---

a little butter and flour
3 eggs plus 2 egg yolks
1¼ cups super-fine sugar
1 tablespoon of vanilla sugar
10 oz semi-sweet chocolate
1 cup all-purpose flour
½ cup potato flour
3 tablespoons cocoa powder
baking powder
⅔ cup milk
2 cups whipping cream
2 oz flaked almonds

SERVES 10
PREPARATION AND COOKING TIME:
ABOUT 1¾ HOURS

Butter a 10 inch round cake pan and sprinkle with flour. Whisk the eggs briskly with ¾ cup of the sugar, a pinch of salt and the sachet of vanilla sugar until they form thick ribbons.

Preheat the oven to 350°F. Melt 3 oz of the semi-sweet chocolate over low heat and leave to cool. Mix the flour with the potato flour, cocoa and a heaped teaspoon of baking powder and sift into the egg mixture, folding in carefully with a wooden spoon. Fold in the melted chocolate and pour the mixture into the prepared pan. Bake in the oven for about 30 minutes.

Meanwhile beat the egg yolks with the remaining flour, sugar and a pinch of salt. Gradually add the milk and bring to the boil, stirring constantly. Remove the pan from the heat and leave to cool, stirring from time to time.

Cut 4 oz of the semi-sweet chocolate into small pieces, melt it over low heat and add it to the mixture, stirring vigorously. Leave to cool.

Turn cake out onto a wire rack. Whisk the cream until stiff then fold it into the chocolate mixture. Cut the cake into three layers and sandwich together with two thirds of the chocolate mixture. Coat top and sides of cake with some chocolate mixture and sprinkle with the remainder of the semi-sweet chocolate, grated. Pipe rosettes of chocolate mixture on the cake and decorate with flaked almonds. Refrigerate and serve within 4–5 hours.

FAR LEFT: *Profiteroles in spun caramel* (top left); *Chocolate gateau* (bottom).

Coffee Ice Cream

Gelato al caffè

¾ cup ground coffee
1 tablespoon of vanilla sugar
1¾ cups sugar
scant 1 cup light cream
1 egg white

SERVES 6

PREPARATION AND COOKING TIME:
30 MINUTES, PLUS FREEZING

In a small saucepan bring 1½ cups of water to the boil, pour in the coffee and, stirring constantly, simmer over very low heat until the foam has disappeared. Leave to infuse for about 15 minutes, so that the ground coffee sinks to the bottom of the saucepan; strain the liquid coffee into a bowl.

Add the vanilla sugar and the sugar, stir until the sugar is dissolved then leave to cool. At this point mix in the cream and place in the refrigerator for at least 1 hour to cool completely.

Pour the mixture into an ice cream machine or container, add the egg white whisked to a froth, with a pinch of salt, so that the ice cream will be smooth and soft. Freeze until required.

Vanilla Ice Cream

Gelato alla vaniglia

2½ cups milk
¾ cup sugar
1 small vanilla bean
5 egg yolks
1 egg white

SERVES 6

PREPARATION AND COOKING TIME:
30 MINUTES, PLUS FREEZING

Heat most of the milk in a saucepan with the sugar, a pinch of salt and the vanilla bean until almost boiling. Remove from the heat and discard the bean.

Meanwhile, beat the egg yolks then add, little by little, first the reserved cold milk, then the hot, stirring constantly. When the ingredients are well blended, pour the mixture back into the saucepan and heat for about 2 minutes, stirring.

Pour the mixture into a bowl and let it cool, stirring occasionally. Pour it into an ice-cream machine or container, pouring it through a fine strainer. Halfway through the process add the egg white whisked to a froth with a pinch of salt so that the ice cream will be very smooth and soft.

Freeze until required.

Pistachio Ice Cream

Gelato al pistacchio

---

4 oz pistachio nuts
1¼ cups sugar
2½ cups milk
1 vanilla bean
5 egg yolks

SERVES 6

PREPARATION AND COOKING TIME:
30 MINUTES, PLUS FREEZING

Plunge the pistachio nuts into salted boiling water for 1 minute, then drain and shell them. Pound them in a mortar, adding a tablespoon of sugar from time to time, until they are reduced to powder.

Heat most of the milk with the remaining sugar and the vanilla bean and bring slowly to the boil, stirring occasionally with a wooden spoon. Remove from the heat and discard the bean.

Meanwhile, beat the egg yolks in a bowl with the powdered pistachio nuts, using a small whisk to obtain a smooth mixture. Add first the reserved cold milk, then the hot, stirring constantly. When the ingredients are well blended, pour the mixture back into the saucepan and heat for about 2 minutes, stirring. Pour the mixture into a bowl and let it cool, stirring occasionally. Pour through a fine strainer into an ice-cream machine or container.

Freeze until required.

Amaretto Ice Cream

Gelato all'Amaretto

2½ cups milk
1 vanilla bean
5 egg yolks
¾ cup sugar
4 oz small macaroons
4 tablespoons Amaretto liqueur

SERVES 6
PREPARATION AND COOKING TIME:
1½ HOURS, PLUS FREEZING

Heat the milk in a saucepan with the vanilla bean and bring slowly to the boil; strain, remove from the heat and discard the bean. Leave to cool.

Meanwhile, beat the egg yolks with a pinch of salt and the sugar until soft and frothy. Stir in the lukewarm milk, pouring it in a trickle, and whisk until well blended. Then pour the mixture back into the saucepan, place over very low heat and, stirring constantly, heat until the mixture is about to boil.

Remove from the heat and pour the liquid through a fine strainer, then leave to cool at room temperature, stirring occasionally. Add the finely crumbled macaroons and Amaretto liqueur. Place in the refrigerator for about 1 hour, then pour the mixture into an ice-cream machine or container. Freeze until required.

Torrone Ice Cream

Gelato al torroncino

5 oz assorted crystallized fruit
1 cup Maraschino liqueur
4 oz torrone (Italian nougat)
2½ cups milk
1 vanilla bean
1 cup sugar
4 egg yolks

SERVES 6
PREPARATION AND COOKING TIME:
1½ HOURS, PLUS FREEZING

Coarsely chop the crystallized fruit, of different colors and flavors, place it in a small bowl and moisten it with the Maraschino. Pound the torrone to a powder.

In a saucepan heat most of the milk with the vanilla bean and the sugar. When the milk is hot and the sugar has dissolved, discard the bean.

Beat the egg yolks in a bowl adding first the reserved cold milk then the hot, pouring in a trickle and stirring constantly. When the ingredients are well mixed, pour back into the saucepan and heat for a couple of minutes, stirring, without bringing it to boil. Remove the saucepan from the heat and strain the mixture into a bowl. Let it cool, stirring occasionally, then leave it for at least 1 hour in the refrigerator.

Just before placing it in an ice-cream machine or container mix in the crystallized fruit and the torrone. Freeze until required.

Peach and Macaroon Pie

Crostata di pesche all'Amaretto

a little butter and flour
1 cup all-purpose flour
¼ cup sugar
grated rind of ½ lemon
1 egg yolk
4 tablespoons butter
1 tablespoon dry vermouth
12 small macaroons
6 tablespoons peach jam
1 tablespoon apricot brandy
2 large yellow peaches
1 tablespoon Amaretto liqueur
redcurrants

SERVES 6–8
PREPARATION AND COOKING TIME:
ABOUT 1 HOUR, PLUS COOLING

Preheat the oven to 375°F. Butter and flour a 10 inch pie dish.

Sift the flour and add a pinch of salt, the sugar and the grated lemon rind. Make a well in the center and add the egg yolk, the softened butter, cut into small pieces, and the vermouth. Knead rapidly into a smooth dough, then roll out and line the prepared dish with it; prick the bottom of the pastry with a fork. Crumble over 7 macaroons. Set aside 2 tablespoons of jam, place the rest in a bowl and stir in the apricot brandy. Spread evenly over the crumbs.

Peel, halve and stone the peaches, then cut them into equal slices and arrange them in a circle, slightly overlapping on the pastry; in the center put the remaining macaroons and sprinkle them with the Amaretto liqueur. Bake for about 40 minutes.

Remove the pie from the oven and let it cool in the dish; then place it on a large round plate. Melt the remaining jam over low heat, pour it through a fine strainer and brush the peach slices and the macaroons with it. As soon as the glaze has cooled and is firm, garnish the pie with sprigs of redcurrants and serve.

Zabaglione Trifle

Dolce al cucchiaio

FOR THE SPONGE CAKE
1 cup all-purpose flour
½ cup super-fine sugar
3 eggs
2 teaspoons vanilla extract
salt
butter and flour for the pan

FOR THE ZABAGLIONE
¼ cup super-fine sugar
¼ cup Marsala wine
3 egg yolks, plus 1 whole egg
salt

TO FINISH
3 Golden Delicious apples
1 tablespoon super-fine sugar
2¼ cups heavy cream
⅓ cup Maraschino
juice of 1 lemon
raspberries
butter for greasing

SERVES 10–12
PREPARATION AND COOKING TIME:
ABOUT 2 HOURS

Preheat the oven to 375°F. Using the listed ingredients, make a sponge mixture: beat the eggs and sugar together until light and fluffy. Sift in the flour, vanilla and a pinch of salt and beat until the mixture makes a smooth batter. Butter and flour an 8 inch cake pan and bake in the oven for about 35 minutes or until the cake springs back when lightly pressed with a finger. Turn out the cake and leave to cool on a wire rack. Increase the oven temperature to 475°F.

Now prepare the zabaglione: combine all the ingredients with a pinch of salt in a stainless steel bowl. Stand the bowl in a water bath of tepid water, place over very low heat and whisk the eggs until risen, creamy and thick. Remove from the water bath and leave to cool. Core two of the apples, peel and slice thinly, then arrange on a greased baking sheet. Sprinkle with the sugar, then cook in the hot oven for about 5 minutes. Whip the cream and fold about 1 cup into the prepared zabaglione. Dilute the Maraschino with a little cold water. Cut the sponge cake into small slices, brush them with the Maraschino, then arrange a few in the bottom of a bowl. Cover with half the zabaglione, and follow with alternate layers of apple, sponge cake, apple and zabaglione. Level the surface carefully.

Thinly slice the remaining apple, without peeling it. Dip the slices in lemon juice, then drain and arrange them around the edge of the trifle. Put the remaining whipped cream in a piping bag with a star tip and pipe decoratively onto the trifle. Finish the decoration with a couple of dozen raspberries, and keep in the refrigerator until you are ready to serve.

Fresh Apricot Compote

Composta di albicocche

1¼ lb firm ripe apricots
4 oz apricot jam
1 tablespoon white rum
1 tablespoon apricot liqueur
grated rind of 1 lemon
1 lime for garnish
7 Maraschino cherries

SERVES 6
PREPARATION TIME: ABOUT 15 MINUTES,
PLUS 1½ HOURS SOAKING

Remove the stalks from the apricots and wipe them with a damp cloth. Halve them, remove the pits, and slice them into a bowl. Strain the jam, dilute it with the rum and liqueur and add the grated lemon rind. Mix well and pour over the apricots, stirring carefully. Cover the bowl with plastic wrap and leave in the warmest part of the refrigerator for at least 1½ hours, giving the mixture a gentle stir from time to time.

Distribute the apricots among six individual bowls. Garnish each one with five wafer-thin rings of lime and five slices of Maraschino cherry. Serve at once.

FAR LEFT: *Peach and macaroon pie.*

Rich Zuccotto

Zuccotto ricco

FOR THE SPONGE CAKE
3 egg yolks
¾ cup super-fine sugar
salt
1¼ cups all-purpose flour
2 teaspoons vanilla extract
flour and butter for the pan

FOR THE PASTRY CREAM
4 egg yolks
¾ cup super-fine sugar
¼ cup all-purpose flour
2¼ cups milk
lemon zest

FOR THE FILLING AND TO FINISH
7 oz semi-sweet chocolate
1¾ cups heavy cream
½ cup crème de cacao liqueur
langue de chat cookies, for serving

SERVES 12
PREPARATION AND COOKING TIME:
ABOUT 2 HOURS, PLUS CHILLING

Preheat the oven to 375°F. Make the sponge cake (you can do this the day before). Beat the egg yolks with the sugar and a pinch of salt until the mixture forms a ribbon (when you lift the whisk, the mixture which falls from it does not sink back immediately into the mixture in the bowl, but remains lightly on the surface). Sift in the flour from a height, then add the vanilla, folding them in carefully with a wooden spoon, stirring from bottom to top and vice-versa. Pour the mixture into a buttered and floured 9 inch cake pan, and bake in the oven for about 35 minutes, or until a skewer inserted into the center comes out clean. Remove from the oven, invert on to a wire rack and leave to cool.

Meanwhile, make the pastry cream: work the egg yolks with the sugar and flour. Heat the milk with a little lemon zest, then pour it into the egg mixture in a thin stream. Set over moderate heat and, stirring continuously, boil for about 5 minutes, then turn off the heat and leave to cool.

Melt 5 oz semi-sweet chocolate and cool until it is tepid. Whip one-quarter of the heavy cream until very firm and mix it with the chocolate and the cooled pastry cream.

To assemble the zuccotto: cut the crusts off the sponge cake and slice it. Moisten with the liqueur diluted with ½ cup water. Use some of the slices to line a large, flat-bottomed bowl. Cut the rest into strips and fill the bowl with layers of chocolate cream and sponge strips. Chill in the refrigerator for at least 3 hours.

Unmold the zuccotto onto a serving plate. Whip the remaining cream, place in a piping bag with a star tip, and pipe it over the zuccotto. Melt the rest of the chocolate, place in an icing bag and decorate the zuccotto as in the photo, finishing with a crown of *langues de chat* cookies. Leave in the fridge until ready to serve: the decorated zuccotto will keep for about 6–8 hours.

Chestnut Cups

Coppette di castagne

---

1 lb chestnuts, boiled and peeled
½ cup super-fine sugar
4 tablespoons Cointreau liqueur
a little vanilla sugar
½ cup whipping cream
6 pistachio nuts

SERVES 4
PREPARATION AND COOKING TIME:
ABOUT 30 MINUTES, PLUS COOLING

Place the chestnuts in a bowl that just holds them. Heat the sugar with 3 tablespoons of water, letting it dissolve gradually then come to the boil. Remove from the heat, add the Cointreau and vanilla sugar, stir and pour this mixture over the chestnuts. Cover the bowl with plastic wrap and leave it to cool completely, during which time the chestnuts will absorb much of the syrup.

Divide the chestnuts between four individual cups. Whip the cream until firm and, using a piping bag fitted with a star tip, decorate each cup with a ring of cream rosettes. Blanch the pistachio nuts for a few seconds in slightly salted boiling water, remove the skins and dry them on paper towels. Chop them finely and sprinkle them on the cream. Serve immediately, since the chestnuts are at their best straight after cooling.

RIGHT: *Rich zuccotto.*

Peaches with Pine Nuts

Pesche ai pinoli

4 equal-sized yellow peaches, perfectly ripe
butter
1 clove
2 inch piece lemon rind
2 tablespoons sugar
6 tablespoons brandy
8 tablespoons pine nuts

SERVES 4
PREPARATION AND COOKING TIME:
ABOUT 45 MINUTES

Remove the stems from the peaches, then wash and dry them; cut them in half with a small sharp knife and remove the pits.

Melt a large knob of butter in a saucepan, then arrange the eight peach halves on the bottom of the pan, cut side down. Fry very gently for a few moments with the pan uncovered, then add the clove and the piece of lemon rind. Sprinkle the fruit with the sugar and moisten with the brandy. Shake the pan slightly to make sure the peaches aren't stuck to the bottom, then lower the heat to the minimum, cover, and cook the peaches for about 20 minutes until they are poached and glazed.

Place the peaches, cut side upwards, on a serving dish and in the hollow of each place a spoonful of pine nuts. Reduce the cooking liquid slightly, then pour it directly onto the fruit.

Serve immediately while still hot — though peaches prepared in this way are also excellent lukewarm.

Baskets of Grapes

Cestini all'uva

---

2 egg whites
6 tablespoons sugar
¾ cup all-purpose flour
6 tablespoons butter
1 lb vanilla ice cream
about 1 cup whipping cream
a large bunch of black grapes

SERVES 6

PREPARATION AND COOKING TIME: 45 MINUTES

Preheat the oven to 425°F. Beat the egg whites in a bowl until stiff then gradually whisk in the sugar and keep beating for 2–3 minutes. Add 2 tablespoons of flour and 4 tablespoons of melted butter, stirring to form a smooth batter.

Grease and flour a baking sheet. Pour about 3 tablespoons of the batter separately onto it, keeping them well apart. Spread the mixture on the sheet with the back of a spoon into three thin disks about 5 inches in diameter. Bake for 6–7 minutes until golden at the edges. Remove them from the oven and, working quickly with a fish slice, transfer each onto an upturned glass.

While soft, press them against the glass bottom to shape into baskets. Repeat with the remaining mixture. Set aside, still on the glasses, to firm up.

When cool and firm, put in a scoop of ice cream in the center of each basket. Decorate with whipped cream and garnish all around with the washed and dried grapes. Serve at once.

Figs with Redcurrants and Ice Cream

Fichi Speziati con ribes e gelato

2¼ lb fresh figs, not overripe
½ cup sugar
½ cup golden raisins
ground cinnamon
ground ginger
a few whole cloves
6 tablespoons brandy
rind of 1 lemon
12 thin slices fruit cake or loaf
redcurrants
6 scoops vanilla ice cream

SERVES 6

PREPARATION AND COOKING TIME: ABOUT 40 MINUTES, PLUS 1 HOUR MARINATING

Using a small, sharp knife, peel the figs. Cut each one into four or six according to size and place in a stainless steel saucepan. Add the sugar, raisins, a large pinch of cinnamon, a pinch of ginger and a few cloves. Pour over 2 tablespoons of the brandy. Cut a 3 inch piece of lemon rind into needle-fine strips and add to the other ingredients. Cover the mixture and leave in a cool place for about 1 hour.

Cook the figs over low heat for about 15 minutes from the moment the liquid begins to simmer. Keep the pan uncovered and stir gently from time to time. Immerse the saucepan in cold water to cool quickly.

Arrange the fruit cake in a glass salad bowl and pour over the remaining brandy. Spread the fig mixture on top and cover. Keep in the refrigerator until it is time to serve. Then sprinkle some stemmed, washed redcurrants on top and decorate with scoops of ice cream.

LEFT: *Baskets of grapes.*

Mother's Day Cake

Torta "festa della mamma"

---

butter
1 cup all-purpose flour
3 eggs plus 4 egg yolks
1½ cups super-fine sugar
2 tablespoons of vanilla sugar
½ cup potato flour
1 tablespoon gelatin
⅔ cup Marsala wine
½ cup Amaretto liqueur
½ cup whipping cream
5 large ripe strawberries

SERVES 10–12

PREPARATION AND COOKING TIME: ABOUT 1¼ HOURS, PLUS AT LEAST 2 HOURS CHILLING

Preheat the oven to 350°F. Butter and flour a round, springform cake pan about 10 inches in diameter. Beat three of the eggs with half of the sugar, half the vanilla sugar and a pinch of salt until frothy. Add the remaining flour and the potato flour sifted together through a fine strainer. Fold them in very gently with an up-and-down movement rather than a circular one using a wooden spoon. Pour the batter into the cake pan and bake in the oven for about 35 minutes, or until a skewer inserted into the center comes out clean. Turn the cake out on to a rack to cool.

Meanwhile, soften the gelatin in a little cold water. In a copper bowl beat the 4 egg yolks together with the remaining sugar and vanilla sugar. When the mixture is frothy add the Marsala, making sure that each tablespoon is thoroughly absorbed before adding the next. Then add 3 tablespoons of the Amaretto liqueur, pouring it in a trickle and stirring all the time. Place the copper bowl over a pan of barely simmering water and, still stirring, heat the zabaglione cream until it is very hot. At this point remove it from the heat and fold in the gelatin. Mix thoroughly until the gelatin has dissolved, then pour the zabaglione cream into a bowl and let it cool.

Cut the cake into three layers of equal thickness and place the lowest one back in the springform pan lined with waxed paper. Sprinkle the cake with a third of the remaining Amaretto liqueur and spread over it a third of the warm zabaglione cream. Repeat the same procedure with the second and third layers of cake. Refrigerate the cake for at least 2 hours, when the zabaglione cream will have set.

Beat the cream until stiff and put it in a piping bag. Wipe the strawberries and hull four of them, then cut them in half lengthways. Slide the blade of a small knife between the side of the pan and the cake, then open the hinge and detach the side of the pan. Slide the cake onto a serving dish by removing first the bottom of the pan and then the waxed paper. Garnish the top with the whipped cream and the strawberries. Serve immediately.

RIGHT: *Mother's Day cake.*

Strawberry Mousse

Turbante rosa fragola

---

2 tablespoons gelatin
a little almond oil
8 oz just-ripe strawberries
½ cup sugar
1¾ cups whipping cream
4 tablespoons Cointreau liqueur
2 tablespoons shredded coconut
10 equal-sized strawberries, with their stalks, for garnish
fresh mint leaves for garnish

SERVES 8–10
PREPARATION AND COOKING TIME:
ABOUT 1 HOUR, PLUS OVERNIGHT CHILLING

Soak the gelatin in cold water. Lightly oil a 1 quart deep mold with the almond oil. Hull the strawberries and wash them rapidly under cold running water. Lay them out to dry on a double layer of paper towels. When they are completely dry, process them in a blender with the sugar and pour the purée into a bowl.

Whip the cream until it is stiff then gently fold it into the strawberry purée, mixing in with a wooden spoon with an up-and-down movement to prevent the cream from deflating. Heat the Cointreau in a small saucepan until it begins to simmer. Remove from the heat and stir in the gelatin until it has dissolved. Add the coconut to the strawberry mixture, then slowly pour in the Cointreau and gelatin in a trickle. Mix constantly with an up-and-down folding movement.

Pour into the mold, bang it gently, cover with plastic wrap and refrigerate overnight. Turn the mousse out on to a serving dish and garnish with the strawberries and the mint leaves. Serve at once.

May Evening Pie

Crostata 'sera di maggio'

1¼ cups all-purpose flour
¾ cup sugar
grated rind of ½ lemon
6 tablespoons butter
1 small egg
2 tablespoons gelatin
1¼ lb ripe strawberries
½ cup Cointreau liqueur
⅔ cup whipping cream
a few mint leaves for garnish

SERVES 8
PREPARATION AND COOKING TIME:
ABOUT 1 HOUR, PLUS 3–4 HOURS CHILLING

Mix the flour, ¼ cup of sugar, the grated lemon rind and a pinch of salt together and make a well in the center. Cut the softened butter into small pieces and place in the well with the egg; mix quickly to a smooth dough. Roll it into a ball, wrap it in waxed paper or plastic wrap and let it rest in the refrigerator for about 30 minutes.

Meanwhile preheat the oven to 350°F. Butter and flour a pie dish 9 inches in diameter. Roll out enough dough to line the dish and prick it with a fork; cover it with a sheet of foil and place a few dried beans on top. Bake the pastry for about 30 minutes. Remove the beans and foil and let the pastry shell cool inside the dish.

Dissolve the gelatin in a little cold water. Remove the stems from 1 lb of the strawberries, wash them in very cold water, drain them, then cut them into small pieces. Place them in a blender together with the remaining sugar and blend them first at low speed then at high speed for a couple of minutes. Heat the Cointreau in a saucepan; remove it from the heat and, while still hot, fold in the gelatin, stirring it until it is completely dissolved; add the strawberries and stir the mixture for a further 30 seconds.

Turn out the pastry shell onto a serving dish and pour over the strawberry mixture, distributing it evenly. Keep the tart in the refrigerator for 3–4 hours or, even better, overnight, to set the filling.

A short time before serving, beat the whipping cream until stiff, put it in a piping bag, and decorate to taste, finishing off with the remaining strawberries, washed but not stemmed, and a few mint leaves. Serve immediately.

Pudding with Almonds and Raisins

Crema sformata con mandorle e uvetta

¾ cup golden raisins
⅔ cup dry white wine
4 oz almonds
2 eggs
¾ cup super-fine sugar
2 slices white bread, crumbled
1¼ cups light cream
1¼ cups milk
ground nutmeg
1 teaspoon ground cinnamon
butter

SERVES 6
PREPARATION AND COOKING TIME:
ABOUT 1½ HOURS

Preheat the oven to 350°F. Soak the raisins in the white wine. Parboil the almonds in a little water for a few minutes, drain and peel them. Toast them in the oven for 3–4 minutes. Chop finely in a food processor.

Reduce the oven temperature to 300°F. Beat the eggs, add the sugar and whisk to the ribbon. Mix in the chopped almonds, the crumbled bread and the drained raisins. Add the cream and milk and flavor with a pinch of ground nutmeg and the cinnamon.

Butter a 10 inch pie dish and pour in the mixture. Cook in the preheated oven for at least 1 hour. The cake is ready when the center springs back when pressed with a finger. Cool in the dish and then turn onto a plate. This dish may be served with whipped cream piped onto the top or served separately.

Fried Ricotta Slices

Crema di ricotta, fritta

---

4 oz ricotta cheese
6 tablespoons sugar
1 cup all-purpose flour
5 eggs
scant 1 cup light cream
1¼ cups milk
oil
a little semolina

SERVES 4–6
PREPARATION AND COOKING TIME:
ABOUT 40 MINUTES

Sieve and mash the ricotta and mix it with the sugar, a little salt and the sifted flour. Stir in the eggs, one at a time, to form a smooth, creamy paste. Whisk in the cream and milk.

Heat the mixture in a small saucepan, stirring constantly with a whisk, and allow it to thicken. Remove from the heat as soon as it starts to boil.

Grease a baking pan with plenty of oil and pour in the mixture, spreading it to a thickness of about ½ inch. Leave to cool and set then cut it into diamond shapes. Coat the diamonds in the semolina.

Heat plenty of oil in a large frying pan and fry the diamonds a few at a time, turning them carefully so that they brown on all sides. Drain on paper towels and arrange on a plate. Serve warm or cold.

Grape and Apple Cheesecake

Crostata di mascarpone all'uva e mela

FOR THE CRUST
1 cup all-purpose flour
¼ cup super-fine sugar
4 oz butter
2 egg yolks
grated rind of 1 lemon
a little butter and flour

FOR THE FILLING
7 oz Mascarpone cheese
½ cup confectioners' sugar
2 egg yolks
2 tablespoons brandy

FOR THE TOPPING
20 small macaroons
a large bunch green grapes
1 apple
5 tablespoons super-fine sugar
5 mint leaves

SERVES 8
PREPARATION AND COOKING TIME:
ABOUT 1½ HOURS

LEFT: *Grape and apple cheesecake.*

To make the crust: put the sifted flour, sugar and a pinch of salt together in a bowl and add the butter, cut into small cubes. Rub it in with your fingers until the mixture resembles coarse breadcrumbs. Add the egg yolks and lemon rind. Roll the dough into a ball, wrap it in plastic wrap and leave it in the refrigerator for 30 minutes.

Meanwhile preheat the oven to 375°F. Grease and flour a 10 inch pie dish with a smooth bottom and fluted sides.

Roll out the pastry and line the pan, pricking the bottom with a fork. Bake in the oven for about 20 minutes or until well cooked and golden. Leave to cool in the pan.

Now prepare the filling: beat the cheese and sugar together, incorporating the egg yolks one at a time. Add the brandy.

Crumble the macaroons finely. When the pie shell is cold, take it out of the pie dish and set it on a plate. Sprinkle the macaroons over the bottom and pour in the filling. Wash and dry the grapes and arrange them on top together with thin slices of apple.

Dissolve the sugar in 1 tablespoon of water over low heat. When it is a thick syrup, brush it, still hot, over the fruit. Decorate the center of the cake with the mint leaves and keep it in a cool place or the warmest part of the refrigerator until required.

Serve the grape and apple cheesecake within a couple of hours.

299

September Fruit Salad

Capriccio settembrino

---

2 apples
juice of 1 lemon
¼ cup sugar
1 peach
12 oz red plums
8 oz green grapes
3 tablespoons Cointreau liqueur

SERVES 4

PREPARATION TIME: ABOUT 30 MINUTES,
PLUS 1 HOUR CHILLING

Peel and core the apples, cut into quarters and then dice. As they are ready, put them into a bowl containing the strained lemon juice. Add the sugar, then mix carefully with a wooden spoon.

Remove the stalks from the peach and the plums and wipe with a damp cloth. Cut in half and remove the stones, then dice and add to the apples in the bowl. Wipe the grapes with a damp cloth and remove stalks and pips if necessary. Cut the larger grapes in half. Add to the rest of the fruit. Mix well and pour over the Cointreau.

Cover with plastic wrap and refrigerate for at least 1 hour. Mix carefully before serving.

Ricotta Pie with Golden Raisins

Torta di ricotta alla panna

---

12 oz prepared pie pastry
a little flour
a little butter
½ cup golden raisins
4 oz candied peel
12 oz full-cream ricotta cheese
3 eggs, separated
½ cup sugar
grated rind of 1 lemon
a little confectioners' sugar

SERVES 8

PREPARATION AND COOKING TIME:
ABOUT 1 HOUR, PLUS THAWING

Roll out the pastry on a lightly floured board and use it to line a buttered, floured 9 inch pie dish. Cut off the excess dough and shape into a ring with which to thicken the sides of the pie; then prick the base with a fork.

Preheat the oven to 350°F. Wash and dry the raisins; cut the candied peel into small cubes. Sieve the ricotta into a bowl and mix in, one at a time, the yolks of the three eggs, then the sugar, the grated rind of the lemon, the diced candied peel and the raisins, stirring vigorously. Beat the egg whites with a pinch of salt until they are quite stiff and fold them into the mixture.

Pour the mixture into the pastry shell and tap the dish to remove air bubbles in the mixture. Bake for about 45 minutes. Finally, turn out and leave it to cool. Before serving, sprinkle with confectioners' sugar.

Meringue Gateau

Torta meringata

FOR THE MERINGUE
a little oil
3 egg whites
2 cups confectioners' sugar
a little vanilla sugar

FOR THE ÉCLAIRS
butter
1/2 cup all-purpose flour
1 egg

FOR THE CUSTARD
3 eggs
1/2 cup sugar
a little vanilla sugar
1/2 cup all-purpose flour
2 1/2 cups milk
1 tablespoon cocoa powder
1 tablespoon Grand Marnier liqueur
1 tablespoon Maraschino liqueur
1/2 cup whipping cream

SERVES 10

PREPARATION AND COOKING TIME:
ABOUT 4 HOURS

To prepare the meringue: lightly grease an 11 inch circle of waxed paper with a little oil and place it on a small baking tray. Preheat the oven to 225°F. Whisk the egg whites with a pinch of salt and sift in most of the confectioners' sugar and the vanilla sugar, a little at a time, beating briskly until the mixture is well risen and firm. Using a piping bag with a plain tip, cover the circle of waxed paper by piping two overlapping spirals. Sprinkle the remaining confectioners' sugar on top and bake for a couple of hours; then turn off the oven and leave an hour before taking it out to cool.

To prepare the éclairs: preheat the oven to 375°F and butter and flour a small baking sheet. Bring 4 tablespoons of water to the boil in a saucepan with 2 tablespoons of diced butter and a pinch of salt. As soon as the butter is completely melted, remove from the heat and sift in the flour, beating briskly with a wooden spoon. Return the pan to the heat and continue to cook, stirring continuously, until the mixture begins to sizzle and come away from the sides of the pan. Turn it onto a plate and spread it out

302

to cool.

Return it to the pan and beat in the egg, making sure the mixture is completely smooth. Using a piping bag with a plain tip, pipe at least 30 finger shapes on the prepared baking sheet, spaced apart to allow them to spread. Bake for 15 minutes then turn them out to cool on a wire rack.

To prepare the custard: beat the eggs, the sugar, vanilla sugar, flour and a pinch of salt together in a saucepan. When smooth, gradually add the milk. Bring to the boil, stirring all the time. Remove from the heat and divide into two, adding the cocoa powder and Grand Marnier to one half and the Maraschino to the other. Let them cool, stirring frequently, then put them into two separate piping bags with plain tips.

To assemble the gateau: whip the cream and pipe it into the eclairs, then sprinkle them with a little confectioners' sugar. Just before serving, set the meringue base on a large plate, make a ring round the edge with the yellow custard and set the eclairs on it. Cover the rest of the meringue with alternate stripes of the two custards and serve.

Stuffed Baked Apples

Mele Golose

---

1 oz almonds, blanched
1 oz hazelnuts, blanched
1 oz peanuts, blanched
1 oz walnuts, blanched
1 oz semi-sweet chocolate, broken into pieces
10 apples, equal in size and not too ripe
butter
1 small cinnamon stick
3 cloves
spiral of lemon rind, 3 in long
⅔ cup sweet white wine
¾ cup super-fine sugar
4 egg yolks
4 tablespoons cornstarch
a little vanilla sugar
2½ cups milk
4 tablespoons Calvados or brandy
1 oz pistachio nuts
⅔ cup whipping cream

SERVES 10

PREPARATION AND COOKING TIME:
ABOUT 1½ HOURS, PLUS CHILLING

Preheat the oven to 375°F. Put the almonds, hazelnuts, peanuts, walnuts, and chocolate into a blender and process at maximum speed for a few seconds until the ingredients are all ground to a paste. Put the mixture in a bowl.

Peel the apples and, using an apple corer, cut into the base, stopping when you reach the stalk: you should hollow out the core just up to the stalk end, leaving it closed at the top. Remove the apple flesh from the cores, chop it and add to the nut paste in the bowl, and mix together well.

Stuff each apple with the mixture, pressing it in with a teaspoon. Butter an ovenproof dish which is just the right size to hold the apples in one layer and arrange them in it. Break up the cinnamon stick and put this in the dish, along with the cloves and the lemon rind. Pour in the wine and sprinkle over ¼ cup of sugar. Bake in the oven for about 45 minutes, basting from time to time with the juices.

Remove the cooked apples from the oven and set them aside while you prepare the custard. Beat the egg yolks in a saucepan with the remaining sugar, cornstarch, vanilla sugar and a pinch of salt. Then pour in the milk in a slow trickle, mixing constantly with a small whisk. Bring to the boil, remove from the heat and add the Calvados. Arrange the cooked apples on a serving dish and pour the custard over it at once.

Blanch the pistachio nuts in boiling salted water, chop them and sprinkle them over the custard-covered apples. Whip the cream until it is stiff and put in a piping bag. Decorate the apples with swirls around the outside and one in the center. Keep in a very cool place or in the warmest part of the refrigerator until you are ready to serve.

Panettone Charlotte

Charlotte di panettone

---

about 1 lb apples
about 1½ lb pears
4 oz butter
½ cup sugar
⅔ cup dry white wine
12 oz slightly stale panettone
2 eggs
⅔ cup milk
½ cup heavy cream

SERVES 8

PREPARATION AND COOKING TIME: ABOUT 2½
HOURS, PLUS COOLING AND CHILLING

Preheat the oven to 350°F. Peel, core and quarter the apples and pears. Heat two frying pans with about half the butter in each. As soon as the butter is hot, put the apples in one frying pan and the pears in the other. Sprinkle each with 1 tablespoon of sugar and pour half the wine into each frying pan. Cook over low heat until the fruit is cooked but still firm and the pieces intact.

Meanwhile liberally butter a 1½ quart deep round ovenproof mold, then cut two foil strips, about 2 inches wide and long enough to place crossways inside the mold with about ¾ inch at the ends to hang over the rim. Butter these too.

Cut the panettone into thin slices. Place a layer of panettone on the bottom of the mold and press it down lightly to make it stick. Then place half the apples on top. Cover with another layer of panettone and then a layer of pears. Continue alternating the panettone, apples and pears in this way, finishing with a layer of panettone. Press down lightly so there are no spaces left.

Beat the eggs with the remaining sugar in a bowl and dilute with the milk and cream. Pour the mixture over the panettone and prick with a skewer to help the liquid penetrate. Leave the charlotte to rest for about 15 minutes, then bake for about 1½ hours. Remove from the oven and leave to cool.

Turn it out onto a serving dish with the help of the strips of foil (which should then be discarded). Refrigerate the charlotte for a couple of hours before serving. This is a particularly good recipe for using up leftover panettone.

Panettone Filled with Tangerine Custard

Panettone farcito al mandarino

---

about 2 tablespoons gelatin
4 eggs
½ cup sugar
1 tangerine
½ cup all-purpose flour
1¼ cups milk
½ cup tangerine juice
1 panettone
4 tablespoons Cointreau liqueur
1¾ cups whipping cream

SERVES 10–12

PREPARATION AND COOKING TIME:
ABOUT 1 HOUR PLUS 6–8 HOURS CHILLING

Dissolve the gelatin in cold water. Whisk together the egg yolks and the sugar in a saucepan until pale and frothy. Grate the tangerine rind and add this, then sift in the flour. Mix again, then dilute with the milk and tangerine juice, adding them in a trickle. Bring slowly to the boil, stirring constantly with a wooden spoon. Remove from the heat and dissolve the gelatin in the mixture. Leave to cool, stirring gently from time to time in order to prevent a skin forming.

Meanwhile, turn the panettone upside down and, using a sharp-pointed knife, cut out a circle from the base, about ¾ inch from the edge. Set the circle aside. Hollow out the inside of the panettone, always keeping about ¾ inch from the edge. Make a large cavity and pour in the Cointreau. Whip the cream and fold it into the cold tangerine-flavored custard. Use an up-and-down movement, not a circular one, to prevent the cream from going flat. Pour the mixture into the panettone and replace the circle in the base to restore its original form. Place it upside-down in a bowl which is just the right size to hold the panettone and cover with plastic wrap.

Refrigerate for 6–8 hours or, better still, overnight. Turn out on to a serving dish and serve. Cut with a sharp, serrated knife to avoid crumbling it.

RIGHT: Panettone filled with tangerine custard (top);
Panettone charlotte (bottom).

Index